Developmental Assets

This book is a resource of Search Institute's Healthy Communities • Healthy Youth initiative. This effort seeks to motivate and equip individuals, organizations, and their leaders to join together in nurturing competent, caring, and responsible children and adolescents. The initiative sponsors research, evaluation, training, technical assistance, networking opportunities, and the development of resource materials based on Search Institute's framework of developmental assets.

Major support for Search Institute's Healthy Communities • Healthy Youth initiative is underwritten by Lutheran Brotherhood, a not-for-profit financial services organization that provides financial services and community service opportunities for Lutherans nationwide, as well as philanthropic outreach in communities. Search Institute's work on asset building has also received support from the Blandin Foundation, the Annie E. Casey Foundation, the Cargill Foundation, The Colorado Trust, the DeWitt Wallace-Reader's Digest Fund, the W. K. Kellogg Foundation, the Lilly Endowment, the Norwest Foundation, and other funders. The initiative is also supported by school districts, city agencies, community collaborations, state agencies, youth organizations, community foundations, and residents in hundreds of communities across the United States.

The research for this resource was funded through the sales of Search Institute's products for communities, organizations, and individuals dedicated to the well-being of children and adolescents.

Peter C. Scales

and Nancy Leffert

Foreword by Richard M. Lerner

Search Institute • Minneapolis

Developmental
Assets

A Synthesis of

the Scientific Research

on Adolescent Development

10   9   8   7   6   5   4   3   2

Printed in the United States of America on acid-free paper

Library of Congress Cataloging-in-Publication Data

Scales, Peter, 1949–
    Developmental assets : a synthesis of the scientific research on adolescent development / Peter C. Scales and Nancy Leffert.
        p.   cm.
    Includes bibliographical references and index.
    ISBN 1-57482-338-8 (acid-free paper)
    1. Adolescent psychology.   I. Leffert, Nancy, 1949–   .
II. Title.
BF724.S327   1999
305.235'5—dc21   98-47379

Search Institute
700 South Third Street, Suite 210
Minneapolis, MN 55415-1138

612-376-8955
800-888-7828

www.search-institute.org

Credits
Editors: Eugene C. Roehlkepartain, Kate Tyler, Kathryn (Kay) L. Hong
Design: Diane Gleba Hall
Production: Becky Manfredini

We dedicate this book to our families, for their love, support, understanding, and encouragement during the writing of this book and for their ability to keep us centered on what is truly important:

Martha R. Roper and Dane R. Roper
Mark, Jonathan, and Jeremy Leffert

Contents

Developmental assets are the positive relationships, opportunities, competencies, values, and self-perceptions that youth need to succeed.

The External Assets

Supported young people know they can rely on positive, fulfilling relationships with many adults in their families, schools, and communities.

Young people are empowered to the extent that they are seen by others as resources, make contributions to society, and feel free of threats to their safety.

Boundaries and expectations are the rules, standards, and norms in families, schools, neighborhoods, and communities that guide young people's choices and regulate their behavior.

A healthy community offers a rich array of constructive, engaging opportunities and activities to all young people.

The Internal Assets

Foreword

It is not news that the youth of America face challenges to their health and positive development that are unique to this century. Drug and alcohol use and abuse, unsafe sex and teenage pregnancy, school failure and dropout, delinquency and often violent crimes, life in single-parent families, and poverty are among the better-known examples of these challenges.

Many people act as if there is little that can be done to address the problems faced by our nation as a consequence of the human and social capital lost—or at least severely compromised—because of these problems. For instance, the status of American youth has not attracted sufficient attention among policy makers to bring them to enact a national youth policy; the United States remains the only Western nation without such a course of action in place. In turn, although excellent prevention research pertinent to youth problems continues to be conducted, the majority of scholars in our nation too often regard research on such problems to be of secondary importance, arguing that the best use of their intellectual resources is to study issues of "basic" scientific importance. As a result, they dismiss work on the contemporary issues facing adolescents as being of "only applied" concern.

This lack of attention allows policy makers and the scholarly community to overlook important news about our nation's youth, including the news contained in this vitally important and excellent book by Peter C. Scales and Nancy Leffert. The news is *not* that youth have problems, *nor* that the problems can be addressed by prevention programs, albeit with often less-than-desired or unsustained effects. Rather, Scales and Leffert present us with a different conception of American youth and their development, one that merges an understanding of the basic processes involved in adaptive (that is, positive, healthy) development with a clear action agenda, with "applications" involving community-based strategies and the engagement of public policy. The vision put forward by Scales, Leffert, and their colleagues at Search Institute in Minneapolis, Minnesota, is one of positive youth development pursued in the scholarship that they have conducted over the past several years.

Karen Pittman, a preeminent voice in the youth development field, has observed that the prevention of youth problems does not represent the provision of resources that enable young people to develop in healthy and positive ways. Consistent with that observation, Search Institute has built a conceptual model of adolescent development based on the strengths of young people and on the resources they and the members of their families and communities can provide to enable these strengths to become the ingredients of positive development across the life span. With this model as a frame, Search Institute researchers have identified the 40 key individual and contextual resources—the 40 internal and external developmental assets—for youth. They demonstrate that the more assets possessed by young people, the less probability of their engagement in problem behaviors. Moreover, they demonstrate that the more assets possessed by youth, the greater the likelihood that health and positive behaviors will characterize their development.

In this volume, Scales and Leffert show that a wealth of literature regarding the behavior and development of adolescents and the interpersonal and institutional influences on their behavior (for example, family, school, and community-based, youth-serving programs) may be integrated and extended by the conceptual and empirical features of the developmental asset model.

The news in this volume, then, is that an approach to youth development based on these assets contributes in three significant ways to understanding and improving the lives of our young people. First, the asset approach crystallizes and extends basic scholarship about the developmental process in general and the adolescent period in particular. Second, this approach builds bridges between basic and applied interests in the study of adolescent development. Scales and Leffert synthesize what basic research has learned about how changes in environments and relationships affect adolescents, and in the process, they point to what, in effect, constitute community-based intervention strategies. Third, the asset approach offers a vision of, and a set of prescriptions for, policy innovations that hold the promise of building in America a system whereby we capitalize on the strengths of our children, families, and communities and work together to maximize the likelihood that all youth will be given an opportunity to demonstrate their best.

In short, the news provided by this book—the integrative conceptual and rigorous empirical work it documents, and the creative, timely, and important message it offers about programs and policies pertinent to our nation's youth—leads me to a conclusion about its substantive significance: The 40 assets for the healthy development of youth that have been identified by Search Institute should be extended by one—Search Institute itself. No institution is doing more to enhance understanding of the bases of positive development of our nation's youth. And no institution is adding more to the momentum building in the United States for the creation of a national youth policy based on developmental assets and their role in promoting positive youth development. The knowledge about strengthening our young people and the impetus to community action and policy innovation that derives from the contributions of Search Institute are critical assets as our nation debates whether and how it will address the historically unprecedented set of challenges facing our youth.

Scholars of youth development owe Scales, Leffert, and their colleagues at Search Institute a great debt for providing an exemplar of applied developmental science—for conducting high-quality scholarship that furthers understanding of youth development while it serves as a vital basis for youth-serving programs and policies. In building a compelling case for a focus on the assets requisite for healthy youth development, the work of Search Institute is making a singular and sustainable contribution to the future of civil society in America.

Richard M. Lerner, Ph.D.

Center for Child, Family, and Community Partnerships

Boston College

Acknowledgments

A book of this scope would not have been possible without the help of a larger team. Searching the literature for relevant research and evaluations, acquiring articles and books, and compiling the references was an arduous task, most capably completed by Renee Vraa, Pat Johnson, Candyce Kroenke, and Ben Nicholson. The comprehensiveness of this review is largely a result of their assistance. We also extend our thanks to Nancy Ashley, Bonnie Benard, Thomas H. Berkas, Ph.D., Carol Breslau, Brett Brown, Ph.D., Holly Halvorson, María Guajardo Lucero, Ph.D., and Rick Jackson, Ph.D., who lent their expertise in reviewing the manuscript, and to Kate Tyler, the substantive editor, who has contributed to the blending of our voices, and engaged and challenged us to think even more deeply about this work. We offer our sincere thanks as well to these Search Institute colleagues, who assisted in the creation and execution of this book: Peter L. Benson, Ph.D., Ann Betz, Dale A. Blyth, Ph.D., Tamra Boyce, Marilyn Erickson, Jennifer Griffin-Wiesner, Kathryn (Kay) Hong, Becky Manfredini, Karen Pladsen, Eugene C. Roehlkepartain, Amanda Seigel, Terri Swanson, Rick Trierweiler, and Jean Wachs.

List of Figures and Tables

Tables

*Developmental assets are
the positive relationships,
opportunities, competencies,
values, and self-perceptions
that youth need to succeed.*

Introduction: The Framework of Developmental Assets

When adults talk about youth, they talk mostly about problems—alcohol and other drugs, adolescent pregnancy, school dropout. The result is that many Americans have both a distorted, negative view of young people and an imbalanced, inaccurate picture of what they need to succeed. In this book, we focus instead on youth assets, the positive relationships, opportunities, skills, and values that help young people grow up healthy. (See Table 1.) We present research that describes the critical influence those assets have on youth development.

For several generations now, policies and programs for and about youth have focused mostly on naming and trying to prevent problem behaviors. But research in the past decade especially has consistently found that this approach has had limited impact. Programs concentrating solely on preventing specific youth problems (without attention to social context) typically have been unable to document any long-term effects (Scales, 1990).

For example, the Drug Abuse Resistance Education (DARE) program is the single most prevalent such program in U.S. schools, and yet a comprehensive meta-analysis of studies on the program showed it did not significantly reduce alcohol and other drug use (Ennett, Tobler, Ringwalt, & Flewelling, 1994). Similarly, while a plethora of programs focus solely on getting young people to "just say no" to sexual intercourse ("abstinence-only" programs that do not include information on contraception), not a single scientifically valid evaluation of such programs has shown them to be effective either in keeping young people from having sex or in reducing the pregnancy rate among teens

Table 1. The Framework of 40 Developmental Assets, with Definitions
Search Institute has identified the following building blocks of healthy development that help young people grow up healthy, caring, and responsible.
External Assets
Support
1. **Family support**—Family life provides high levels of love and support.   2. **Positive family communication**—Young person and her or his parent(s) communicate positively, and young person is willing to seek advice and counsel from parents.   3. **Other adult relationships**—Young person receives support from three or more non-parent adults.   4. **Caring neighborhood**—Young person experiences caring neighbors.   5. **Caring school climate**—School provides a caring, encouraging environment.   6. **Parent involvement in schooling**—Parent(s) are actively involved in helping young person succeed in school.
Empowerment
7. **Community values youth**—Young person perceives that adults in the community value youth.   8. **Youth as resources**—Young people are given useful roles in the community.   9. **Service to others**—Young person serves in the community one hour or more per week.   10. **Safety**—Young person feels safe at home, at school, and in the neighborhood.
Boundaries and Expectations
11. **Family boundaries**—Family has clear rules and consequences and monitors the young person's whereabouts.   12. **School boundaries**—School provides clear rules and consequences.   13. **Neighborhood boundaries**—Neighbors take responsibility for monitoring young people's behavior.   14. **Adult role models**—Parent(s) and other adults model positive, responsible behavior.   15. **Positive peer influence**—Young person's best friends model responsible behavior.   16. **High expectations**—Both parent(s) and teachers encourage the young person to do well.
Constructive Use of Time
17. **Creative activities**—Young person spends three or more hours per week in lessons or practice in music, theater, or other arts.

Table 1. The Framework of 40 Developmental Assets, with Definitions (cont.)

18. **Youth programs**—Young person spends three or more hours per week in sports, clubs, or organizations at school and/or in the community.

19. **Religious community**—Young person spends one or more hours per week in activities in a religious institution.

20. **Time at home**—Young person is out with friends "with nothing special to do" two or fewer nights per week.

Internal Assets

Commitment to Learning

---

21. **Achievement motivation**—Young person is motivated to do well in school.

22. **School engagement**—Young person is actively engaged in learning.

23. **Homework**—Young person reports doing at least one hour of homework every school day.

24. **Bonding to school**—Young person cares about her or his school.

25. **Reading for pleasure**—Young person reads for pleasure three or more hours per week.

Positive Values

---

26. **Caring**—Young person places high value on helping other people.

27. **Equality and social justice**—Young person places high value on promoting equality and reducing hunger and poverty.

28. **Integrity**—Young person acts on convictions and stands up for her or his beliefs.

29. **Honesty**—Young person "tells the truth even when it is not easy."

30. **Responsibility**—Young person accepts and takes personal responsibility.

31. **Restraint**—Young person believes it is important not to be sexually active or to use alcohol or other drugs.

Social Competencies

---

32. **Planning and decision making**—Young person knows how to plan ahead and make choices.

33. **Interpersonal competence**—Young person has empathy, sensitivity, and friendship skills.

34. **Cultural competence**—Young person has knowledge of and comfort with people of different cultural/racial/ethnic backgrounds.

35. **Resistance skills**—Young person can resist negative peer pressure and dangerous situations.

36. **Peaceful conflict resolution**—Young person seeks to resolve conflict nonviolently.

Table 1. The Framework of 40 Developmental Assets, with Definitions (cont.)
Positive Identity
37. Personal power—Young person feels he or she has control over "things that happen to me."
38. Self-esteem—Young person reports having a high self-esteem.
39. Sense of purpose—Young person reports that "my life has a purpose."
40. Positive view of personal future—Young person is optimistic about her or his personal future.
This table may be reproduced for educational, noncommercial uses only. Copyright ©1997 by Search Institute, 700 S. Third Street, Suite 210, Minneapolis, MN 55415; 800-888-7828; www.search-institute.org.

who do have intercourse (Kirby et al., 1994; Haffner, 1995). It has been known for more than a decade that the programs that seem to work are multifaceted, involving the varied contexts of young people's lives and the adults who figure prominently in those lives—including parents, religious leaders, peers, and teachers—as well as the media (Dryfoos, 1990; Pentz et al., 1989; Schorr, 1997; Schorr & Schorr, 1988; Vincent, Clearie, & Schlucter, 1987). Successful prevention programs also include content that goes beyond admonitions and slogans; instead, they use social learning theory (i.e., that young people are heavily influenced by their social relationships in acquiring attitudes and learning behaviors) to help youth build social competencies and positive values, understanding the complex ways in which youth are influenced by their relationships and by the experiences they have every day. Those programs are personal and inviting, they are flexible and informal in responding to young people's needs, and they are comprehensive. In short, successful prevention programs also put great emphasis on broader supports, opportunities, and competencies in young people's lives (Petersen, Leffert, Graham, Alwin, & Ding, 1997).

Not surprisingly then, research over the past two decades has shown that young people who successfully face many challenges in navigating through adolescence—young people who are resilient—have positive things in their lives beyond exposure to special prevention programs. The luckiest children start out with innate dispositions and traits that lead them to be curious, happy, outgoing, and confident babies who then attract adult attention and caring. But whether born with a happy disposition or not, children who have caring adults in their lives develop competencies and self-perceptions that attract additional friends, both peers and adults, and raise the chances of further successes (Garmezy, 1991; Rutter, 1979; Werner & Smith, 1992).

The Developmental Asset Approach

Since 1989, Search Institute has been conducting research—grounded in the vast literature on resilience, prevention, and adolescent development—that has illuminated the positive relationships, opportunities, competencies, values, and self-perceptions that youth need to succeed. The institute's framework of "developmental assets" grows out of that research, which has involved more than 500,000 6th- to 12th-grade youth in more than 600 communities across the country (for more complete descriptions of the framework and its conceptual and research origins, see Benson, 1997; Benson, Leffert, Scales, & Blyth, 1998). Developmental assets are the building blocks that all youth need to be healthy, caring, principled, and productive. The developmental asset framework includes many of the "core elements of healthy development and . . . community actors (family, neighborhood, school, youth organizations, congregations, and so on) needed to promote these essential building blocks" (Benson, 1997, p. 27).

The original framework identified and measured 30 assets. Subsequent research (including focus groups to deepen understanding of how the developmental assets are experienced by urban youth, youth living in poverty, and youth of color) led to a revision of the framework to its current 40-asset structure. The 40 assets are grouped into eight categories representing broad domains of influence in young people's lives: support, empowerment, boundaries and expectations, and constructive use of time are external assets (relationships and opportunities that adults provide); commitment to learning, positive values, social competencies, and positive identity are internal assets (competencies and values that youth develop internally that help them become self-regulating adults). (See Table 2.)

The developmental assets have been measured using Search Institute's *Profiles of Student Life: Attitudes and Behaviors*, a 156-item self-report survey that is administered to 6th- to 12th-grade students in public and private schools. The instrument measures each of the 40 developmental assets as well as a number of other constructs, including developmental deficits (e.g., whether youth watch too much television or are the victims of violence), thriving indicators (e.g., school success and maintenance of physical health behaviors), and high-risk behaviors (e.g., alcohol, tobacco, and other drug use, sexual intercourse, and violence). Communities or school districts self-select to complete the survey, the data from which are then used to generate a report on the community's youth.

The data cited in this book represent the aggregate of 99,462 youth in grades 6 through 12 in public and/or alternative schools from 213 U.S. towns and cities who took the survey during the 1996–97 school year. This sample is made up of approximately equal numbers of males and females, and included 40% 6th to

5

Table 2. The Eight Categories of Developmental Assets

External Assets

Support	The support assets refer to the ways in which children are loved, affirmed, and accepted. Ideally, children experience an abundance of support not only in their families but also from many people in a variety of settings, such as in school or religious congregations, among extended family, within the family's social network, and in other areas in which socialization occurs.
Empowerment	An important developmental need is to feel safe and valued. The empowerment assets focus on community perceptions of youth and the opportunities they have to contribute to society in meaningful ways.
Boundaries and Expectations	Clear and consistent boundaries complement support and empowerment. Ideally, young people experience boundary assets in the family, at school, in after-school programs, and in the neighborhood. They provide a set of consistent messages about appropriate behavior and expectations across socializing contexts.
Constructive Use of Time	Healthy communities provide a rich array of constructive after-school opportunities. Whether through schools, community organizations, congregations, or for-profit centers, structured activities stimulate positive growth and contribute to the development of the other assets.

Internal Assets

Commitment to Learning	Developing an internal intellectual curiosity and the skills to gain new knowledge is essential for both school and work success. The commitment-to-learning assets reflect how connected young people are to their schools, how motivated they are to achieve, and whether they express their curiosity and work ethic in homework and reading for fun.
Positive Values	Positive values are important "internal compasses" that guide young people's priorities and choices. Although there are many values that American society cherishes and seeks to nurture in youth, the asset framework focuses on several widely shared values that affect youth behavior.
Social Competencies	These assets are important personal and interpersonal skills youth need to negotiate the maze of choices, options, and relationships they face. These skills also lay the foundation for independence and competence as adults.
Positive Identity	This category focuses on young people's views of themselves—their own sense of agency, purpose, worth, and promise. Without a positive sense of who they are, youth may feel powerless, without a sense of initiative and direction.

Note *Adapted from* Starting Out Right: Developmental Assets for Children *(pp. 17–18), by Nancy Leffert, Peter L. Benson, and Jolene L. Roehlkepartain, 1997, Minneapolis: Search Institute. Copyright 1997 by Search Institute.*

8th graders and 60% 9th to 12th graders. The self-reported race/ethnicity of the sample was predominantly White (86%), with 5% multiracial, 4% Latina/Latino, and 2% each African American, Asian/Pacific Islander, and Native American. Most of the respondents were from small- to medium-size towns and cities; only 4% were from major metropolitan areas. Although the sample is not nationally representative, it is nonetheless large and diverse and provides a sense of how adolescents in a large number of communities describe their lives. (For more on the measurement, reporting, reliability, validity, and predictive power of the developmental assets, see Leffert et al., in press.)

This research has shown that the more of these assets young people have, the less likely they are to engage in risky behavior (such as using alcohol or other drugs, or having early, unprotected sexual intercourse; see Table 3), and the more likely they are to engage in positive behaviors (such as succeeding in school or helping others; see Table 4). These relationships between assets and youth well-being remain fairly consistent for adolescents across differences of race and ethnicity, gender, age, socioeconomic background, community size, and region.

Consistent with the problem-focused approach prevalent in the youth development field, a greater number of studies show the negative effects of accumulated deficits and risky behaviors than show the importance of protective factors or assets. Nonetheless, some researchers have shown, as we have, the cumulative power of assets in young people's lives. Among these is Garmezy (1991), who also observed that positive or protective factors in young people's lives often worked indirectly, making them more difficult to detect, whereas risk factors were often easier to study and understand because they seemed to operate more directly to cause negative outcomes. Jessor, Van Den Bos, Vanderryn, Costa, and Turbin (1995) also reported that the higher the number of protective factors youth had, the fewer the risky behaviors in which they engaged. In addition, the effect of the protective factors was proportionately more powerful for youth in high-risk situations. Finally, and importantly, these researchers found that having protective factors as a young adolescent was even more influential in later positive outcomes than having risk factors as a young adolescent; in other words, assets were stronger than risks.

Disturbing Findings

Search Institute data show, however, that the average adolescent surveyed has fewer than half of the 40 assets we have defined. This disturbing finding is confirmed by a wide range of recent research.

For example, many young people's lives do not include the structured activities that stimulate positive growth and contribute to the development of the other assets. Search Institute data show that only 50% of youth spend even three hours a week in constructive after-school activities. The Carnegie Council on Adolescent Development (1992a) found that at least one third of 8th graders spend two hours every school day home alone after school with nothing con-

Risk Behavior Pattern	Definition	No. of Assets			
		0–10	11–20	21–30	31–40
Alcohol	Has used alcohol three or more times in the past month or got drunk once or more in the past two weeks.	53	30	11	3
Tobacco	Smokes one or more cigarettes every day or uses chewing tobacco frequently.	45	21	6	1
Illicit drugs	Used illicit drugs three or more times in the past year.	42	19	6	1
Sexual intercourse	Has had sexual intercourse three or more times in lifetime.	33	21	10	3
Depression/ suicide	Is frequently depressed and/or has attempted suicide.	40	25	13	4
Antisocial behavior	Has been involved in three or more incidents of shoplifting, trouble with police, or vandalism in the past year.	52	23	7	1
Violence	Has engaged in three or more acts of fighting, hitting, injuring a person, carrying or using a weapon, or threatening physical harm in the past year.	61	35	16	6
School problems	Has skipped school two or more days in the past month and/or has below a C average.	43	19	7	2
Driving and alcohol	Has driven after drinking or ridden with a drinking driver three or more times in the past year.	42	24	10	4
Gambling	Has gambled three or more times in the past year.	34	23	13	6

Table 3. Patterns of Assets and High-Risk Behavior among Adolescents (in %)

Note *From unpublished Search Institute data on 6th- to 12th-grade students in public and/or alternative schools who completed the institute's* Profiles of Student Life: Attitudes and Behaviors *survey during the 1996–97 school year; N = 99,462 students in 213 U.S. communities.*

structive to do, while much larger proportions, especially among youth of color, have limited access to structured activities.

Large numbers of youth also lack other assets essential to their positive development. Both Search Institute data and other studies (cited in Scales, 1996) show that only about half of youth feel engaged in schoolwork and connected to their schools. Fully 80% of youth think adults in their communities do not value them, according to Search Institute data. They evidently are right: A recent national survey of U.S. adults reported that more than 60% did not think youth would make the country a better place to live, and 20% felt they would make the country worse (Farkas, Johnson, Duffett, & Bers, 1997). Search Institute data also show that 64% of youth spend one hour or more each week in activities of a congregation, while another study found that only 35% attended religious services weekly (Role of Religion, 1996). (It would seem that youth in our sample are more connected to religious organizations, but there are no comparable figures that, like ours, add together time spent in

Table 4. The Relation of Assets to Thriving Indicators among Adolescents (in %)					
Thriving		**No. of Assets**			
Behavior	**Definition**	**0–10**	**11–20**	**21–30**	**31–40**
Succeeds in school	Gets mostly As on report card.	7	19	35	53
Helps others	Helps friends or neighbors one or more hours per week.	69	83	91	96
Values diversity	Places high importance on getting to know people of other racial/ethnic groups.	34	53	69	87
Maintains good health	Pays attention to healthy nutrition and exercise.	25	46	69	88
Exhibits leadership	Has been a leader of a group or organization in the past 12 months.	48	67	78	87
Resists danger	Avoids doing things that are dangerous.	6	15	29	43
Delays gratification	Saves money for something special rather than spending it all right away.	27	42	56	72
Overcomes adversity	Does not give up when things get difficult.	57	69	79	86

Note *From unpublished Search Institute data on 6th- to 12th-grade students in public and/or alternative schools who completed the institute's* Profiles of Student Life: Attitudes and Behaviors *survey during the 1996–97 school year; N = 99,462 students in 213 U.S. communities.*

religious services, youth groups, recreation, or any other activity sponsored by a congregation.)

The developmental assets do not include everything youth need. Young people also need adequate food, shelter, clothing, caregivers who at the minimum are not abusive or neglectful, families with adequate incomes, schools where both children and teachers feel safe, and economically and culturally vibrant neighborhoods—not ones beset by drugs, violent crime, and infrastructural decay. For example, young people who are disadvantaged by living in poor neighborhoods are consistently more likely to engage in risky behavior at higher rates than their more affluent peers, and they show consistently lower rates of positive outcomes (Brooks-Gunn & Duncan, 1997). Moreover, young people who live in abusive homes or in neighborhoods with high levels of violence are more likely to become both victims and perpetrators of violence (Garbarino, 1995). Young people's individual temperaments also matter: Babies who are cuddly and affectionate not only elicit smiles from their caregivers but also seem to have a better chance of attracting the nurturance of adults and are less likely to be abused (Werner & Smith, 1992).

Not all children who confront great challenges in their lives are destined to poor developmental outcomes, however. The literature on resilience suggests that as many as 30–40% of multiply disadvantaged children and youth "make it." By any reasonable definition (Rutter, 1979; Werner & Smith, 1992), neither genetics nor geography is destiny.

Rationale for the Asset Framework

Young people need more than economic and infrastructural supports. Our focus on the developmental assets suggests that the 40 assets together have the potential to weave a strong fabric that supports and guides positive youth development, even in the face of multiple adversities; that is, the assets can promote resilience among young people. The work of many researchers over the past two decades has shown that resilient youth have at least one adult who cares deeply for them. In Bronfenbrenner's (1991) words, they have adults who give them "irrational love." Luckier still are youth who have a loving parent or other related adult and at least one adult friend or mentor who care about them, act as role models, and often, connect them with other resources and opportunities. McLaughlin and Irby (1994) called such adults in disadvantaged urban settings "wizards" for their almost magical ability to create for the youth they care for an oasis in the midst of despair, a connection to resources, and a reason to hope. The luckiest of all live in communities where the adults in their lives talk with each other and support each other, creating a "web of influence" (Price, Cioci,

Penner, & Trautlein, 1993) that supports youth even under great adversity. Youth can overcome the circumstances of economically disadvantaged neighborhoods if the adults in those communities—parents, teachers, religious leaders, neighbors—share norms and values about what they want youth to believe and do and about how adults should help youth live out those expectations (Connell, Spencer, & Aber, 1994).

Most clearly articulated by Bronfenbrenner (1979), the overarching theme in the work of these researchers and theorists is that young people live in multiple, overlapping ecologies and that helping them create and maintain successful pathways to adulthood requires simultaneous attention to and marshaling of supports across all those ecologies. Werner and Smith's 30-year study of the children of Kauai (1992) showed how those multiple ecologies not only operated to promote positive outcomes at given developmental stages, but also worked cumulatively and circularly to build for fortunate youth an ever-expanding number and variety of supports and competencies. Supports experienced in infancy have a profound effect on resiliency experienced in adulthood. At the same time, Garmezy (1991) demonstrated the importance to developmental outcomes of young people establishing a sense of their basic competence across their diverse ecologies—social competence in general, and specific competencies in dealing with their families, their schools, and their peers. Jessor (1993) constructed an understanding of how adolescent risk behaviors that seemed distinct—delinquency, substance abuse, school failure, early sexual intercourse—actually clustered together; youth engaged in one of those risky behaviors were far more likely than other youth to be engaged in one or more of the other risky behaviors. Jessor concluded that a considerable degree of shared causation, which he labeled unconventionality, explained the co-occurrence of those risks. Hawkins, Catalano, and Miller (1992) derived from this growing body of research a number of risk and protective factors that seemed consistently to appear together in the lives of youth. More recently, Resnick et al. (1997) reported the first of many planned studies of a longitudinal sample of more than 12,000 youth; they found that how connected young people were to their families and schools was significantly related to their likelihood of engaging in a variety of health-compromising behaviors.

That many studies have demonstrated the importance of multiple and interacting influences on the well-being of youth confirms the validity of a multifaceted approach to youth development, "prevention," health promotion, and resilience. In addition, the consistent identification of certain similar constructs as fundamentally important underscores the need to focus efforts on how these variables work together in young people's lives:

- The relationships and connections young people have with caring others;
- The development of various skills and competencies such as planning and decision making;
- The effective occupation of young people's time;
- The establishing of consistent norms and expectations for behavior;
- The positive connection to social institutions such as schools and religious congregations; and
- The development of positive self-perceptions.

All these elements occur repeatedly in the scientific literature as critical elements in the healthy development of youth.

The Importance of the 40 Assets

The 40 developmental assets reflect those crucial categories of influence that time and again have been shown to meaningfully shape young people's developmental pathways.

Unlike the overall employment or crime rate in a community, these assets reflect primary socialization processes that every resident can do something about. They represent the everyday acts of involvement and nurturing that are within the grasp of all caring adults and youth, not just trained youth workers. Equally as critical as the scientific validity of the developmental asset structure is its mobilizing dimension. McKnight and Kretzmann (1990) have observed that the dominant approach to working with low-income communities has been to focus on deficits and "needs," but that "in neighborhoods where there are effective community development efforts, there is also a map of the community's assets, capacities, and abilities" (p. 3). Such a process of naming and counting a community's strengths helps local residents take ownership of their collective direction: "Significant community development only takes place when local community people are committed to investing themselves and their resources in the effort" (p. 2). Cardenas Ramirez (1992) goes further, calling for naming the assets that are not as easily quantified as the number of clubs, congregations, and civic groups. At the neighborhood level, those would include the neighborhood's history and the pride residents feel about living there, as well as the value they attach to various infrastructural assets. In the same way, the 40-asset framework includes readily quantified assets, such as hours youth volunteer, and less easily grasped assets, such as their perceived values and sense of identity and their perception about whether their schools are caring places. Successful community development initiatives are resident driven, grassroots, and optimistic. They are based on the understanding residents have of their community's strengths and their own capacity to make a difference. As Walker (1997) notes, an initiative will endure only if it is widely known and respected by residents, and if "it is continuously replenished by the ideas, energy, and commitment of new individuals" (p. ii). The 40-asset structure encourages all residents to become involved because it makes it clear that informal, everyday acts of asset building by ordinary citizens are equally as important as, if not more important than, efforts by skilled professional youth workers.

For example, although not everyone can offer youth a well-designed experience that builds their planning and decision-making skills, everyone can talk with adolescents, keep an eye on them when their parents are not around, protect them, and give them help when they need it. Everyone can help make youth feel valued and supported. The philosophical belief that everyone can and should help support the well-being of children and youth undergirds a number of current community mobilization efforts. As of 1998, Search Institute's national Healthy Communities • Healthy Youth initiative has helped more than 300 U.S. communities to enlist individuals and institutions to build developmental assets for youth. Other examples are Public/Private Venture's Community Change for Youth Development initiative in several urban communities, the Communities That Care initiative of the Social Development Research Group, Chapin Hall Center for Children's neighborhood cluster initiative in Chicago, the Kellogg Foundation's 20-year investment in three Michigan communities in the Kellogg Youth Initiative Project, and the Annie E. Casey Foundation's Plain Talk initiative to reduce adolescent pregnancy in several cities. These use language similar but not identical to the asset framework to describe what youth need, and they all base their efforts on a commitment to the mobilization of all sectors of the community—schools, families, neighborhoods, congregations, businesses, media, government, youth organizations, and residents—to promote positive youth development. Important in all these initiatives is the meaningful involvement of youth themselves. One significant example is the Center for Youth Development and Policy Research's program of youth mapping, in which young people are trained to map their community's assets and to work with adults to interpret their data and use the research to spark united community action for youth development.

Why This Book?

We have several reasons for writing this book. First, although the developmental asset framework has been shown to be empirically convincing in demonstrating a link between youth assets and youth behavior, it was developed initially out of the lessons of research done by many others in the 1970s and 1980s. We have since revised the framework on the basis of our own research, but it also must be refreshed and reinvigorated by the lessons of hundreds of new studies, new ways of thinking about how youth develop, and new lessons from working with youth. Our primary interest in writing this book is to conduct a deep examination of the latest research so that we can gain a richer understanding of the developmental asset framework. It is unlikely, for example, that the 40 assets included in the framework are the only 40 "things" that youth need, and they might not even be the best 40. We know they are powerful, but our assumption is that the framework can always be improved. By examining the relation of the asset framework to other current research on adolescent development, this book clarifies the extent to which the asset model accurately describes what youth need and identifies areas in which it might be strengthened.

Second, as more individuals and communities use the asset framework to deepen their own understanding of youth and to stimulate asset-building activities, programs, and policies, we have received an increasing number of requests for a more elaborate background than we have as yet published on the scientific basis for the framework. This book pulls together the scientific literature on the assets so that those involved in mobilizing their communities on behalf of youth will have confidence in the fundamental scientific credibility of the asset framework—even as they understand the limitations of this or any other framework that attempts to depict in relatively simple terms the wonderful complexity and contradictions of human development.

Finally, as awareness of the asset framework has grown among both social scientists and those who work with youth, useful and legitimate questions have been raised about the quality of the concepts and how we measure them. We hope that this book, in showing how the assets are reflected in the scientific literature on adolescent development, will speak clearly to many of those questions. Even more important, we hope it will encourage careful review of the framework and dialogue about it among our colleagues, both scientists and practitioners. The developmental asset framework is a research-based theory that we continually test. Like any other theory, the asset model should not be immune to testing, criticism, and revision as the emerging research dictates. This process is at the heart of credible social science, and we are committed to taking it where it leads.

Our Process

To synthesize the related scientific literature, we have conducted extensive literature searches for each of the 40 developmental assets, searching for the terms in the asset's definition as well as numerous other synonyms and key words in computerized databases such as PsychLit and the Educational Resources Information Center (ERIC). Less systematically, we have included unpublished papers recently presented at professional conferences.

We applied several criteria to select the studies included for the review. First, the sample size generally needed to be 50 or greater to prevent overgeneralization. Second, we concentrated on studies that relied on quantitative methods, which would allow greater validity in generalizing results. Third, we focused on studies of middle and high school–age youth, but occasionally included studies of younger children and young adults if studies of adolescents were not numerous. Fourth, we included other reviews of the research literature and occasional "thought pieces," even though those researchers did not collect new data. Fifth, we focused mainly on recent studies, published between 1990 and 1998. We did not include studies whose measures or statistical analyses we thought were inappropriate to their study's questions and sampling. We concentrated mainly on studies of U.S. youth but included studies of youth in other industrialized countries where appropriate.

More than 1,200 articles, chapters, books, and research reports were identified and reviewed. More than 800 of these are actually cited in this book. Overall, our selection of studies is biased toward larger-sample, survey-based, quantitative research. This means that we may have sacrificed being able to describe some of the rich variation in how the assets work across different contexts in favor of being able to make more generalizable conclusions about how assets work in most young people's lives.

Despite the comprehensiveness of our search, we make no claim that this is an exhaustive review. We have attempted, however, to review a sufficient number and variety of studies to give us confidence that the conclusions we draw accurately and validly represent the available research. In addition, we do not discuss every study cited but provide details on studies selectively and purposefully. Our goals are not only to clarify the ways in which a given asset seems to have the effects we have hypothesized, but also to describe how the asset works in as many contexts as there are data from which to draw reasonable conclusions.

In each chapter, we first define the asset category and present the overall results of our search, showing the studies that indicate support for the category's positive effects on youth, as well as any studies with neutral or contradictory findings. Next, we describe variations in the data based on gender; race, ethnicity, and other cultural differences; socioeconomic circumstances; age or grade; or family, school, or neighborhood contexts. (Terms used to identify racial/ethnic groups reflect the variety of terms used by researchers.)

We then expand this discussion with an examination of how the asset category seems to operate in young people's lives—directly as well as indirectly, in combination with other factors—noting exceptions and uncertainties along the way. In the chapter sections that summarize the research findings and how the assets work, we discuss the assets, with a few exceptions, in order. (In several instances, the findings or the conceptualization of the assets dictated that another order would be more logical.) We follow these descriptions with a summary of what Search Institute data on the 40 assets (collected during the 1996–97 school year) indicate about the level of the assets among young people, and a consideration of what seems to be missing conceptually from our definition of the asset category or lacking in our measurement. Then we provide a brief description of how the research suggests each asset category might be built and the role of individuals, families, neighborhoods, programs, and policies in that task of asset building. Finally, each chapter ends with a selected reading list. We have selected a few significant readings from the scientific literature on the developmental importance of each asset category for young people. This is not intended as an exhaustive list of all relevant or important work on the subject, but rather offers a sampling of useful research.

Conclusion

Ultimately, healthy adolescent development is not only about ensuring that the developmental pathways adolescents take help them become self-sufficient adults who have positive and responsible family and social relationships, and who are good citizens (National Clearinghouse on Families and Youth, 1997). It is not just about becoming, it is also about being. Adults have a responsibility to create the conditions under which adolescents, while they are adolescents, can be healthy, productive, caring, and happy. It is our responsibility to help all adolescents—male or female, of whatever racial or ethnic origin, with disabilities or not, rich or poor, gay or straight—answer yes to compelling developmental questions: Am I normal? Am I competent? Am I lovable and loving? (Scales, 1991). The evidence we review in this book demonstrates that building youth assets helps adolescents answer those questions in the affirmative, and helps them grow up healthy, productive, caring, and happy. And yet, the evidence also suggests that we are not taking full advantage of the developmental effectiveness of those assets: Too few youth have sufficient numbers of the assets, which means that too few adults and too few communities are committed to doing all they can to promote positive youth development.

This book shows that the scientific evidence for the strength of the developmental asset framework is compelling. Building youth assets does not replace or diminish the need for focused prevention or for timely intervention when youth already are experiencing problems. Asset building, prevention, and treatment are all necessary components of a healthy community for youth. The asset-building approach is not a substitute for prevention and treatment; it is a different way of thinking about youth development, an approach that stresses strengths more than deficits, opportunities more than risks. Asset building is what good prevention is all about, but based on a different, more positive and holistic view of youth and their environments. Philosophically, asset building represents a hopeful, optimistic perspective. The research we present in this book suggests that hope is well founded.

Selected Readings

In this list are significant scientific articles and books that offer more in-depth information on the theory and research behind Search Institute's framework of developmental assets, as well as other major books that offer comprehensive perspectives on adolescent development. This is not an exhaustive list of all relevant or important work on the subject, but rather a sampling of useful readings.

Benson, P. L. (1997). *All kids are our kids: What communities must do to raise caring and responsible children and adolescents.* San Francisco, CA: Jossey-Bass.

Benson, P. L., Leffert, N., Scales, P. C., & Blyth, D. A. (1998). Beyond the "village" rhetoric: Creating healthy communities for children and adolescents. *Applied Developmental Science.*

Benson, P. L., Scales, P. C., & Roehlkepartain, E. C. (1999). *A fragile foundation: The state of developmental assets among American youth.* Minneapolis: Search Institute.

Blyth, D. A., & Leffert, N. (1995). Communities as contexts for adolescent development: An empirical analysis. *Journal of Adolescent Research, 10,* 64–87.

Czikszentimhalyi, M., & Larson, R. (1984). *Being adolescent: Conflict and growth in the teenage years.* New York: Basic Books.

Feldman, S. S., & Elliott, G. R. (Eds.), (1990). *At the threshold: The developing adolescent.* Cambridge, MA: Harvard University Press.

Leffert, N., Benson, P. L., Scales, P. C., Sharma, A. R., Drake, D. R., & Blyth, D. A. (in press). Developmental assets: Measurement and prediction of risk behaviors among adolescents. *Applied Developmental Science.*

Millstein, S. G., Petersen, A. C., & Nightingale, E. O. (Eds.). (1993). *Promoting the health of adolescents: New directions for the twenty-first century.* New York: Oxford University Press.

Scales, P. C., Benson, P. L., Leffert, N., & Blyth, D. A. (1998). The strength of developmental assets as predictors of positive youth development outcomes. Manuscript submitted for publication.

Werner, E. E., & Smith, R. S. (1992). *Overcoming the odds: High risk children from birth to adulthood.* Ithaca, NY: Cornell University Press.

The External Assets

Supported young people know they can
rely on positive, fulfilling relationships
with many adults in their families,
schools, and communities.

1

The Support Assets

Every child needs love, affirmation, and acceptance. That is what we mean by the term *support* (Benson, 1997). In this chapter, we review research that shows how important support is for the healthy, positive development of young people. We do not include material assets (money, possessions) in the definition or the review of support because, as stated in the Introduction, our primary concern is with the developmental infrastructure, not the economic or physical infrastructure, of the environments in which young people live. Clearly, family or community wealth does have an effect on specific assets. (For example, see Chapter 4, on constructive use of time, and Chapter 5, on commitment to learning.) However, even where the influence of wealth is apparent, it often seems to be less considerable than the influence of the support, expectations, values, and competencies derived from relationships with others.

Support may be especially important for adolescents because the physical, emotional, social, spiritual, and intellectual changes they are going through may make it more difficult for adults to feel close to them. As part of their normal developmental "work," adolescents spend less time with their parents, often seeming embarrassed to be seen in public with them and other family members. They tend to reject adult opinions about the clothes they wear, the music they listen to, and how late they should stay out. They exert more independence and are more willing to voice viewpoints that are in conflict with those of parents and other adults. An adult who demonstrates caring and support despite the adolescent's apparent physical and emotional distancing becomes someone the youth deeply knows he or she can count on. The real challenge for adults, of course, is to provide support while simultaneously encouraging the adolescent's emerging autonomy and self-regulation. That kind of balance communicates respect for the adolescent as someone who is becoming an autonomous young adult, while at the same time letting that young person know he or she is not alone.

How important is support? Numerous studies in the 1970s and 1980s confirmed that social support is associated with better physical and mental health among adults (Turner, Frankel, & Levin, 1983). A large and growing number of studies since that time also have confirmed that a caring and supportive relationship with an adult remains "the most critical variable" predicting health and resiliency throughout childhood and adolescence (Benard, 1991; Garmezy, 1993). More recently, a national study of more than 12,000 7th–12th graders reported that a high degree of connectedness to families and schools significantly protected youth from seven of eight behaviors risky to their health, such as suicidal thoughts and behaviors, violence, substance use, and having their first sexual intercourse at a young age (Resnick et al., 1997).

Unfortunately, large proportions of young people do not seem to experience either enough support or the right kinds of support in their families, schools, or communities. By the "right kinds" of support, we mean caring and love that are offered to a child regardless of her or his behavior, not only as a reward for "good" behavior. We mean unconditional love of the kind the psychologist Urie Bronfenbrenner had in mind when he said that all children need someone in their lives who is simply "crazy" about them (Bronfenbrenner, 1991). To the extent that any child does not have that kind of support, he or she does not have the "right" kind. The research we review in this chapter makes it clear that too many youth in America fail to experience this kind of support. The research also holds hope, however, for it tells us how families, schools, and communities can overcome the gaps in support and provide all young people with the love, affirmation, and acceptance they need to succeed.

What Is Support?

Support is the first of the eight categories of developmental assets. (See Table 5.) Price, Cioci, Penner, and Trautlein (1990) define support as the provision of material benefits (aid), feedback that strengthens identity (affirmation), and caring or nurturance (affect). Youth who feel supported feel that they are connected to people they value and that adults know them and care for them. They also feel that they have adults they can turn to for help of various kinds, such as dealing with emotional problems, learning new skills, or obtaining financial resources. Supported youth know they are not alone; they know they can rely on positive, fulfilling relationships with numerous adults in their families, schools, and communities.

Support as a social-psychological construct has both quantitative, easily observable aspects and qualitative, less apparent aspects. For example, the research literature shows that young people's satisfaction with the support they receive is at least as important as the numbers of adults to whom they feel they can turn for help (reviewed in Scales & Gibbons, 1996). Some youth may need several adults they can turn to; others may need only one truly dependable, caring adult for support. For youth who feel they are getting the support they need, when they need it, one adult may be enough. At the same time, youth who can name several adults to whom they can turn for guidance, advice, or comfort may not have sufficient support if they don't feel loved deeply enough or accepted unconditionally—for example, if they get lectures when they seek advice or are made to feel embarrassed or stupid by adults. Whether a young person feels a sense of support also can vary depending on the issue or need of immediate importance. A youth who feels loved and cared for by parents or extended family might feel that he or she has no adult to turn to for advice on sexuality or that he or she is poorly supported (e.g., treated impersonally) at school.

Summary of Research Findings

Studies are abundant on this asset category and reflect a wide variety of research instruments, methods, and samples. Researchers consistently have found that a person's feeling of being supported, connected, and cared about is strongly related to a variety of positive outcomes. The influence of support from parents clearly is greater than support from school or neighborhood, but each kind of

Table 5. The Support Assets	
Family support	Family life provides high levels of love and support.
Positive family communication	Young person and her or his parent(s) communicate positively, and young person is willing to seek advice and counsel from parent(s).
Other adult relationships	Young person receives support from three or more nonparent adults.
Caring neighborhood	Young person experiences caring neighbors.
Caring school climate	School provides a caring, encouraging environment.
Parent involvement in schooling	Parent(s) are actively involved in helping young person succeed in school.

support increases a young person's overall sense of support and builds relation-ships with different positive outcomes. Moreover, the studies we review here have suggested that the interplay among the support from various sources—parents, school, neighborhood, and peers—can be significant and that young people benefit from indirect as well as direct sources of support.

Family Support, Positive Family Communication, and Parent Involvement in Schooling

Parental support has been associated with positive outcomes such as lower levels of substance abuse, delinquency, and early sexual intercourse, higher lev-els of academic performance, and better mental health. Support from parents (including parent involvement in schooling) has been associated, directly or indirectly, with:

- **Lower substance abuse** (particularly alcohol use) among middle to late adolescents (Anderson & Henry, 1994; Bailey & Hubbard, 1990; Barnes, 1984; Barnes & Farrell, 1992; Bogenschneider, Small, & Tsay, 1997; Brook, Whiteman, & Finch, 1993; Cochran & Bø, 1989; Coombs, Paulson, & Richardson, 1991; Hawkins, Catalano, & Miller, 1992; Kumpfer & Turner, 1990/1991; Lempers, Clark-Lempers, & Simons, 1989; Moore & Glei, 1995; Resnick et al., 1997; Whitbeck, Hoyt, Miller, & Kao, 1992; Wills, McNamara, Vaccaro, & Hirky, 1996; Wills, Vaccaro, & McNamara, 1992; Windle, 1992);
- **Higher adolescent self-esteem, self-concept, academic self-concept, self-worth, positive feelings about self, and perceived competence** (Blyth & Traeger, 1988; Cauce, Felner, & Primavera, 1982; Coates, 1985; Cotterell, 1992; Cotton & Savard, 1982; Delaney, 1996; Grolnick & Slowiaczek, 1994; Lackovic-Grgin, Dekovic, & Opacic, 1994; Lamborn, Mounts, Steinberg, & Dornbusch, 1991; Leung & Leung, 1992; Nielsen & Metha, 1994; Palmer, Dakof, & Liddle, 1993; Ryan, Stiller, & Lynch, 1994; Shulman, 1993; Wenz-Gross, Siperstein, Untch, & Widaman, 1997; Williams & McGee, 1991; Zimmerman, Salem, & Maton, 1995);
- **More positive development of other psychosocial traits such as lower acceptance of unconventionality** (not adhering to social norms in areas such as substance use, school achievement, sexual behavior, delinquency) (Brook et al., 1993); **less anxiety and depression** (Delaney, 1996; Eccles, Early, Fraser, Belansky, & McCarthy, 1997; Harter, Marold, & Whitesell, 1992; Hartos &

Power, 1997; Herman-Stahl & Petersen, 1996; Lempers et al., 1989; McKeowan et al., 1997; Procidano, Guinta, & Buglione, 1988; Resnick et al., 1997; Steinberg, Mounts, Lamborn, & Dornbusch, 1991; Walker & Greene, 1987; Whitbeck, Conger, & Kao, 1993; Windle, 1992; Zimmerman, Salem, and Maton, 1995); **less psychological distress or a "buffering" of the effects of stress** (DuBois, Felner, Brand, Adan, & Evans, 1992; Eisenberg & McNally, 1993; Frey & Röthlisberger, 1996; Hershberger & D'Augelli, 1995); **fewer "false" presentations of self to others** (Harter, Marold, Whitesell, & Cobbs, 1996); **greater ego and identity development and identity exploration** (Cooper, Grotevant, & Condon, 1983; Grotevant & Cooper, 1985, 1986; Hauser et al., 1984; Palmer et al., 1993); **less aggressive conflict resolution** (Kashani & Shepperd, 1990); **greater prosocial values and moral reasoning** (Kasser, Ryan, Zax, & Sameroff, 1995; Eisenberg & McNally, 1993; Walker & Taylor, 1991); **greater psychosocial competence, interpersonal relationships, or social self-efficacy** (Kurdek & Fine, 1994; Mallinckrodt, 1992; McFarlane, Bellissimo, & Norman, 1995; Peterson & Leigh, 1990; Romig & Bakken, 1992); and **greater sense of coherence in life** (things will work out well) (Margalit & Eysenck, 1990);

- **Less delinquency and school misconduct** (Barnes & Farrell, 1992; Bogenschneider et al., 1997; Cochran & Bø, 1989; Davey, 1993; Eccles, Early, Fraser, Belansky, & McCarthy, 1997; Henderson & Berla, 1994; Kurdek, Fine, & Sinclair, 1995; Lamborn et al., 1991; Moore & Glei, 1995; Smith & Krohn, 1995; Steinberg et al., 1991; Vazsonyi & Flannery, 1997; Wang, Fitzhugh, Westerfield, & Eddy, 1995; Warr, 1993); **fewer eating disorders** (Leon, Fulkerson, Perry, & Dube, 1994); **less casual, unprotected sexual intercourse** (St. Lawrence, Brasfield, Jefferson, Allyene, & Shirley, 1994; Whitbeck et al., 1993); and **greater self-efficacy for using condoms** (Hutchinson & Cooney, 1998); and

- **Higher school engagement, motivation, aspirations, attendance, personal responsibility for achievement; more hours spent on homework, higher grades, and higher standardized test scores** (Astone & McLanahan, 1991; Bisnaire, Firestone, & Rynard, 1990; Bogenschneider et al., 1997; Cauce et al., 1982; Chavkin & Gonzalez, 1995; Christenson, Rounds, & Gorney, 1992; Cotton & Savard, 1982; Davey, 1993; Eccles, Early, et al., 1997; Epstein, 1987; Feldman & Wentzel, 1990; Glaser, Larsen, & Salem

Nichols, 1992; Glasgow, Dornbusch, Troyer, Steinberg, & Ritter, 1997; Grolnick & Slowiaczek, 1994; Harnish, 1985; Henderson & Berla, 1994; Keith, Reimers, Fehrmann, Pottebaum, & Aubey, 1986; Kurdek et al., 1995; Lamborn et al., 1991; Marjoribanks, 1990; Masselam, Marcus, & Stunkard, 1990; McDonald & Sayger, 1996; Otto & Atkinson, 1997; Palmer et al., 1993; Paulson, 1994; Rosenthal & Feldman, 1991; Ryan et al., 1994; Scott & Scott, 1989; Steinberg, Lamborn, Darling, Mounts, & Dornbusch, 1994; Steinberg, Lamborn, Dornbusch, & Darling, 1992; Steinberg et al., 1991; Steinberg, Elmen, & Mounts, 1989; Stevenson & Baker, 1987; Swick, 1988; Taylor, Phillip, Hinton, & Wilson, 1992; Visser, 1987; Wang et al., 1995; Wentzel, 1994; Yap & Enoki, 1994).

Caring School Climate

Not surprisingly, support provided by the school environment has been associated with better academic performance; it also has been linked to better mental health and lower delinquency among adolescents. Support provided by teachers and the school environment has been associated, directly or indirectly, with:

- **Higher grades, engagement, attendance, expectations and aspirations, sense of scholastic competence; fewer school suspensions; and nondelayed progression through grades** (Davis & Jordan, 1994; DuBois, Felner, Meares, & Krier, 1994; Eccles, Lord, Roeser, Barber, & Jozefowicz, 1997; Eccles & Harold, 1993; Felner, Ginter, & Primavera, 1982; Goodenow, 1993a, 1993b; Gottfredson & Gottfredson, 1989; Graham, Updegraff, Tomascik, & McHale, 1997; Grossman & Garry, 1997; Hawkins & Lam, 1987; Hayward & Tallmadge, 1995; Lunenburg & Schmidt, 1989; Marjoribanks, 1990; Maryland State Department of Education, 1990; Noguera, 1995; Patrick, Hicks, & Ryan, 1997; Roeser, Midgley, & Urdan, 1996; Rutter, 1983; Ryan et al., 1994);
- **Higher self-esteem, higher self-concept** (Felner et al., 1982; Hoge, Smit, & Hanson, 1990; Knight, 1991; Ryan et al., 1994; Simmons & Blyth, 1987);
- **Less anxiety and depression, lower feelings of loneliness** (DuBois et al., 1992; Graham et al., 1997; Pretty, Andrewes, & Collett, 1994); and
- **Less substance use** (DuBois et al., 1994; Eggert & Herting, 1991; Grossman & Garry, 1997; Hawkins, Catalano, & Miller, 1992).

Other Adult Relationships and Caring Neighborhood

Although there is much less research on neighborhood support than on support offered by families or schools, the research does suggest that support from adults in the neighborhood can lower adolescents' substance use and exposure to violence, as well as strengthen their connection to school, academic performance, and helping behaviors. Support provided by other adults, neighbors, and the neighborhood environment has been associated, directly or indirectly, with:

- **Higher grades, more liking of school, higher IQ score, higher school completion rates, and higher math test scores** (Cochran & Bø, 1989; Coon, Carey, & Fulker, 1992; Duncan, 1994; Entwisle, Alexander, & Olson, 1994; Wenz-Gross et al., 1997; Werner, 1993);
- **More prosocial behavior and fewer behavior problems** (Cochran & Bø, 1989; Svedhem, 1994);
- **Reduced experience of violence** (Levine & Rosich, 1996; Melton, 1992; Sampson, Raudenbush, & Earls, 1997);
- **Less substance use** (Hawkins, Catalano, & Miller, 1992; Werner, 1993);
- **Fewer feelings of loneliness, anxiety, or depression** (Pretty et al., 1994; Rhodes, Ebert, & Fischer, 1992); and
- **Greater self-esteem, hopes for the future, and cheerfulness** (Talmi & Harter 1998).

Variations in Findings

Although the research certainly has confirmed the significant positive role that parent, school, and neighborhood support can play in adolescents' lives, findings from these studies have by no means been universal. Some studies have found that parental support did not predict better school performance (DuBois et al., 1992; Reynolds & Gill, 1994), lower adolescent drug use (McGee, 1992), or higher self-esteem (Paterson, Pryor, & Field, 1995). In other studies, support has been found to be more important for some youth than others. For example, Margalit and Eysenck (1990) found that Israeli male adolescents perceived more coherence in their lives if their parents emphasized their personal growth more than support, whereas females felt their lives were more coherent if parents emphasized support more than personal growth. In another study, DuBois et al. (1994) found that high levels of school support were related to better grades and lower alcohol use only among youth with multiple disadvantages (such as living in poverty and experiencing family breakup), not among youth who had no serious disadvantages in their lives.

Finally, studies occasionally report a finding contrary to what is expected, given the weight of the research. For example, Knight (1991) found that support from teachers had a slight negative relationship with motivation among 6th graders; Knight reasoned that if these young adolescents saw themselves defined as needing extra help, that self-perception could have lowered their expectations of themselves and lessened their motivation to try. Similarly, Otto and Atkinson (1997) found that a high level of parental monitoring of the schoolwork of high school juniors was associated with lower grades and test scores. These older teenagers may have perceived monitoring not as an expression of support but as evidence of overcontrol and perhaps of their own inabilities, again contributing to lessened motivation to succeed.

Another contrary example is found in Weist, Freedman, Paskewitz, Proescher, and Flaherty (1995), who reported that for a small sample of 9th graders, family cohesion (i.e., emotional closeness) seemed to protect males from stress, but not females; in fact, family cohesion was associated with greater vulnerability in females. Cauce et al. (1982) also reported that for Black females in low-income families (but not for males or White females in low-income families), high levels of family support were related to poorer scholastic self-concepts, contrary to what we might expect. Although these studies did not address it, one possibility for these odd findings was posed in Grotevant and Cooper's (1985) research: Adolescent ego development may be best fostered when adolescents are in the process of connecting to fathers and separating from mothers. Perhaps overresponsive mothers smother females in their reaching for autonomy and so prevent optimal development of a strong identity and self-efficacy that is critical to resilience. On the other hand, it may be that close identification with their low-income families makes it harder for females to separate from them by doing well in school, an accomplishment that will likely lead them out of low-income status.

Context Matters

These examples of somewhat inconsistent or even contrary studies are a helpful reminder that even in those studies reporting significant positive associations of support with a variety of desirable outcomes, context matters. Although our general conclusions about the strong positive benefit of support seem sound, it would be wrong to conclude that the same kind of support that has a positive impact for a 6th-grade male with no serious life disadvantages would necessarily and inevitably have the same impact when provided to a 10th-grade female trying to overcome multiple disadvantages. Moreover, as Jessor (1993) noted, adolescents are simultaneously embedded in multiple contexts—specifically, family, school, and neighborhood—and the impact of these contexts on adolescents varies both with the degree of interaction among the contexts and with the adolescent's developmental stage.

In looking specifically at the effects of gender, race/ethnicity, and other similar variables, it is important to keep in mind that these variables are interacting in ways that may not always be clear. Each individual adolescent's development is complex.

Gender   Overall, the research suggests the power of the six support assets for most youth, but there seem to be some differences as well. For example, females and younger adolescents (usually measured in the 5th–7th grades) seem to be more positively affected by support and connectedness in general, especially by parent support (Bailey & Hubbard, 1990; Clark-Lempers, Lempers, & Ho, 1991; Cotterell, 1992; Eccles, Early, et al., 1997; Leon et al., 1994; Margalit & Eysenck, 1990; Windle, 1992). Females also seem to have larger possible networks of support, including more adults and more connections across family, school, and neighborhood (Coates, 1987; Svedhem, 1994). Some research, however, suggests that males may be even more sensitive to and helped by support offered outside the family, in the neighborhood and wider community (Entwisle et al., 1994; Werner, 1993).

Sometimes the differences are subtle. One study reported that a high level of family cohesion was related to more intimate friendships only for females, but that for males, satisfaction with the level of family cohesion was the more critical factor (Romig & Bakken, 1992). Females do seem to suffer more in the transition to a junior high setting (Simmons & Blyth, 1987), but school can offer an important source of support for both females and males. Goodenow (1993a) found that teacher support was more important for females' motivation than for males'. On the other hand, Williams and McGee (1991) found that school attachment had a positive relationship to males' assessments of their personal strengths but not to females' assessments of their own strengths. The two studies may have come to different conclusions because one was about the effect of a personal relationship with teachers, whereas the other concerned attachment to or caring about school more generally. It may be that the personal relationship with teachers is more influential for females and the quality of the broader school environment more important for males. This would be consistent with other findings (which we report later) that suggest males are more affected by community-level factors such as poverty and crime than are females.

Race and ethnicity   There are fewer studies on differences in support by race or ethnicity than by gender, and the available studies focus largely on Latina/ Latino and African American youth. One large study, however, suggested that attachment to parents, although important for White, African American, and Latina/Latino youth, is particularly important in helping prevent delinquency among Latina/Latino youth: Level of attachment to parents explained twice as much of the delinquency of Latina/Latino youth as it did the delinquency of African American and White youth (Smith & Krohn, 1995). In contrast, another large study (Vazsonyi & Flannery, 1997) reported that family and school support influences were important for both White and Latina/Latino youth in preventing delinquency, but that family support was somewhat more important for White youth and school support somewhat more important for Latina/Latino youth. Finally, living in a neighborhood where proportionately more residents are of one's own race or ethnic background has been found to be a better predictor of the mental health of Latina/Latino youth than of White or African American youth (McLeod & Edwards, 1995). The researchers concluded that for African American youth, a high proportion of African Americans in the same neighborhood was associated with higher rates of poverty, and the detrimental effects of high poverty rates outweighed the advantages of a homogeneous culture. In contrast, rates of poverty among different Latina/Latino populations were more varied. For these youth, having a high concentration of other Latinas/Latinos in their neighborhood potentially may offer a net positive: a familiar cultural oasis within the dominant majority culture.

Other contextual variables   Another example of the complexity of the support assets is provided by Gauze, Bukowski, Aquan-Assee, and Sippola (1996). They found that closeness and flexibility within a family played a bigger role in young adolescents' feelings of personal competence for youth who did not have close friends than those family dynamics did for youth with close friends. Family support did not have as large an impact on youth feeling competent if they already had close friends. Similarly, Wenz-Gross et al. (1997) found that family emotional support lessened depression only if young adolescents were highly stressed in their relationships with friends, and that problem-solving help from nonfamily adults increased positive feelings about school only for adolescents whose relationships with teachers were highly stressful. In the absence of high stress, those influences were not significant. Finally, Hershberger and D'Augelli (1995) studied gay, lesbian, and bisexual teenagers and young adults, and reported that family support helped lessen the effects of low levels of victimization (e.g., verbal taunts) on mental health, but did not sustain the mental health of gay youth in the face of physical aggression or other forms of discrimination.

Moreover, what is considered "supportive" may best be determined from the perspective of those receiving the support, not those providing it; one study found that it was adolescents' reports of parent support, not parents' reports, that were related to various positive outcomes (Paulson, 1994). Consider also the illustration provided by Davis and Jordan's (1994) large study of African American males followed from the 8th grade to the 10th grade: Teachers whose African American male students got the highest grades in middle school had the highest expectations for their students' success and assigned the greatest amount of homework. In high school, the highest-scoring Black male teens had teachers who had a strong sense of personal responsibility for the quality of their teaching. At both middle and high school levels, the students perceived the teachers' behaviors—assigning lots of homework and being concerned with quality—as supportive and caring, although they were not necessarily "supportive" in the sense of being warm, nurturing, or emotionally available. This study suggests how the 40 assets often operate together and how difficult it can be to tease out the impact of a single asset. Being forced by their teachers to do a lot of homework (a commitment-to-learning asset) and to meet high teacher standards (a boundaries-and-expectations asset) led these students to define their teachers as caring (a support asset). Thus, "support" from teachers may not be neatly separable from those other assets.

How Support Works

Young people want support. In a study of 15 local affiliates of national organizations such as Girls, Inc., the YMCA, and Boys and Girls Clubs, Gambone and Arbreton (1997) reported that one of the main reasons youth participated in the programs of those organizations, beyond having fun and learning a lot, was that "adults here care about me" (p. 43). Similarly, in a review of research on young adolescents and schools, Kramer (1992) observed that the need for love and belonging so frequently described as crucial in psychological writings and research was "startlingly apparent" (p. 42) in what young people said best defined a good school: nurturing relationships. And yet our own data from 6th- through 12th-grade youth (see Figure 1), as well as other research, suggest that only a minority of young people actually experience abundant support across all parts of their lives—in their families, their schools, and their communities. Adults also sense that youth do not receive enough support. A Search Institute study of more than 500 religious youth workers, for example, found that 65% thought it an important goal of youth work to build caring relationships among youth and adults in the congregation, but just 25% thought they actually did very well in this respect (Roehlkepartain & Scales, 1995). The National Education Longitudinal Study of 8th graders (National Center for Education Statistics, 1990) reported mixed data. On the one hand, about 66% of students said teachers and students got along, discipline was fair, teachers were interested in students, teachers really listened to them, and similar indications of a caring and supportive school climate. On the other hand, nearly half of the students said that their parents never or seldom talked with them about what they were learning at school (Cross, 1991).

Family Support and Positive Family Communication

Parental support is most often conceptualized as having several dimensions: warmth, firmness, and democracy (Steinberg et al., 1989). Supportive parents (also called "authoritative") are emotionally close with their children, communicate openly with them, engage them in democratic discussions about family rules and decisions, and provide clear but sometimes negotiable boundaries and norms. (For more on parenting styles, see Table 6.) However, Steinberg et al. (1991) reported that less than 20% of a sample of 10,000 9th- through 12th-grade students said they had such supportive parents.

Adolescents who see their parents airing disagreements "within a basic context of connectedness" (Grotevant & Cooper, 1986, p. 94) are aided in their own identity formation. Unfortunately, marriages in distress are likely to contribute to problems among adolescents, in part because when parents are engaged in frequent conflict, adolescents perceive them as being more hostile to them personally. Adolescents in such situations tend to have more depression, anxiety, delinquency, and aggressiveness than adolescents whose parents are not in marital conflict (Harold & Conger, 1997).

Table 6. Descriptions of Common Parenting Styles

Over the past 25 years, a rich trove of research has yielded several commonly accepted descriptions of parenting styles that repeatedly are associated with differing youth outcomes:

- **Authoritarian** parents are strict to a fault, overemphasizing control of their adolescent and infrequently demonstrating warmth.

- **Permissive** parents show plenty of love but also are quite lax in their rule setting and enforcing.

- **Authoritative** parents, in contrast, are both firm and loving. They encourage their adolescent's emerging autonomy, but through gradual expansion of the decisions they allow youth to make, not through indulgence. As Glasgow et al. (1997) expressed it:

  Authoritative parents maintain an effective balance between high levels of demandingness and responsiveness. These parents establish and firmly enforce rules and standards for their children's behavior. They consistently monitor conduct and use nonpunitive methods of discipline when rules are violated. Socially responsible and mature behavior is expected and reinforced. Authoritative parents are also warm and supportive. They encourage bi-directional communication, validate the child's individual point of view, and recognize the rights of both parents and children. (p. 508)

Supportive parents are those who, in their children's perceptions, are close, intimate, nurturing, and less likely to be punitive than parents rated as non-supportive (Eisenberg & McNally, 1993; Lackovic-Grgin et al., 1994; Scott & Scott, 1989). Supportive parents may offer protection to adolescents both by blocking the effects of exposure to risk and by strengthening other protective factors or developmental assets. For example, supportive parents may diminish the influence of drug-using friends on an adolescent. Alternatively, supportive parents may strengthen an adolescent's belief in and adherence to conventional norms (e.g., abstaining from alcohol and other drugs, achieving in school), which has been shown to prevent drug use (Hawkins, Catalano, & Miller, 1992). Another possibility is that parenting style may enhance adolescent ego development, which in turn is related to positive outcomes. Best, Hauser, and Allen (1997) supported the notion of complex relationships among parenting style, adolescent development, and outcomes in their longitudinal study of 14-year-olds followed until they were age 25. Both educational attainment (number of years of schooling) and resiliency were predicted by parents' simultaneous encouragement of adolescent autonomy and connection. The effect of child-rearing style on both educational attainment and resiliency was mediated, however, by the adolescent's level of ego development (impulse control, cognitive complexity, interpersonal style). That is, when the adolescent's level of ego development was included, the influence of parenting style decreased, even losing its significance as a predictor of resiliency. Hartos and Power (1997) also reported that parental closeness could operate to reduce adolescents' anxiety and depression. In their study of 9th graders, mothers generally had little idea how much stress their adolescent children were experiencing. Nonetheless, adolescents reported better adjustment if their mothers communicated more with them and were more aware of the stressors on their children. Although single parents may face more challenges financially and in balancing work and family life, parents who are married are not automatically able to give their children the support they need. Moreover, one study found that adolescents who perceived that their parents had a poor relationship—whether the parents are married or divorced—had lower life satisfaction, greater sense of failure, and higher anxiety, regardless of the support they received from parents (Grossman & Rowat, 1995).

Supportive parents promote the successful developmental maturation of their adolescent children by being both separate from them and connected to them. Some evidence suggests that adolescent ego development is promoted by fathers and adolescents increasing their mutual connectedness while mothers and adolescents increase their mutual separation (Grotevant & Cooper, 1985). This line of research acknowledges that adolescents have an impact on parent behavior, so that a cycle of either positive or negative communication and relatedness is created: Adolescents whose parents are both warm and demanding have greater social competence, and parents (and others) respond to this greater social competence with still more warmth, caring, and effective negotiation of rules (Peterson & Leigh, 1990). Similarly, adolescent openness to parents' influence appears to contribute to parents' feeling competent. In turn, children of parents who feel competent report more parental monitoring and emotional responsiveness, and fewer attempts at psychological control, which is the profile of an authoritative parent (Bogenschneider et al., 1997).

Within this atmosphere of open communication, acceptance, and emotional warmth, adolescents may be more likely to talk and to express opinions. This elaboration of ideas may be an important way adolescents develop their identities and personal competencies (Hauser et al., 1984). Several other studies suggest that families promote positive adolescent outcomes when they have a balance of cohesiveness (feeling connected and being expressive) and adaptability (being flexible). Just as families that are overpermissive or excessively strict produce negative outcomes, families that are too close (enmeshed) or too flexible (chaotic) also fail to provide the optimal structure for positive adolescent development (Gauze et al., 1996; Masselam et al., 1990; Walker & Greene, 1987). Those parenting styles have both direct and indirect effects. For example, a large study of high school students (Glasgow et al., 1997) found that non-authoritative parents seemed to contribute to a feeling in adolescents that their poor school achievement stemmed from low ability or external causes rather than from their own inadequate effort. The more the youth felt a lack of responsibility for their academic success, the less engaged they were and the less homework they did one year later.

Parent Involvement in Schooling

Unquestionably, parental support affects adolescents' perceptions about their own abilities; these perceptions in turn can facilitate or impede progress in school. For example, in studying 6th-grade males, Wentzel (1994) and Feldman and Wentzel (1990) demonstrated that parental support (defined in these studies as warm parental control) indirectly promoted better grades by building sons' self-restraint and self-worth and by decreasing their emotional distress at school. Because of their parents' child-rearing practices, those males were better behaved, less anxious, and more confident, and so more ready to learn. Teachers may be motivated to give extra attention to those children, and may feel more capable as teachers, which circularly increases children's sense that teachers care for them and sustains their motivation to learn. A longitudinal study of nearly 600 children followed from preschool through 6th grade also concluded that mothers' calm discussion of conflicts, as well as the level of their concern and involvement in their child's life, predicted academic performance in grade 6 (Pettit, Bates, & Dodge, 1997). Steinberg et al. (1989) also concluded that warm, democratic, and firm parents seemed to promote in adolescents a positive attitude and belief about their ability to achieve. As part of the developing autonomy they are nurturing in their adolescent child, those parents help the adolescent acquire a healthy orientation to work, a quality that is related to doing well in school.

When parents more specifically provide support by becoming involved in their child's schooling, the positive effects can be profound. Although most of the research has been with elementary school children, the data from studies of middle and high school–age youth are quite similar. Palmer et al. (1993), after reviewing scores of studies, concluded that parent involvement promotes student success at all grade levels. Furthermore, they noted that almost the entire typically strong association between a family's socioeconomic status and children's academic achievement disappears when parent involvement enters the picture: Poor parents who are highly involved with helping their children succeed academically promote academic success almost to the degree that wealthier parents do. Chavkin and Gonzalez (1995) concluded that parent involvement was twice as predictive of academic learning as socioeconomic status. More recent analysis of National Assessment of Educational Progress data comparing 1973 math scores with 1992 scores has indicated that the scores of Latino youth increase significantly, even while the median Latino family income is shrinking (Lawton, 1998). The researchers attributed the finding in part to greater involvement by these parents.

Paulson (1994) also concluded that although child-rearing style (e.g., authoritative) was a more powerful predictor of student achievement, levels of parent involvement in schooling added significantly to the researchers' ability to predict levels of student achievement. Much of the effect of parent involvement may be indirect. For example, one study found that parent involvement had no direct effect on seniors' achievement, but had a strong indirect effect through the influence parents had on the time students spent on their homework (Keith et al., 1986). Moreover, differences in parenting styles are still critical, even for parents who are already engaged with their children's schooling. A large study of adolescents and school achievement found that involvement by nonauthoritative parents (those who were either too rigid or too permissive) actually weakened the positive effects of parent involvement on student engagement and achievement: Achievement was much more likely when the parents who were involved also had a more generally authoritative style of child rearing (Steinberg et al., 1992). Although the measurement of parent involvement has often included parental attendance at school functions, the much more important attitudes and behaviors seem to be having high expectations for their children's success, encouraging and expressing interest in what their children are doing at school, monitoring and talking with their children about homework and school activities, making sure there is a place to study at home, making sure children attend school, and encouraging children to read (Cotton & Savard, 1982; Epstein, 1987; Grolnick & Slowiaczek, 1994; Henderson & Berla, 1994; Palmer et al., 1993; Wang et al., 1995; Yap & Enoki, 1994).

Other Adult Relationships

In general, Scales and Gibbons's review (1996) reports that most youth prefer parents and peers as sources of support and that the majority of youth can at least name an adult they could turn to for help if they need it. Youth of color and those from low-income backgrounds also seem to use extended family members such as grandparents, aunts, uncles, and cousins as sources of support more than do White youth or youth who are financially better off. Moreover, females seem to have larger networks with more unrelated adults than do males and to have closer relationships with those adults. Further, on some issues, such as school concerns or sexual issues, nonparental adults often are preferred sources of advice. The literature indicates that while unrelated adults such as teachers, coaches, and clergy (e.g., ministers, priests, and rabbis) are listed by only a small proportion of youth as globally important sources of support, they become important in particular settings and for meeting specific needs. The literature is mixed about whether relationships with other adults become less or more common as youth get older.

Talmi and Harter (1998) showed how social support from other adults interacts with adolescent self-perceptions to contribute to positive outcomes. Among more than 300 mostly White middle school students, the young adolescents who had the highest self-worth, most positive hopes for the future, and the most cheerfulness were those who had social support from "special adults." They also had higher perceived competence in domains other adolescents feel are important, such as scholastic competence, behavior, physical appearance, and peer likability. The researchers concluded that examining only social support is inadequate; one must simultaneously look at other variables that affect adolescent adjustment.

Caring School Climate

The support adults provide to adolescents at school is similar, but not identical, to the support adults provide in neighborhoods: being caring and friendly, as well as holding high expectations for youth's behavior. Largely because of the

Carnegie Council on Adolescent Development's influential report, *Turning Points* (1989), which highlighted the vulnerabilities of young adolescents, most of the recent research we cite on school support and youth refers to the middle school years. Although teachers are infrequently mentioned when adolescents are asked to list important sources of support (Scales & Gibbons, 1996), their influence and that of the school environment are clear and consistent in numerous studies. A "caring" or supportive teacher is one who has high expectations for students' success, is considered "fair" in dealing with a variety of students, is friendly and approachable, and shows care and concern about the student as a person. These teachers create a climate in which students feel respected and valued, and have a psychological sense of membership or belonging in the school (Goodenow, 1993a, 1993b). Teachers who are controlling and punitive have students who are less satisfied with school and less committed to their class work (Lunenburg & Schmidt, 1989). In fact, one study reported that young adolescents' confidence in their ability to relate to their teachers is itself related to students' confidence in their ability to do academic work, especially among females (Patrick et al., 1997).

Supportive teachers also have a high degree of confidence in their own ability as teachers: A profound research finding is that high-achieving young people moving from elementary school to junior high school are likely to drop dramatically in their motivation and school performance if they also go from having teachers who believe in themselves to teachers who are less confident (Eccles, Lord, et al., 1997). Unfortunately, 7th-grade teachers in general, compared with 6th-grade teachers, are seen by young adolescents as less supportive, friendly, and fair. Seventh graders are more likely to be controlled, insufficiently challenged academically, and tracked into high- and low-ability groups; all these practices weaken young people's sense that teachers and schools "care" for them (Eccles & Harold, 1993). The result is that young adolescents may begin to "turn away from the adults in the school as a source of emotional support" (Eccles, Lord, et al., 1997, p. 312).

On the other hand, students in middle schools that have teacher-based advisory programs and small teacher-student ratios feel more positive about school, have fewer mental health and behavior problems, and achieve at higher levels (Felner et al., 1997). Teacher teaming, another practice intended to promote student bonding to school, has been found to have a greater effect on students in schools with low socioeconomic status, where at least 25% of the students receive reduced-price or free lunch (Arhar & Kromrey, 1993). The researchers concluded that the resources available to students at schools with higher average family socioeconomic status provided greater support for student growth. The teaming practice had little effect in that environment, whereas it provided welcomed additional support resources for students in the more impoverished environment.

Caring neighborhood　The research on the effects of neighborhood support is neither as plentiful nor as conclusive as studies on parental and school support. Indeed, the National Research Council's Committee on Youth Development concluded recently that the study of neighborhood influences was a field "in its infancy" (National Research Council, 1996, p. 16) and that cause-and-effect relationships among neighborhood factors and adolescent development had not yet been conclusively identified. Nevertheless, some studies suggest the potential role that neighborhoods can play in youth development.

Blyth and Leffert (1995) reported that vulnerable youth in the healthiest communities studied (communities with lower rates of adolescent problem behavior such as substance use) had better outcomes than vulnerable youth in the least healthy communities. The reason for this result, however, seemed to be that youth in the healthiest communities more often reported constructive after-school activities, a caring school environment, and connections to a religious organization. These are all situations in which youth can have positive relationships with supportive adults (one of the six support assets), and for many youth, those relationships occur within their neighborhoods. Duncan (1994) studied longitudinal data to see how neighborhood affected school completion rates; while family characteristics such as family income and mother's education were "consistently" more powerful in explaining school completion than any neighborhood characteristics, the presence of affluent neighbors nevertheless had a significant additional positive contribution, especially for White males and for both White and Black females, a finding also reported by Brooks-Gunn, Guo, and Furstenberg (1993).

Barber and Olsen (1997) studied a diverse sample of more than 900 5th through 8th graders and found that only a little over 20% of 5th graders and a little over 10% of 8th graders had significant interaction at least weekly with neighbors, friends' parents, community leaders, or congregational leaders. Given these limited connections, it is not surprising that neighborhood connection was found to have little relationship to school grades, depression, or antisocial behavior among these youth. Blyth and Leffert (1995) reported that more pervasive effects on large numbers of youth could be seen only when the asset of a caring neighborhood was experienced by a relatively large proportion of youth (more than the 10–20% in this study).

Entwisle et al. (1994) looked at neighborhood effects on the gender gap that occurs in math scores between males and females by the end of middle school. They concluded that both White and African American males' math achievement responded positively to higher median neighborhood income and higher average levels of parents' education. They interpreted their data to suggest that males were more cognizant of and responsive to neighborhood resources than females. Pretty et al. (1994) found that although school support was a stronger predictor of adolescent loneliness, adolescents' sense of their neighborhood support was significantly associated with how lonely they felt. In this study, youth were less lonely if they had larger numbers of people in the neighborhood they felt they could count on.

In research on the effects of violent neighborhoods, studies not only highlight the deleterious effects of exposure to violence but also suggest that such neighborhood circumstances can be overcome. DuRant, Cadenhead, Pendergrast, Slavens, and Linder (1994) found that children who lived in a violent neighborhood but who had a strong sense of purpose in life were less likely to be violent themselves. In another study of elementary school children in a dangerous neighborhood, Richters and Martinez (1993) found that 80% of the small sample were not failing socially, emotionally, or academically and that "adaptational failure" was explained more by instability, guns, and drugs in the home than by violence in the community, as perceived by mother or child. Parents may be able to help their children overcome violent settings; when the neighborhood is viewed as dangerous, their parenting styles may be most effective if they are controlling and authoritarian rather than authoritative (Earls, McGuire, & Shay, 1994; Jarrett, 1995).

In a study of nearly 350 Chicago "neighborhood clusters," Sampson et al. (1997) showed that the neighborhood's rate of violence was strongly related to the likelihood of neighbors intervening if neighborhood children were misbehaving, as well as helping each other more generally (a measure of "collective efficacy"). A neighborhood's taking "informal social action" greatly reduced both the perceived and actual levels of violence, even in neighborhoods with significant concentrations of poverty. Collective efficacy also reduced the role of concentrated poverty, the proportion of immigrants in the neighborhood, and residential mobility in explaining perceived and actual violence. Unfortunately, collective efficacy may not be very common. In one South Carolina study, for example, residents were asked on a 7-point scale (with 7 being the highest) how involved they were with other people's children; the average resident scored just 2+ (Garbarino & Kostelny, 1994; also see Farkas et al., 1997).

Sampson (1997) found that neighborhood control (taking collective action against misbehavior, not levels of support or connection to youth) had positive effects on violence and delinquency. He also speculated that neighborhood effects on individual youth (e.g., reducing delinquent behavior) probably occurred indirectly, through how the neighborhood influenced friends, school, and family to more directly encourage positive behavior. While control and support have been found to be essentially independent measures of positive family functioning, Herman, Dornbusch, Herron, and Herting (1997) found those measures to be moderately correlated (correlations between .30 and .40) in a diverse sample of more than 3,900 12- to 18-year-olds. This finding poses challenges for researchers. If control and support are related to each other at the neighborhood level, then neighborhood regulation of young people's behavior may also be felt by youth as a form of caring. As a result, it would be difficult to separate the influence of neighborhood control from that of neighborhood support.

The Interactive Nature of Support

Clearly, when children and adolescents are developing positively, they have an adequate number of resources for support, they are satisfied with the support they receive, and they are surrounded by caring everywhere they turn—at home, in school, and in their neighborhoods. If they have these support assets, then they have a good chance of overcoming the tremendous odds against them if they are poor or live in drug-ridden, violent neighborhoods.

But the research shows that children and adolescents are not simply spectators in this process of "receiving" support. From birth, their individual temperaments put children on different developmental paths because of their capacity to attract support. Werner and Smith's classic 30-year study of children born on the Hawaiian island of Kauai (1992) illustrates these interactions. Infants who were cuddly and affectionate attracted more care and emotional support from parents, especially mothers, from ages 2 to 10 and were able—especially males— to build a larger network of supportive relationships within and outside the family than were infants who had less "easy" temperaments (i.e., who cried a lot or did not smile frequently). In turn, those with more emotional support and larger support networks in childhood had a greater sense of their scholastic competence at age 10, which in turn was associated with their having more sources they could turn to for help at age 18. The link between their infant behavior and their assets at age 18 was that their "individual dispositions led them to select or construct environments that, in turn, reinforced and sustained their active, outgoing dispositions and rewarded their competencies" (Werner, 1993, p. 508). Similarly, Stice and Gonzales (1998) studied more than 600 mostly White 16- to 19-year-olds, concluding that parental control and support were even more important influences on antisocial behavior and substance use when adolescents were temperamentally more emotionally negative, and especially when they had less self-control. Youth who had little self-control and poor parental control and support consistently had the worst levels of antisocial behavior and substance use in the study.

Adolescents can receive—and attract—direct support from parents, school, and neighbors. Price et al. (1990) pointed out, however, that the indirect support created by linkages across those arenas in their social environments may be equally important. Adults' consistent communication of norms and values and awareness of how adolescents are doing in their various areas of life, as well as conscious discussion among caring adults in different life domains about how best to reinforce and support one another, all may make it more likely that adolescents feel well supported by adults—that they experience a pervasive and enduring adult commitment to their well-being. For example, Henderson and Berla (1994) reported that when parents were highly involved with their children's schooling, teachers and parents had better opinions of each other, and teachers had higher expectations for student success, an important ingredient in students actually being successful at school. Similarly, Svedhem (1994) showed that young adolescents with behavior problems at school (especially males) were more likely to have "fragmented" networks, in which family, school, and neighbors in the young people's worlds did not know or connect with one another.

Many adolescents' support systems also change, necessitating caution in interpreting data from only one point in time. For example, Weigel, Devereux, Leigh, and Ballard-Reisch (1998) studied more than 350 9th through 12th graders and found that, over a seven-month period, the identity of the person who was their primary support provider changed for 42% of the adolescents. Youth who experienced such a change were under greater stress at both times in the study and were more likely initially to have chosen best friends or other family adults than parents as primary support providers. Students who chose parents did not perceive as much family conflict, were not under as much stress, and did not change their view of parents as primary support providers. Once again, the lesson is to look at a multitude of factors simultaneously to get a dynamic and accurate picture of the context in which support works for some adolescents differently than it does for others.

Adolescents' Experience of Support

Given the research showing the powerful impact of parent, school, and neighborhood support, it is shocking how few youth report that they receive such support. While the majority of youth surveyed by Search Institute during the 1996–97 school year say they receive love and support from the family, more than one third report that they do not experience even this basic asset. Even more troubling, instead of seeing the proportion of youth with support assets increasing, we see a significant decrease across the middle school and high school years

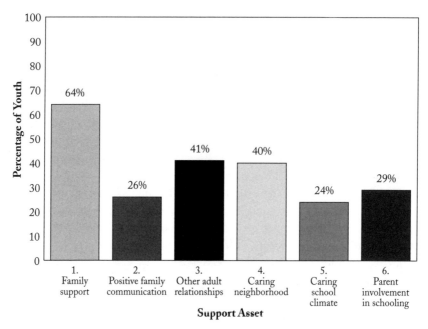

Figure 1 *Adolescents' experience of support: percentage of 6th- to 12th-grade students who report experiencing each of the support assets. From unpublished Search Institute data on youth in public and/or alternative schools who completed the institute's* Profiles of Student Life: Attitudes and Behaviors *survey during the 1996–97 school year;* N = 99,462 *students in 213 U.S. communities.*

in all but one of these six assets, that of adolescents' having several adults outside the family they can turn to. About three out of every four adolescents say they do not have positive family communication or a caring school or feel their parents are involved with their schooling. (See Figure 1.) Sixth graders almost always have the highest proportion of each of the assets, but even for them the asset in addition to family support that is experienced by half or more is caring neighbors, which 50% of 6th graders report having. So, even at the most positive developmental point, it is safe to say that the majority of adolescents in Search Institute's sample are not receiving adequate levels of support at home, in school, in their neighborhoods, or other places they spend time.

What Is Missing from Our Definition of Support?

Together, the six assets captured by our measures represent the support young people feel they are receiving or can potentially receive from their parents, their schools, and their neighborhoods. The research suggests that both the number of sources of support and the quality of support provided are important; these six measures cover both those dimensions. The measures appear to tap many of the same operational definitions found in the relevant research. From these perspectives, the measures appear adequate.

Nonetheless, the support assets may not be "pure" measures independent of and unrelated to other asset categories. For example, there is some potential conceptual and measurement overlap between the asset category of support and the asset category of boundaries and expectations. The research suggests that many youth consider high expectations by parents and teachers (and for some youth, by other adults) to be evidence of caring. In addition, some of the studies suggest that one way parents "support" the development of their adolescents is by becoming more separate from them while maintaining emotional connection and availability. For many adolescents, parents who are oversupportive may not be good. Moreover, the studies on the impact of parents' child-rearing practices suggest that levels of caring, control, and democracy are both independently important and systematically related. If a parent provides high levels of support but too little control (boundaries and expectations), then the child is merely indulged. Even though the support asset would appear to be high, only by examining support in relation to the level of boundaries parents provide can we appropriately conclude that parents are promoting positive development— we cannot draw that conclusion from examining support alone.

Finally, there are some possible domains or aspects of support that we do not measure. Support from peers shows up often in the research as important, although sometimes it has been found to help lessen and sometimes to increase the chances of negative outcomes. In the asset category of boundaries and expectations, we do measure whether the young person's best friends model responsible behavior, but this is not the same as whether they are perceived to provide various kinds of support.

As we mentioned earlier, the research indicates that the style of interaction within a family is important. Whether a family exhibits balanced levels of cohesion and adaptability or is unbalanced to either extreme is related to a variety of positive academic, social-psychological, and behavioral outcomes. In addition, families that practice shared decision making, in which adolescents play a meaningful role, also are more likely to have youth who achieve those positive outcomes. Although we do not explicitly measure and examine the interaction of the qualities of family cohesiveness, adaptability, and decision making, they are indirectly reflected in two assets in the support category (family support and positive family communication), and in three assets in the category of boundaries and expectations (family boundaries, adult role models, and high expectations). Together, these reflect the characteristics of authoritative parenting (loving and firm, neither too strict nor too permissive) that have been found, among other positive outcomes, to promote academic achievement and self-esteem, and to reduce depression and high-risk behavior among youth.

Finally, we ask about support given to youth by the family, but not whether the parent(s) or family as a whole experience sufficient support—such as jobs, housing, food, child care, and education—so that parents are able to provide the support youth need. For example, Hunter (1997) studied a national sample of nearly 500 African American parents of children under 18. Just as the research shows that adolescents of color tend to call on extended family for support, so Hunter also discovered that for both Black mothers and fathers, grandmothers were a common source of child-care assistance and—especially for mothers—parenting advice: More than half of both mothers and fathers used grandmothers for help. We do not assess whether parents desire and use this kind of support.

Research also suggests that siblings can play an important role in adolescents' adjustment, a factor we do not measure. For example, Conger, Conger, and Scaramella (1997) reported that attempts by siblings to control 7th graders psychologically (make them feel guilty, criticize them, get into arguments with them) were associated with lower self-esteem and antisocial behaviors (and for males, depression) three years later.

Two other aspects of Search Institute's measure of support deserve a comment: school and neighborhood. A "caring" school climate clearly is important. While we do measure young people's perceptions of how caring a place their school is, what about the overall quality of the schools youth attend? We do not directly measure, for example, whether the schools young people attend are helping all children succeed academically, diminishing the achievement gap between low-income and middle- to upper-income youth, exceeding district, state, or national scores on normed tests, or other measures of school quality. We do not directly measure whether teachers have been specially trained to teach the age-group they teach, the degree to which the school uses recommended practices (such as teacher-based guidance programs, interdisciplinary curricula, cooperative learning, limited tracking), or similar indicators that a school is restructuring to promote higher achievement for all youth. It is unclear how much additional value would be added to our measurement of caring by having additional information on issues such as these. This kind of overall school quality is perhaps best approximated by looking at a measure made up of assets 5, 10, 12, and 16 (combining caring school climate, safety, school boundaries, and high expectations).

Finally, we do measure the degree to which young people feel many people in their neighborhood care about them. That is probably as good a measure of neighborhood support as any. As we summarized earlier, research does suggest the positive effects of neighborhood support, but the studies are neither as numerous nor as clear and consistent as they are for school or parent support as to what the effects are and what definition of a "caring" neighborhood makes the most conceptual and measurement sense.

Given these caveats, our six measures of support, separately and together, seem to have a reasonable degree of validity and can be considered an acceptable measure of perceived support.

How Can Support Be Built?

Support clearly is important for positive youth development, and too few youth seem to experience it. One of the challenges to building support for young people is simply lack of time. Young people today experience 10–12 hours less parental contact each week than in 1960, both because of the increase in divorce and because of the change in employment patterns that have occurred since then. Parents in the majority of two-parent families now are working for most of a child's first 18 years (Fuchs & Reklis, 1992). Although one study of single parenting concluded that the risk to children's well-being from living in single-parent families was attributable less to lack of time for supervision than to the conflicts involved in divorce and remarriage (Dawson, 1991), time may be more of an influence on parents' support and connectedness with children (Resnick et al., 1997). Csikszentmihalyi and Larson (1984) found that just 19% of an adolescent's week typically was spent with family and 2% with other adults, compared with 23% with classmates, 29% with friends, and 27% alone. Policies that would enable parents to spend more time with their adolescent children without losing job security or income may be crucial to any set of recommendations for building support for youth.

As adolescents mature, the time they spend with parents also can increasingly be a function of choice. Parents who use warm and democratic yet firm methods of child rearing seem to encourage their children to want to spend more time with them; this effect is especially significant for males (Fallon & Bowles, 1997). Providing family support that helps parents use effective child-rearing practices clearly is an important measure for strengthening the support youth can get from their parents.

In reviewing 26 qualitative studies on what contributes to resilience among African American youth from low-income families, Jarrett (1995) concluded that a process of "community bridging" stimulated by family was present in most cases. Typically observed in the lives of these resilient youth were supportive adult networks, limits that parents placed on going out into the community, stringent parental monitoring, and participation in adult-sponsored youth development activities. In other words, those families were trying to carve out what McLaughlin and Irby (1994) called "urban sanctuaries." In their study of 60 organizations reaching more than 24,000 young people, McLaughlin and Irby reported that sanctuaries have these attributes: a family-like environment in which the individual is valued and rules are clear; opportunities for active participation and real challenges; explicit program planning and assessment; a commitment to being youth driven; a belief that youth are resources to be nurtured, not problems to be solved; flexibility; "rootedness" in the local area; a tradition of challenging youth to develop competence; and active reaching out to those not yet connected.

It may seem too simple to state that organizations that want to provide support to youth have to have that as an explicit goal. Nonetheless, our study of religious youth workers (Scales et al., 1995) found that the congregations that were the most successful in keeping youth involved past bar or bat mitzvah or confirmation were those that deliberately focused on nurturing caring adult-youth relationships, as well as providing opportunities for youth service and dealing with values. Those supportive relationships didn't just happen; they formed because the congregation was committed to fostering them. Morrow and Styles (1995) pointed to an important component of successful adult-youth relationships in concluding that "prescriptive" adult-youth mentoring relationships (ones in which the adult had a specific goal, such as school success, and geared all interactions with the youth to achieving that goal) were actually less effective in achieving positive outcomes than "democratic" relationships, those based on the needs of the youth, which varied over time. Youth in those democratic relationships reported considerable feelings of support from their mentors—feelings not reported nearly as much by youth in the prescriptive mentoring relationships. This suggests that mentors need to be trained to accept and value youth for who they are, to guide them but to share with them decision making about activities, and to let the youth set the agenda for their relationship. In the end, those youth probably will feel more supported and be more successful in reaching the goals that both the youth and adult want them to attain. In a study of the Big Brothers/Big Sisters program, Tierney, Grossman, and Resch (1995) found that to be the case. Over the 18-month study, "littles" (young people paired with older mentors) who had that kind of friend rather than a "preacher" relationship with their mentors, and who had a high level of contact with those mentors (about 12 hours or more a month, on average), were significantly less likely than counterparts without those supportive relationships to start alcohol or other drug use, use physical violence, or skip school, and were more likely to feel competent about schoolwork, get better grades, and trust their parents.

Schools, too, need to create smaller learning communities that nurture caring relationships among teachers and students and that have developmentally responsive and challenging curriculum for all students. Felner et al. (1997) reported in a study of more than 15,000 middle school students that math, language, and reading achievement scores are highest for schools that fully implement recommended middle school practices. Among other steps, those schools promote caring by having teacher-student advisory periods four or five times a week, small teams of no more than 120 students or about 20–25 students per teacher, and four or five periods a week in which teachers on teams plan together. All this helps teachers really know and respond to their students.

Connell, Aber, and Walker (1995) have proposed that the key to promoting supportive sanctuaries wherever youth need them is to help neighborhoods develop networks of competent adults with shared values and norms. This is very similar to the observation by Price et al. (1990) that the indirect ties that bind families, schools, and neighborhoods—ties that develop through neighbors' talking with each other, learning each other's names and children's names and a little of what's going on in each other's lives, and helping each other out—are the usually invisible elements that take up where official programs leave off. Without them, even young people with access to formal positive youth development programs and services can experience significant gaps in the care and guidance they get from those around them. For those fortunate enough to experience both formal programs that build their support assets and the informal relationships that unite the adults in their worlds with a common purpose of nurturing the youth, the foundation has been set for the remaining developmental assets they need for success in life.

Conclusion

As youth navigate through the developmental changes of adolescence, perhaps no asset category is more important than support. At the most fundamental level, young people need to know that others care for them and want to help them, no matter how mightily those adolescents seem to be struggling for independence from adults. Support has both direct and indirect effects on a wide range of adolescent outcomes. Youth who feel supported achieve more, get into trouble less, enjoy better physical and mental health, and give more to others. The breadth of those associations strengthens the sense that support is a foundational asset category.

Selected Readings

Blyth, D. A., & Leffert, N. (1995). Communities as contexts for adolescent development: An empirical analysis. *Journal of Adolescent Research, 10,* 64–87.

Eccles, J. S., Lord, S. E., Roeser, R. W., Barber, B. L., & Jozefowicz, D. M. H. (1997). The association of school transitions in early adolescence with developmental trajectories through high school. In J. Schulenberg, J. L. Maggs, & K. Hurrelmann (Eds.), *Health risks and developmental transitions during adolescence* (pp. 283–320). Cambridge: Cambridge University Press.

Grotevant, H. D., & Cooper, C. R. (1986). Individuation in family relationships: A perspective on individual differences in the development of identity and role-taking skill in adolescence. *Human Development, 29,* 82–100.

Pettit, G. S., Bates, J. E., & Dodge, K. A. (1997). Supportive parenting, ecological context, and children's adjustment: A seven-year longitudinal study. *Child Development, 68,* 908–923.

Price, R. H., Cioci, M., Penner, W., & Trautlein, B. (April, 1990). *School and community support programs that enhance adolescent health and education* (Carnegie Council on Adolescent Development, Working Papers). Washington, DC: Carnegie Council on Adolescent Development.

Scales, P. C., & Gibbons, J. L. (1996). Extended family members and unrelated adults in the lives of young adolescents: A research agenda. *Journal of Early Adolescence, 16,* 365–389.

Smith, C., & Krohn, M. D. (1995). Delinquency and family life among male adolescents: The role of ethnicity. *Journal of Youth and Adolescence, 24,* 69–93.

Steinberg, L., Elmen, J. D., & Mounts, N. S. (1989). Authoritative parenting, psychosocial maturity, and academic success among adolescents. *Child Development, 60,* 1424–1436.

Steinberg, L., Mounts, N. S., Lamborn, S. D., & Dornbusch, S. M. (1991). Authoritative parenting and adolescent adjustment across varied ecological niches. *Journal of Research on Adolescence, 1,* 19–36.

Werner, E. E., & Smith, R. S. (1992). *Overcoming the odds: High risk children from birth to adulthood.* Ithaca, NY: Cornell University Press.

Young people are empowered
to the extent that they are seen
by others as resources, make
contributions to society, and feel
free of threats to their safety.

2

The Empowerment Assets

> Youth are segregated from adults by the economic and
> educational institutions created by adults, they are deprived
> of psychic support from persons of other ages, a psychic
> support that once came from the family, they are subordinate
> and powerless in relation to adults, and outsiders to the
> dominant social institutions. (Coleman, 1974, p. 125)

James Coleman wrote those words more than a generation ago, as chair of the
President's Panel on Youth. Yet the words still resonate with truth and accuracy.
Most young people today are not "empowered," even though, as Coleman also
noted then, they have "money, they have access to a wide range of communica-
tions media, and control of some, and they are relatively large in number" (p. 125).

What Is Empowerment?

Few terms have come to have so many different meanings as *empowerment*. The
word has been used to denote having a personal sense of feeling powerful (I am
empowered), as well as making others feel powerful (we empowered them). It
can mean helping people feel involved in a process (e.g., the "empowerment
evaluation" approach, which tries to equalize the decision-making relationship
between researchers and those studied), or it can describe a setting in which
power is developed (economic "empowerment zones," usually set up in urban

49

areas, that use tax breaks and other incentives to entice businesses to open or expand). Sometimes the help others offer to increase a person's or group's sense of empowerment is perceived simply as support, the caring and affirmation that bolsters strength, courage, and the will to succeed. At other times, however, attempts to increase others' sense of empowerment are perceived as patronizing and demeaning, and are seen as suggesting that a person, group, or neighborhood lacks the capacity to take control of her, his, or its own destiny. The result of deficit-oriented thinking in many low-income neighborhoods, for example, is that after years of efforts by well-meaning helpers to "empower" those communities with programs and services, "residents come to believe that their well-being depends upon being a client. They see themselves as people with special needs to be met by outsiders" (McKnight & Kretzmann, 1990, p. 1).

In contrast, effective community building "has always depended upon mobilizing the capacities and assets of a people and a place" (McKnight & Kretzmann, 1990, p. 17). Extending this thinking specifically to youth leads to a focus on empowerment as mobilizing young people's capacities and assets. To paraphrase Cardenas Ramirez (1992), who was talking about poor communities, empowerment in this sense would mean that adults trust that "solutions to" young people's "problems must be fashioned not for" them, "but with, of, and by" them (p. 55). Thus, adults empower youth when youth feel they have meaningful roles to play in their families, schools, and communities. *Empowerment* was perhaps best defined several years ago by a young adult, a recent college graduate: "experiences that make [youth] feel powerful" (Tate, 1991, p. 91).

Developmentally, adolescents are at a crossroads where the relative powerlessness of childhood intersects with the relative freedom of adulthood. Adolescents are attempting, as part of their development of a stable identity, to construct an understanding of themselves and their roles in the world. Although all children and adults must feel that others value them, in adolescence there is heightened importance for believing that one can make a contribution, play a meaningful role, and have a place in society where one fits. The essential tension between individuation and connection, between autonomy and dependence, can be profound during adolescence. Young people who feel they are valued generally and who feel they can make specific desirable contributions to society have achieved a healthy balance of those developmental pushes and pulls. The challenge for adults is explicitly to communicate their belief in the value of youth to youth themselves; too often, adults simply assume that youth know that adults value them. Moreover, adults need to provide opportunities for youth leadership and participation in school and community life that are truly young people's to direct—and that will not be taken over by adults if the process moves too slowly or if the ideas youth generate seem too naive and unrealistic. These are considerable challenges for many adults, even those specially trained in youth work.

Empowerment suggests the gradually increasing freedoms and responsibilities young people should acquire as they mature. Adults empower youth by ensuring that they have a chance to add their voices to decisions that affect them and that they have opportunities to define and act on the priorities in their lives. In short, youth who are empowered feel they can make a difference. Among the terms researchers associate with empowerment are *autonomy, self-regulation, roles, helping, giving, contributing, youth leadership, youth involvement,* and *youth participation.* (In contrast, terms associated with the absence of empowerment include *helplessness, violence,* and *threats.*)

In Search Institute's conceptualization, empowerment has several dimensions. (See Table 7.) Feeling empowered is not merely feeling capable of reaching individual goals or sufficiently powerful to resolve personal problems. Empowerment is also a social act.

Youth are empowered to the extent they feel valued, feel that others view them as resources, make contributions to a larger whole to which they belong, and feel free of fundamental physical and emotional threats to their safety.

Significantly, empowerment involves two levels of youth perceptions. One level is distinctly personal: how safe a youth feels and what kind of role the youth feels he or she has in making her or his community a better place in which to live. The other level is more abstract: how a young person perceives adults' views of youth generally. A young person might feel valued at home and in school, where he or she is known, but feel ignored or even treated with hostility by strangers in the community. This disparity between personal and general levels of feeling valued would diminish that young person's sense of empowerment and undermine her or his sense of connection to the broader community. Moreover, older youth might be more sensitive to any disparities between the personal and more general senses of empowerment because of their better-developed cognitive capacities.

Table 7. The Empowerment Assets	
Community values youth	Young person perceives that adults in the community value youth.
Youth as resources	Young people are given useful roles in the community.
Service to others	Young person serves in the community one hour or more per week.
Safety	Young person feels safe at home, at school, and in the neighborhood.

This example underscores the importance of a basic principle of asset development: All adults in the community have a role to play in empowering youth (Benson, 1997). If only those adults who already know a youth show that they value that young person or provide opportunities for her or him to contribute, then that young person is not fully connected to her or his community; moreover, the community is the poorer because it does not reap the full benefit of that young person's talents and interests. Indeed, as Chaskin and Hawley (1994) conceptualize it, caring is a two-way street of connectedness and mutuality, in which adults protect and invest in young people and in which young people themselves then "protect the rights and interests of others, and ultimately support the ongoing development of their social and civic communities" (p. 2).

"Safety" is listed as the fourth empowerment asset, but in terms of Abraham Maslow's framework of developmental needs (1962), safety is the most basic human need once adequate food, water, and shelter have been acquired. Basic needs must be met before it is possible for individuals to love, feel esteem, or in other ways realize their full potential. Ideally, every young person ought to be able to say, in her or his family, school, and neighborhood, "I am safe and secure." Research (some presented in Chapter 1, on support) does suggest that effective parenting can buffer some of the negative effects of living in a violent, dangerous neighborhood, but it is more difficult for children to compensate for unsafe neighborhoods if they are surrounded by threatening, "socially toxic environments" (Garbarino, 1995) in their families and schools.

The rest of the empowerment assets build on the degree of safety or toxicity children experience. If young people feel safe, valued, and have plentiful opportunities to contribute, including being able to help other people, then it is reasonable to expect that they will feel more connected, be more influenced by adult norms and expectations, and be more likely to be productive, caring citizens.

Summary of Research Findings

Our literature search produced relatively few quantitative studies of youth empowerment. Zeldin and Price (1995) noted that there are "few studies to monitor how youth are connected to their community" (p. 8). Maton (1990) asked youth about the "meaningful instrumental activity" they engaged in, such as how often youth contributed to the goals of a group they believed in, helped people in need, or made an important contribution—behaviors that suggest empowerment. Zeldin and Price (1995) posited that empowerment is participation in adult roles, such as leadership and advocacy, earned income, and service. All those activities speak to youth being of use, feeling valued, and helping others.

Much of the research literature, however, is anecdotal and exhortatory; it describes how youth ought to be empowered or discusses theoretically the developmental importance of young people feeling valued and useful. For example, an important report on youth who are not bound for college takes it for granted that young people who make decisions and solve problems "develop not only a sense of belonging and a strong ethic of responsibility, but also an understanding that they are accountable to themselves, their families, and their communities" (William T. Grant Foundation Commission on Work, Family, and Citizenship, 1988, p. 51). Similarly, projects or programs that enable youth to solve community problems are said to "give young people a chance to gain self-esteem, practice leadership, and direct their lives positively" (p. 52). Although those effects are quite reasonable to expect, only a handful of studies are cited in that report documenting such positive outcomes; none used an experimental research design with control groups.

The bulk of the studies regarding youth safety are found in the vast literature on the effects of child abuse and neglect and related studies on the causes and prevention of delinquency. Few studies exist, however, on the implications of how middle and high school–age youth actually perceive their safety. In general, most of the data-based studies on empowerment are about the effects of community service and service-learning programs. Except for those studies of service or service-learning and a number of studies on the effects of adolescents working long hours, there are few other studies on youth as resources or on the impact of youth perceptions about whether they are valued by the community.

Community Values Youth, Youth as Resources, and Service to Others

For youth who do feel valued and useful, the research clearly shows many positive outcomes, including better mental health, higher levels of moral reasoning, and more involvement in the community. In addition, the evidence suggests that empowerment also is associated with reduced substance use, violence, and delinquency. Youth feeling valued and having useful roles have been associated, directly or indirectly with:

- **Higher self-esteem, self-concept** (Benard, 1990; Hill, 1983; Kurth-Schai, 1988; Price et al., 1993; Strother and Associates, 1990);
- **Greater sense of personal control, sense of optimism about the future** (Kurth-Schai, 1988; Nettles, 1991);
- **Greater achievement of self-actualization** (Karnes, Deason, & D'Ilio, 1993);
- **Reduced delinquency** (Bilchik, 1995; Coordinating Council on Juvenile Justice and Delinquency Prevention, 1996; Linquanti, 1992);

- **Reduced violence and fighting; greater perception of safety at school; increased social skills** (Bilchik, 1995; National Crime Prevention Council, 1995);
- **Higher levels of moral reasoning; higher levels of thinking** (Benard, 1990; Kurth-Schai, 1988);
- **Greater social and personal responsibility** (Conrad & Hedin, 1981; Hill, 1983);
- **Decreased school failure, school suspensions; increased school attendance; increased academic performance** (Coordinating Council on Juvenile Justice and Delinquency Prevention, 1996; Linquanti, 1992; National Crime Prevention Council, 1995);
- **More effective parent-child relationships; more complex relationships** (Benard, 1990; Linquanti, 1992);
- **Reduced substance abuse** (Bilchik, 1995; Linquanti, 1992); and
- **Greater participation in community activities** (Benard, 1990; Hill, 1983; Hodgkinson & Weitzman, 1996 [more likely to volunteer if asked]; Price et al., 1993).

Work   A subset of "useful roles" is part-time work, which has been associated, directly or indirectly, with both positive and negative outcomes. As a risk factor, part-time work has been shown to have detrimental effects on school performance, mental health, family life, and delinquency. On the other hand, part-time work has also been found to function positively, being associated with better mental health, happier family life, fewer behavior problems, and less substance use, as the following summary indicates.

Negative work outcomes:

- **Lower school attendance, homework completion, participation in extracurricular activities, school engagement, grades; increased dropout,** if working more than 15 hours/week (Hill, 1983; Kablauoi & Pautler, 1991);
- **Increased psychological distress, depression,** if working more than 20 hours/week (Shanahan, Finch, Mortimer, & Ryu, 1991; Steinberg & Dornbusch, 1991 [for males, only if work stress and self-direction at work were high; for females, only if responsible for things one could not control and if work interfered with school]);
- **Lower family and peer group involvement,** if working more than 15 hours/week; **less parental monitoring** (Hill, 1983; Shanahan, Elder, Burchinal, & Conger, 1996 [findings are based on amount

of earnings, strongly related to—but not strictly identical with—hours worked]);

- **Increased alcohol use; decreased investment in and performance at school** (if working more than 20 hours/week) (Mortimer, Finch, Ryu, Shanahan, & Call, 1993; Steinberg & Dornbusch, 1991);
- **Increased delinquent behavior** (Kablauoi & Pautler, 1991); and
- For 15- to 16-year-old females, more hours worked, **less life satisfaction** (Yamoor & Mortimer, 1990).

Both negative and positive work outcomes:

- For males, **increased traditional gender roles;** for females, **decreased traditional gender roles** (Stevens, Puchtell, Ryu, & Mortimer, 1992).

Positive work outcomes:

- **Increased positive emotional tone in family, increased seeking of parental advice, increased parental seeking of adolescent's advice** (based on earnings, not hours worked) (Shanahan et al., 1996);
- **Higher self-esteem, self-reliance** (Lennings, 1993; Steinberg, Greenberger, Vaux, & Ruggiero, 1981 [total lifetime exposure to work, not current hours]);
- For females, **higher internal orientation,** if working less than 11½ hours/week (Mortimer, Finch, Shanahan, & Ryu, 1992);
- For females, **less problem school behavior,** if working less than 11½ hours/week (Mortimer et al., 1992);
- For 11- to 14-year-old males, but not females, more hours worked, **less teacher perception of them as behavior problems** (Yamoor & Mortimer, 1990);
- For 11- to 14-year-old males, but not females, more hours worked, **greater life satisfaction** (Yamoor & Mortimer, 1990);
- For females, **less alcohol, cigarette use,** if working less than 11½ hours/week (Mortimer et al., 1992); and
- For males, **higher perceived well-being,** if working less than 11½ hours/week (Mortimer et al., 1992).

Service   One specific vehicle for youth to feel they have a useful role in society is through community service or service-learning programs provided through schools and religious organizations and in other settings. Although based on a variety of methods, samples, and instruments, numerous studies have reported positive relationships of service with personal and social responsibility, and to a lesser but still common extent, with personal development. Least well documented have been positive effects on academic performance, although recent studies are beginning to demonstrate positive findings in this domain as well. Community service, volunteering, and service-learning have been associated, directly or indirectly, with:

- **Decreased school failure, suspension, dropout; increased reading grades; increased performance; increased grades, increased school attendance; increased commitment to class work; increased working for good grades** (Allen, Philliber, Herrling, & Kuperminc, 1997; Cohen, Kulik, & Kulik, 1982; Dewsbury-White, 1993; Luchs, 1980 [if 30 hours or more]); Moore & Allen, 1996; Scales, Blyth, Berkas, & Kielsmeier, 1998 [if more than 30 hours and if a lot of reflection is included]; Shumer, 1994; Yates & Youniss, 1996; Yogev & Ronen, 1982);
- **Decreased behavior problems at school** (Calabrese & Schumer, 1986);
- **Reduced teenage pregnancy** (Moore & Allen, 1996; Yates & Youniss, 1996);
- **High levels of parents talking with young adolescents about school** (Scales et al., 1998);
- **Increased sense of developmental opportunities at school** (Hecht & Fusco, 1995; Scales, Blyth, et al., 1998 [if a lot of reflection is included]);
- **Increased self-concept, self-esteem, self-efficacy; decreased alienation; increased sense of competence, efficacy** (Calabrese & Schumer, 1986; Cohen et al., 1982; Conrad, 1980; Conrad & Hedin, 1981; Crosman, 1989; Luchs, 1980 [if 30 hours or more]; Moore & Allen, 1996; Switzer, Simmons, Dew, Regalski, & Wang, 1995 [boys only]; Yates & Youniss, 1996);
- **Reduced violent delinquency** (Coordinating Council on Juvenile Justice and Delinquency Prevention, 1996);
- **Less depression,** for males only (Switzer et al., 1995);
- **Increased prosocial reasoning, moral reasoning** (Batchelder & Root, 1994 [college students]; Conrad, 1980; Conrad & Hedin, 1981);
- **Increased self-disclosure** (Middleton, 1993);
- **More positive attitudes toward adults; better development of mature relationships; increased social competence outside of**

school; increased empathy (Conrad, 1980; Conrad & Hedin, 1981; McGill, 1992; Newmann & Rutter, 1983; Yogev & Ronen, 1982);

- **Increased problem-solving skills** (Conrad, 1980);
- **Increased community involvement as adult; increased political participation and interest; increased positive attitudes toward community involvement, positive civic attitudes, belief that one can make a difference in community, leadership positions in community organizations** (Beane, Turner, Jones, & Lipka, 1981; Conrad, 1980; Giles & Eyler, 1994 [college students]; Hamilton & Zeldin, 1987; Marsh, 1973; O'Connell, 1983; William T. Grant Foundation, 1988); and
- **Increased personal and social responsibility; increased perceived duty to help others; increased efficacy in helping others; increased altruism; increased concern for others' welfare; increased awareness of societal problems** (Conrad & Hedin, 1981; Crosman, 1989; Giles & Eyler, 1994 [college students] Hamilton & Fenzel, 1988; Markus, Howard, & King, 1993 [if 20 hours or more]; Scales, Blyth, et al., 1998; Stockhaus 1976 [if 20 hours or more]; Williams, 1993 [if more than 10 hours]; Yogev & Ronen, 1982).

Safety

Least well represented in the literature are studies about young people's feelings of personal safety and the relationship of those feelings to developmental outcomes. The available data do suggest, however, that young people who feel unsafe or who are victimized suffer socially, emotionally, and academically; this is in addition to the physical harm they may suffer from victimization. Being victimized or feeling unsafe has been associated, directly or indirectly, with:

- **More skipping of school** (Chandler, Nolin, & Davies, 1995; Kann et al., 1998);
- **Lower academic achievement** (Gottfredson & Gottfredson, 1989);
- **More bringing weapons to school** (Gardner, 1995);
- **More violence,** if exposed to violence (DuRant et al., 1994);
- For 8th-grade students in grades 6–8 or 7–9 schools (compared with 8th-grade students in K–8, K–12, or 3–8 schools), **perception that their schools are less safe** (Anderman & Kimweli, 1997);
- **Having fewer friends, less popularity** (Slee & Rigby, 1993 [with greater victimization]); and
- **Less happiness at school** (Slee & Rigby, 1993 [with greater victimization]).

Variations in Findings

How safe, useful, and valued a young person feels, and how much youth contribute service to the community, may vary more than other assets by gender, age, socioeconomic status, and ethnicity. The quantitative research literature on empowerment most often highlights gender differences; other differences, especially variations by race and ethnicity, are only marginally represented.

Gender

Young people of both genders experience significant threats to their safety. For example, the violent victimization rate for teenagers is twice as high as for any other age-group; with the exception of rape, teenage males, especially those who are African American, have the highest violent victimization rates of all (National Crime Prevention Council, 1995). The homicide rate for teenage males, while still less than that of 20- to 24-year-olds, jumped more than 150% between 1985 and 1991, the largest increase of any age-group (Portner, 1994). Males, especially African Americans, are more likely to die between the ages of 12 and 17 than are females, and also more likely to engage in fighting and other serious offenses, and to be arrested. In a large study of U.S. 8th graders, Anderman and Kimweli (1997) found that females were victimized by peers less often than males, and Native American students more often than students in other racial or ethnic groups. Females, however, are more likely than males to be physically abused by adults, and especially to experience sexual abuse (Carnegie Council on Adolescent Development, 1992b). Moreover, a nationwide survey of nearly 7,000 5th–12th graders reported that about 20% of high school females had been sexually or physically abused, including 8% who said they had been forced by a date to have sex against their will (Portner, 1997).

Of the more than 16,000 9th–12th graders surveyed as part of the U.S. Centers for Disease Control and Prevention's 1997 Youth Risk Behavior Surveillance Survey (Kann et al., 1998), nearly 20% stated they had carried a weapon during the preceding 30 days; nearly 40% said they had been in a physical fight in the past year; and 33% reported that they had personal property stolen or vandalized at school in the past year. Males were more likely than females to report all these behaviors.

Females and males may also be affected by work in differing ways. The central issue for females seems to be whether work is supportive of school—that it does not interfere with doing well in school. If it interferes, females have more feelings of depression and self-derogation, lower self-esteem, and lessened feelings of well-being (Mortimer et al., 1993; Shanahan et al., 1991). Among males, however, negative outcomes result if they experience a high degree of work stress, but positive outcomes result if they feel work is providing them with useful skills for the future (Mortimer et al., 1992).

Age

Blyth and Leffert (1995) did not report gender data, but did find that for risky behaviors that become developmentally typical for the majority of youth as youth get older (such as ever drinking alcohol or ever having sexual intercourse), differences between youth in healthy versus less healthy communities decreased at higher grades. In contrast, differences widened on high-risk behaviors that are not common for the majority of young people (such as using drugs). In other words, healthy communities did not provide much protection against common risky behaviors but did protect against less common risky behaviors. There may be a combination of factors operating to produce this finding. As they become older, obtaining driver's licenses and part-time jobs, youth may increasingly be treated more like adults in both expected and permitted behaviors, especially youth who mature physically earlier than their peers (Scales, 1996). Ironically, being treated as more adultlike may increase young people's feelings of being valued and respected while at the same time it actually decreases their safety by allowing or condoning participation in risky behaviors. Although those dynamics apply to all youth, the extra resources and assets youth have in healthy communities work to lessen their chances of taking unusual risks.

A large sample of more than 100,000 youth studied in Dade County, Florida, found that younger children felt safer at school than in their neighborhoods, but middle and high school–age youth perceived school as less safe than their neighborhoods; overall, just 56% of those 3rd–12th graders said they usually felt safe at school (Gardner, 1995). Outside school, about 14% of children under age 18 were substantiated as victims of child abuse or neglect in 1996 ("NCPCA Reports," 1997). Compared to 1986 data that showed the risk of maltreatment increased with a child's age, the most recent data show that middle and high school students are somewhat less likely to be maltreated, but that the proportion of 6- to 11-year-olds being maltreated has sharply increased ("Child Abuse and Neglect," 1996).

School Environment

Anderman and Kimweli (1997) reported that 8th graders in schools comprising grades K–8, K–12, and to a lesser extent, grades 3–8, perceived their schools as safer and also were victimized less than were 8th-grade students in schools comprising grades 6–8 or 7–9. These results may in part have been related to how schools with younger students responded to infractions: Those schools dealt more harshly with repeat infractions of lesser offenses (e.g., using profanity, disturbing the class) and with any serious violations (possessing alcohol or other drugs or possessing weapons), perhaps in part to protect the younger children in the school. Ultimately, swift and certain responses probably contributed to all students in those schools feeling and being safer.

Work Environment

Along with the family and school settings, adolescents' workplaces are among the most studied developmental arenas. The effects of part-time work are mixed. The great majority of studies report that working more than 20 hours per week clearly has negative effects. Some studies report contrary findings, however. For example, Mortimer et al. (1993) followed up their 9th-grade sample one year later and reported that students who worked more than 20 hours per week did not show higher depression, lower self-esteem, or more "external control" orientations (being more influenced by others than by one's own values). They were more likely to use alcohol, but there was "no evidence" that a high number of work hours increased cigarette smoking and "scant" evidence that such workloads negatively affected school. Only seniors in high school who worked long hours spent less time on their homework than their peers. In fact, contrary to what many would predict, Yamoor and Mortimer (1990) found that, for young adolescent males, the more hours they worked, the greater their life satisfaction and the less teachers considered them to be behavior problems.

Vulnerable Youth

The effect of providing the empowerment assets may vary depending on how vulnerable youth are. Vulnerable youth—those with the fewest developmental assets—seem to be helped more than are youth with average or high levels of assets by the broader opportunities available in healthy communities (communities where youth problem statistics are low). Vulnerable youth in healthy communities are less likely to engage in risky behaviors than are equally vulnerable youth in unhealthy communities (Blyth & Leffert, 1995).

The success of the I Have a Dream program illustrates the importance of both empowerment and support for vulnerable youth. Through the program, inner-city 6th graders in New York City were guaranteed money for college if they graduated from high school; the school dropout rate for the first cohort of youth fell from an anticipated 75% to just 2%. Moreover, half the students went on to college—a rate unheard of in their neighborhood. Each student had a mentor who would do anything to support her or his doing well in school. The scholarship money and mentors were evidence that "each student's dream is believed in by powerful people in their environment" (Price et al., 1993, p. 51).

How Empowerment Works

Several of the empowerment assets use the "community" as a reference point. There are legitimate questions about how youth define community. Which adults in the community are the ones whose perception of the "value" of youth matters? How much does a stranger's ill treatment of a young person contribute to her or his sense of being valued or not—compared with the treatment the youth experiences from one or two close neighbors, teachers, clergy, and her or his parents? Similarly, do the kind of service and the context matter (the people, organization, or idea involved), or is any service helpful? Is all service interchangeable? Except for data suggesting that the effects of directly helping others differ from the effects of more anonymous service (Blyth, Saito, & Berkas, 1997), the answers to these questions generally are not found in the available research.

Moreover, our four measures of youth empowerment may not be truly independent of other youth assets. For example, some researchers conceptualize empowerment to include a variety of attributes we include in the asset category of social competencies, such as decision making and planning skills (Galan, 1988). Pittman and Wright (1991) went even further, defining empowerment as the meeting of six basic human needs (e.g., safety, belonging, competence) plus special needs particular to the developmental stage of early or late adolescence (e.g., supervision, exploration of self and environment). By this definition, empowerment is an outcome of having assets more than it is an asset category per se. Empowerment also may overlap conceptually and in measurement with youth participation in organized activities and constructive use of time. One way a community shows that it "values" youth may be that it offers plentiful constructive opportunities for youth after school and on evenings and weekends. Furthermore, if being empowered ultimately means feeling capable of making desired things happen, then empowerment may have some correlation with the assets of positive identity, especially personal power; it could be that "personal power" and "empowerment" measure some of the same things. Similarly, if a mentor provides affirmation, that support may well contribute to a young person's feeling that the "community" values her or him. The question would then be, what level of support (a separate asset category) might get confounded with this aspect of the empowerment asset? Does "adult support" effectively become "empowerment" when three, five, or seven other adults care? If the adolescent says he or she has a caring school?

More broadly, what is it that leads youth to feel valued by the community (the first empowerment asset)? If a young person has useful roles, is protected and safe, and helps others (the other three empowerment assets), do these more or less cumulatively cause the youth to feel valued? How independent from these empowerment assets is "feeling valued" as a separate asset? Our own data suggest that these assets are indeed moderately, but not strongly, related to each other. There are correlations in the mid to upper .30s of young people's feeling valued with their sense that they live in a caring neighborhood and go to a caring school, and correlations in the mid .20s of young people's feeling valued with all the positive-identity assets (Scales, Benson, Leffert, & Blyth, 1998).

Safety

Four percent of students in the 1997 Youth Risk Behavior Surveillance Survey skipped at least 1 day of school in the preceding 30 days because they felt unsafe, with Latina and Black male students more likely to feel unsafe at school (Kann et al., 1998). Similarly, the National Household Education Survey of more than 6,500 youth (Chandler et al., 1995) reported that half of 6th–12th graders had personally witnessed bullying, robbery, or physical assaults at their schools; 7% admitted to having skipped a day of school because of fears for their safety. A national survey of 8th–11th graders (Barringer, 1993) reported that more than 70% of females had received sexual comments or looks or had been touched or grabbed in a sexual way (about 50% of males reported similar experiences). The result of not feeling safe in this way was that about 33% of females did not want to go to school or even talk in class (only a little more than 10% of males felt that way).

It is perhaps more surprising that the proportions skipping school are not even higher. An Australian study of 7- to 13-year-olds, for example, found that students who were victimized felt less safe, less happy about school, and had fewer friends. Whether that lack of social support among peers contributed to their being victimized in the first place was unclear. Kuther and Fisher's (1998) study of young adolescents suggested that lack of social skills may contribute to victimization. Young adolescents who were assertive with others were less likely to be victimized, while those who tried to cope with experiences by keeping their feelings to themselves actually were more likely to be victimized by peers. Nevertheless, victimized children are more socially isolated. The double negative of victimization and social isolation likely constitutes a powerful incentive to dislike and even avoid school.

Moreover, perceptions may count just as much as, if not more than, reality. Fewer youth say they have been victimized at school than say they worry about that possibility: Nearly 1 in 5 middle school youth and 1 in 10 high school youth report that they personally have been victimized. Including both youth who have been victimized and all other youth, one quarter of youth overall and one third of middle school youth say they worry about becoming victims (Nolin,

Davies, & Chandler, 1995). The effect of worry alone on attitudes toward school, friendship formation, participation in after-school activities, or other attitudes and behaviors is unclear, but it is unlikely to have a positive influence.

The findings relating victimization to a variety of effects on adolescents' school attendance, engagement, and performance are consistent. Moreover, those effects occur as early as kindergarten. Ladd, Kochenderfer, and Coleman (1997) studied 200 5- and 6-year-olds, and found that those who were victimized (picked on, hit or kicked, or talked to—or about—unkindly) were significantly less likely to like school and more likely to stay home from school. Because the dimensions of adolescents' commitment to learning build up cumulatively across family, school, and peer experiences beginning in early childhood (see Chapter 5, on commitment to learning), these research results are an especially troubling indication that lack of safety early in life has profound consequences later on.

Community Values Youth

If the key to helping youth feel empowered is that adults believe in their capacities, then it is not surprising that so few youth report experiences of empowerment in our Search Institute surveys (discussed later in this chapter). Speaking of empowerment in low-income communities, Cardenas Ramirez (1992) warned that "deeply held biases about the populations of interest have often been just below the surface, and these biases have prevailed over attempts to paint [low-income residents] as reservoirs of human potential" (p. 49). The same might be said of efforts to empower youth.

How adults view young people's capacities can be a major obstacle to youth empowerment. One study of 1,600 elementary, middle, and high school students in Minnesota (Hedin, Hannes, & Saito, 1985) found that two thirds of young people felt that parents, police, teachers, and senior citizens thought negatively of them; nearly half thought adults viewed them with extreme negativity. Older youth felt adults viewed them negatively more than did younger youth. When compared by gender and by urban versus rural location, young people's views of adult perceptions did not vary much. The researchers concluded that education and the media are among the social influences that have produced a climate for youth that in many ways is "indistinguishable across geographic settings" (p. 4). Popowski's (1985) survey of Chicago youth found that even more youth—97%—thought adults viewed them negatively.

Are those findings outdated? It would appear not. A study of more than 800 11- to 16-year-olds found that young people think the media too often portray them in negative terms, often having to do with crime: 60% of youth overall, and 75% of Black youth, said what they read and hear on the news about young people is negative ("Children Want the Good News," 1994). A recent survey by Public Agenda (Farkas et al., 1997) confirmed what earlier studies have shown: Most adults seem not to place a high degree of value or confidence in youth. In the Public Agenda survey of U.S. adults, nearly 60% thought that today's youth would not, as adults, make the United States a better place in which to live; 21% thought today's youth would make the country worse. A survey of more than 900 adults in Colorado found far fewer adults thinking youth would make that state a worse place in the future (just 6% had that extremely negative view), but 66% felt that youth today did not respect adults, and only 15% strongly agreed that youth were doing volunteer service work in their communities (Scales, 1998). In reality, about 60% of youth contribute to such volunteer service annually (Hodgkinson & Weitzman, 1996). Clearly, a great deal of misinformation about what youth actually are doing and feeling fuels adults' negative attitudes.

In their review of youth development literature, Pittman and Wright (1991) concluded that adults too infrequently conceived of youth as actors in their own development—that is, adults inconsistently grasped that youth development really was "in the hands of youth" themselves (p. 8). When programs do not enable youth to play meaningful roles, they may drop out of or avoid those programs, if they have that choice. In nonschool programs, youth participation is almost always voluntary; young people do "vote with their feet." Half of a group of youth who dropped out of 4-H, for example, said they did so because there were too few leadership opportunities for them (Ladewig & Thomas, 1987, cited in William T. Grant Foundation, 1988).

For many adults, empowering youth may be threatening, because it turns upside down what might have been a relationship based on adults' authority. Penuel (1995) noted, for example, that putting adolescents in decision-making positions forces adults to win by argument, not by the exercise of power: They must "appeal to youths' motivations, interests, and values" (p. 3). The Carnegie Council on Adolescent Development (1992a) observed that even youth-serving organizations often failed to empower youth in a number of ways. These included skirting issues such as sexuality education (not supplying information youth need), not giving youth enough opportunities to participate in real decision making about the organization's goals and programs, and too often keeping the decisions about program activities in the hands of adults (not enabling autonomy).

Religious congregations are frequent exceptions to those trends. The Carnegie Council on Adolescent Development (1992a) concluded that congregations were more enabling of empowerment because of their traditional emphasis on youth as resources and their typical "otherdirectedness" (their concern with service to others) (p. 52). Indeed, according to a Search Institute study of more than 500 religious youth workers (Roehlkepartain & Scales, 1995), one of the striking differences between congregations that maintain young people's involvement after their confirmation or bar/bat mitzvah and those that do not is that successful congregations provide many opportunities for youth to serve others. The traditional Black Christian church in particular often has been the "only institution that black people had access to" (Dassance, quoted in Roehlkepartain, 1998, p. 15); in addition to its cultural and religious emphasis on valuing children and being concerned for their welfare, it has been a principal institution to combat the injustice and powerlessness experienced by many African Americans. Indeed, one reason why African American youth in a national study were found to have higher than average levels of overall well-being, despite also having higher than average levels of poverty, was their dual connection to religious institutions and their greater commitment to working for equality—that is, their sense of being resources and playing useful roles (Moore & Glei, 1995).

Youth as Resources

Petersen, Leffert, and Hurrelmann (1993) concluded that the "freedom of adolescents is embedded in their lack of a social role, their marginality" (p. 613). If that is true for most youth, it may especially be true for youth who, because of their socioeconomic status, race, ethnicity, disability, religion, or sexual orientation, are already marginalized by the majority society. For example, the Cook County, Illinois, sheriff's office found that youth with lower than C averages in school wanted to volunteer in the community as much as better students did, but that the community rarely asked those underachieving students to contribute (Popowski, 1985). Similarly, a small study of young African American adolescents from low socioeconomic backgrounds demonstrated that those children felt capable of helping others—they saw themselves having leadership strengths to the same degree as the more diverse sample on which the leadership instrument was normed (Riley & Karnes, 1994).

A much larger study was the evaluation of the Neighborhood Program sponsored by the Ford and Eisenhower foundations. The researchers found that strategies of "empowering residents of high-crime communities, improving services, or expanding opportunities for high-risk youth," or a combination of these approaches, were related to improved youth self-esteem and neighborhood social cohesion in 8 of the program's 10 demonstration cities. The greatest impact on antisocial behavior, however, occurred in Washington, D.C., and Boston, the two cities that had the most "sustained focus on empowering youth" (Strother & Associates, 1990, p. 25). An example of the impact of youth playing such a valued role is the Project Northland alcohol use prevention program (Komro et al., 1996). Seventh-graders who helped plan alcohol-free activities such as open gyms, ski trips, or roller-skating outings—compared with youth who either simply attended those events or did not participate at all—were significantly less likely to report using alcohol during the previous year and during the month preceding the postsurvey. The effects were strongest for youth who already had used alcohol during the 6th grade, suggesting that vulnerable youth especially may benefit from feeling empowered. Finally, in Werner and Smith's classic longitudinal study of Hawaiian youth followed into adulthood (1992), those who were the most resilient as adults tended to have taken on various kinds of helping responsibilities as adolescents, whether paid work or caring for ailing family members.

Service to Others

The effect on later resilience of having a valued role as an adolescent suggests that connection to other adults and social institutions has important developmental benefits. In a study of more than 3,000 high school seniors, Youniss, Yates, and Su (1997) found that youth who already had been most active in political campaigns or writing to government officials, and who attended religious services regularly, were more likely to contribute community service as well. Moreover, community service participation for most youth was in turn associated with lower use of marijuana. The researchers suggested there may be an "integrated youth syndrome" (p. 259) that is a counterpoint to the syndrome of multiple problems some youth experience. Those youth who are more involved with social institutions not only are less likely to violate social norms but also are more likely to reinforce community norms by their participation. Their social connection thus has positive effects both for the individual young people and for their communities.

Studies on community service or service-learning, taken as a whole, show that participation in service contributes to youth having numerous positive attitudes and behaviors, but the effects are modest at best and most of the research designs have not been rigorous (Scales & Blyth, 1997). Although young people are probably even more likely to do service within a religious organization than a school (Hodgkinson & Weitzman, 1996), most of the better quantitative data have been collected through school settings. Moore and Allen (1996) concluded that there was little or no evidence of the impact of service-learning on social competence, career exploration, problem-solving abilities, attitudes toward school, or belief in the individual's responsibility to help those in need. Scales and Blyth (1997) reached a somewhat different conclusion, noting that adolescents' sense of personal and social responsibility is one of the more commonly observed effects in studies of service-learning. In fact, in a study of more than 1,000 6th–8th graders, Scales, Blyth, et al. (1998) found that service-learning students' concern for others' welfare was maintained over the school year, while control students' concern for others decreased, such that service-learning students had significantly higher concern for the welfare of others by the end of the school year, compared to controls.

The degree of exposure to helping behavior seems to matter: In reviewing literature on youth volunteering, Moore and Allen (1996) concluded that positive effects occurred most often in programs of at least 12 weeks' duration in which youth were involved at least two days each week. Several studies of community service and service-learning also have concluded that effects from service experiences differ depending on student participation (Melchior, 1997; Scales & Blyth, 1997; Scales, Blyth, et al., 1998).

What do youth themselves say about helping others? A Gallup survey found that one of the main reasons young people volunteered was their desire to do something about a cause that was important to them (Hodgkinson & Weitzman, 1996). They wanted to be useful and feel valued. Perhaps surprisingly, healthy communities—those with lower levels of youth engaged in risky behavior—are only marginally more likely to have youth engaged in such prosocial behaviors as community service. The reason seems to be that few communities of any kind do a good job of engaging young people's energies and idealism—of activating their potential as community resources. In a study of 112 communities, youth avoidance of negative behaviors was much more significant in differentiating communities, largely because so few youth in any community (the average was 16%) engaged in prosocial behaviors (Blyth & Leffert, 1995).

Moreover, it is not enough for youth to want to help others; for the positive impact of prosocial dispositions to be realized, young people have to act prosocially. In Blyth and Leffert's (1995) study of 112 communities, young people's prosocial behaviors were much more related to community health than were their values about helping. This finding takes on particular importance in view of a Gallup poll that found that adolescents were four times more likely to volunteer and help out in the community if they were asked than if they were not, but that only half of a national sample of 12- to 17-year-olds said that adults did, indeed, ask them to help out (Hodgkinson & Weitzman, 1996). When the cable television channel Nickelodeon sponsored its annual Big Help-a-Thon in October 1997, 8 million young people called in pledges of community service totaling more than 85 million hours, working with organizations such as Habitat for Humanity, Youth Service America, and Boys and Girls Clubs of America ("Philanthropy," 1997). This suggests the high level of interest youth have in contributing to their communities.

Finally, adolescents who have role models of service and community connection are more likely to contribute service. Reviewing the literature on youth community service, Yates and Youniss (1996) concluded that youth who served voluntarily were more likely than were nonserving youth to have parents who volunteered and to be stronger in their religious attachments, another source of support for serving others. Indeed, adolescents whose parents are involved in the community are more likely to be involved than are their peers whose parents are uninvolved, regardless of how warm the parents are or how much they encourage community service. Parental warmth is not irrelevant, however. Youth with parents who are warm in their relationships with their adolescent sons and daughters are more likely than the youth of less warm parents to be involved in the community, even when the parents are less involved (Fletcher, 1997). Warm parents, regardless of their own community involvement, seem to encourage their children's community connections. Csikszentmihalyi and Henshaw's (1997) large study of 6th, 8th, and 10th graders in 13 communities also found parental encouragement to be the most important factor in whether adolescents participated in extracurricular activities.

What is it that makes certain experiences empowering for youth? Empowering programs include components in which youth reflect about the meaning of their activities; do and not just observe; work with accepting and uncriticizing adults; have adult responsibilities; have a sense that they can make a contribution; and have the freedom to explore their own interests and develop their own ideas (Hill, 1983). Similarly, Price et al. (1993) noted that successful support programs for youth provide opportunities for growth and mastery, specifically through "roles and activities" that encourage active participation and that provide opportunities to learn new skills in a predictable environment (p. 49). Even more simply, young adolescents themselves, in focus groups convened on behalf of the Carnegie Council on Adolescent Development, told that blue-ribbon commission that they wanted programs that engaged their interests and communicated respect for youth (Carnegie Council on Adolescent Development, 1992b). A study in which nearly 7,000 Philadelphia 9th graders (Ginsburg et al., 1995) explained why they would or would not seek health care supports those findings. Although confidentiality was an important factor, how well the health-care provider communicated honesty and respect to the young person (such as by sharing information directly with them and not just with their parents) was as or more important.

Those attributes should operate in any opportunity or program that aims to empower youth, but they may be particularly effective for traditionally disenfranchised youth. Reviewing successful programs for disadvantaged urban young males, Jones (1990) concluded that they created a safe and protective family-like environment and linked the young men with "real opportunities" in the community (p. 1). Strother and Associates (1990) used almost the same language—extended family–like places and jobs—to describe what helped reduce criminality in the Neighborhood Program's multisite demonstration project.

Adolescents' Experience of Empowerment

Our data show, not surprisingly, that older youth feel safer than younger adolescents. Unlike most assets, which seem to decline when comparing 6th graders with 12th graders, sense of safety increases steadily from 45% of 6th graders to 68% of 12th graders. This may be because older youth experience fewer threats (although the consequences of those threats may be greater at older ages) and because they usually feel more physically capable of handling those threats than do younger youth. It is less likely that older youth also may feel more emotionally and cognitively able to deal with those threatening situations in a nonviolent manner. Our data show that 6th graders have more confidence in peaceful conflict resolution skills than 12th graders do (see Chapter 7, on social competencies).

Empowerment also involves significant gender differences: By 55% to 45%, females are more likely than are males to contribute community service one hour per week or more, but males, by a margin of 65% to 49%, say they are more likely than are females to feel safe in their homes, schools, and neighborhoods. Because females are more socialized to help others and males to be able to defend themselves and fight, these figures likely reflect some gender-related reporting bias.

The most pronounced and disturbing trend in our data, however, is that three of the four empowerment assets decline substantially when comparing 6th graders with 12th graders. The degree to which youth feel valued by the larger community, the opportunities they have to play useful roles, and especially, the amount of service they typically contribute, all drop steadily across the middle school and high school years. The majority of American youth in our surveys are less empowered and less connected to the community as they get older and move closer to the assumption of adult responsibilities. (See Figure 2.)

What Is Missing from Our Definition of Empowerment?

The four assets that make up the empowerment category are found repeatedly in the youth development literature. There seems to be consensus among researchers that how prepared youth are to influence their own destiny is related to how valued, useful, and safe they feel and how connected they feel to a larger community to which they contribute. Yet it is possible to imagine other measures of empowerment that may be equally valid, such as:

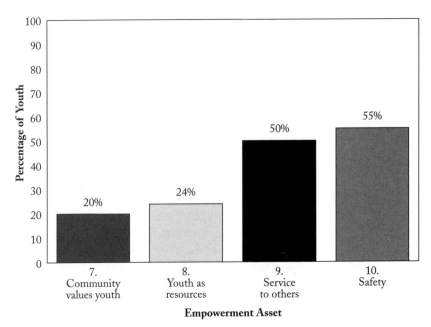

Figure 2 *Adolescents' experience of empowerment: percentage of 6th- to 12th-grade students who report experiencing each of the empowerment assets. For all but "safety," the percentages decline meaningfully when comparing 6th graders to 12th graders. From unpublished Search Institute data on youth in public and/or alternative schools who completed the institute's* Profiles of Student Life: Attitudes and Behaviors *survey during the 1996–97 school year; N = 99,462 students in 213 U.S. communities.*

- Seeing results from one's actions, not just feeling good about giving or service;
- Protecting others (not just experiencing one's own safety), or serving as an advocate or voice for others;
- Being responsible and accountable (not just playing "useful" roles); and
- Being able to change something wrong or ineffective in a socially constructive way.

We might also reasonably ask in what way economic and employment opportunity in the wider community is a form of empowerment. For youth living in impoverished areas, is the economic status of the community (both young people's awareness of the economy and direct economic effects on opportunities for them) more important than a sense of personal efficacy? That is, is current employment of adults more, as, or less important than young people's belief in their own possibility of meaningful employment now and in the future?

In addition, is there a contradiction in terms when we define "youth as resources" to mean that youth are "given" useful roles? Is it not even more empowering for youth to be expected and encouraged to ask to contribute or otherwise to initiate their useful contribution? If youth wait until adults "give" them useful roles, is that not a kind of second-class empowerment compared with the effect of asserting their own roles on their own terms? These are among the many questions for research on empowerment to pursue.

How Can Empowerment Be Built?

If adults simply asked youth their opinions more often, listened to them, and acted on those views, young people would probably view that as a major achievement. At the most basic level of empowerment, for example, are the terms adults use to describe young people. As one young adult described it: "The word 'teen' seems to imply immaturity or childishness . . . 'young adult' and 'young person' suggest more maturity . . . let's not keep calling our young people and young adults 'kids,' 'children,' or worst of all, 'teens'" (Tosiello, 1994, p. 51).

Benson (1997) warns that asset building in general is less about programs than it is about community members mobilizing to "build sustained, informal, positive relationships" (p. 93) with young people. This caveat is as true for the empowerment assets as it is for the other categories of assets. Empowerment is built through the daily experiences young people have, the numerous affirmations of their value and countless small gestures that communicate a desire for their contributions. The "programs" that best promote young people's sense of empowerment are those that are activated by adults who believe in youth and the power of those informal relationships.

Gambone and Arbreton (1997) studied 15 Girls Inc., YMCA, and Boys and Girls Clubs affiliates; they found that key components for success were young people's sense of safety, challenging and interesting activities, a sense of belonging, social support from adults, input into decision making, leadership opportunities, and volunteer and community service. Only one quarter of youth in those settings participated in community service (the lowest ranked of those seven developmental qualities), but those who participated in the greatest variety of activities reported having more leadership opportunities.

Similarly, the Coordinating Council on Juvenile Justice and Delinquency Prevention (1996) reviewed existing data and reported that effective programs for reducing violent delinquency among youth of all races combined efforts at truancy reduction, mentoring, conflict resolution training, after-school tutoring, vocational training, cultural development, recreation, and youth leadership.

In addition, a number of "rites of passage" programs have been developed specifically for African American youth to help them feel valued, useful, and capable by exposing them to traditional values and ceremonies, with an emphasis on the importance of kinship ties, community, and collective responsibility (Carnegie Council on Adolescent Development, 1992a). Finally, religious organizations representing many faiths are engaged in the reinvention of their youth "programs." Instead of youth programs being islands set apart from the congregation, those congregations are adopting the basic asset-building principle that youth work is everybody's job; that informal adult-youth relationships that express interest, respect, caring, and support are the foundation for all formal program activities, whether leadership, service, or the study of sacred texts and traditions (Roehlkepartain, 1998).

The Youth as Resources program now operates in at least 20 cities. Community boards have provided funds and young people have, among almost countless other contributions, "designed and built a playground at a shelter for abused children, established a peer counseling program, painted anti-drug murals in their neighborhood, and produced a video to educate their peers on the effects of drug abuse" (National Crime Prevention Council, 1995, p. 27). In more than 200 Wisconsin communities, teenagers have served on town steering committees that generate questions about youth that they want youth to answer in a subsequent survey. The results then point the way to community-based strategies to promote positive youth development. The "teen assessment project" has been credited with spawning 45 new school or community policies on youth, 43 new youth programs, 24 new community coalitions, and 112 grants awarded for more than $850,000 (Small, 1996). Similarly, 11- to 14-year-olds in Kansas City were hired to find out what opportunities were available for youth in that city; the data are being used to set up a referral bank so that young people can call and find out what is available near where they live (Benson, 1997).

The results of youth participation were demonstrated in a San Jose campaign to reduce the amount of tobacco advertising visible in local stores. Youth were involved in the campaign as planners, community mobilizers, and data collectors. After a three-month campaign, there was a significant drop in tobacco signage; the researchers concluded that youth involvement was among the "critical" reasons the project succeeded (Rogers, Reighery, Tencati, Butler, & Weiner, 1995, p. 440). Kurth-Schai (1988) reported on an unusual study in which 6th graders were asked to describe their ideal future and tell how it might be created. Among other outcomes, the researchers concluded that playing this role increased young people's self-esteem and sense of community spirit. A well-evaluated example of the impact of youth service is the Teen Outreach Program. Middle and high school students each contribute an average of more than 30 hours volunteer work in the community over the academic year, in addition to participating in a classroom life skills class. An eight-year longitudinal evaluation showed that program participants had 5% less course failure, 8% fewer suspensions, and, even more impressive, 33% fewer pregnancies and 50% fewer dropouts than comparison students (Moore & Allen, 1996).

Numerous other examples have been documented of efforts in which adults have helped young people take the lead, in both school- and community-based initiatives, to better their communities—such as mentoring younger children, designing substance abuse prevention programs, providing peer counseling, setting up youth credit unions and youth-oriented exhibits in museums, and galvanizing support for broad community change by developing recommendations for community improvement to submit to civic leaders in dozens of communities (O'Neil, 1990; Scales, 1991). Today, major institutions from private foundations such as the W. K. Kellogg Foundation (Checkoway, 1996) to government agencies such as the U.S. Family and Youth Services Bureau (National Clearinghouse on Families and Youth, 1996) are investing in training and materials development to tap young people's idealism, energy, and desire to be resources and to make contributions to widespread community improvement.

Conclusion

The examples we have discussed of how empowerment can be built point to a fundamental philosophical commitment that underlies this chapter's central ideas: Empowerment is built by those who believe that young people grow up in communities, not programs, and that young people are both the producers and the beneficiaries of community development (Center for Youth Development and Policy Research, 1994). Opportunities that empower young people, families, and communities to help themselves focus on their "capacities, skills, and assets, rather than . . . their deficits, weaknesses, and problems" (Linquanti, 1992, p. 3). Empowerment in this spirit is less about preparing youth for tomorrow and more about equipping them for engagement, connection, and contribution today. Empowerment then ultimately rests on the conviction that youth are truly empowered only when they contribute to their community and not just live in it.

Selected Readings

Center for Youth Development and Policy Research (1994). *Definitions of youth development, youth participation and community development.* Notes from the Wingspread Conference on Youth Participation and Neighborhood Development. Washington, DC: Author.

Chaskin, R. W., & Hawley, T. (1994). *Youth and caring: Developing a field of inquiry and practice.* Chicago: University of Chicago, Chapin Hall Center for Children.

Gambone, M. A., & Arbreton, A. J. A. (1997). *Safe havens: The contributions of youth organizations to healthy adolescent development.* Philadelphia: Public/Private Ventures.

Garbarino, J. (1995). *Raising children in a socially toxic environment.* San Francisco: Jossey-Bass.

Hedin, D., Hannes, K., & Saito, R. (1985). *Minnesota youth poll: Youth look at themselves and the world.* St. Paul: University of Minnesota, Minnesota Report AD-MR-2666.

Scales, P. C., Benson, P. L., Leffert, N., & Blyth, D. A. (1998). The strength of developmental assets as predictors of positive youth development outcomes. Manuscript submitted for publication.

Strother and Associates (1990). *Youth investment and community reconstruction: Street lessons on drugs and crime for the nineties. Final report.* Rochester, NY: Author. (ERIC Document Reproduction Service No. ED 372 149)

Zeldin, S., & Price, L. A. (1995). Creating supportive communities for adolescent development: Challenges to scholars—An introduction. *Journal of Adolescent Research, 10,* 6–14.

Boundaries and expectations are the rules, standards, and norms in families, schools, neighborhoods, and communities that guide young people's choices and regulate their behavior.

3

The Boundaries-and-Expectations Assets

To successfully navigate through adolescence, young people need a clear sense of the rules or limits in the various settings in which they live and interact (e.g., family, school, neighborhood). As adolescents grow and mature, these rules and limits change. Youth also need adults who model healthy and constructive behaviors, particularly as adolescents begin to "try on" adult roles themselves. In addition, young people need to interact with peers who are engaged in positive behaviors, and they need adults who expect them to do their best.

What Are Boundaries and Expectations?

Boundaries and expectations are the rules, standards, and norms pertaining to behavior. Specifically, they are the rules and regulations that address what young people can and cannot do and the consequences for breaking those rules in both the family and school contexts. Boundaries and expectations also relate to the presence of adults in the adolescent's life who model helping and other prosocial behaviors, friends who model positive behaviors (e.g., doing well in school, not getting into trouble), parents and teachers who expect the adolescent to be the best he or she can be, and, finally, the neighborhood awareness of, and responses to, adolescent behavior. Boundaries and expectations are more than family boundaries, because rules and standards are essential across all of the socializing systems in which adolescents interact. Recent accounts of what shapes adolescent development have noted that social control strategies exerted in the community are no less important for the development of children and youth than are the controls exerted in their families (Furstenberg, 1993; Sampson, 1997).

Boundaries and expectations are an important aspect of a young person's life. Ideally, they will change over the course of adolescence. In early adolescence, adolescents are more like children; boundaries set for young adolescents (5th through 8th graders) are appropriately more similar to those of middle childhood than they are to the boundaries set for older adolescents. For example, in early adolescence, the parent will be setting and monitoring the adolescent's curfew, probably based on some combination of family rules and what might be appropriate given the type of activity the adolescent is involved in on a particular night. The parent will probably be monitoring homework as well, or at least asking about or "checking in" with the child about homework assignments and test schedules.

As young people develop, they have an increasing need for autonomy and become capable of taking on more responsibility. Responsibility for boundaries is then appropriately shared between the parents and the adolescent and, in other contexts, between teachers and other adults and the adolescent. The same process most likely occurs with respect to expectations. Adults will have expectations for young adolescents that are much like those of middle childhood. Gradually, the adolescent should begin to internalize these expectations as part of a normal developmental process.

To return to the curfew example, by the time the adolescent is a senior in high school and preparing to leave home for a job or college, most parents will have slowly withdrawn from monitoring curfews as closely as when the adolescent was younger. The adolescent increasingly monitors herself or himself within the context of the family environment, rather than wanting to take on these responsibilities only after leaving home. Young people will vary considerably, however, in terms of maturity and have other developmental or contextual differences that might alter the normative course of development in this area. Although one adolescent might be ready for increasing responsibility quite early, another may be less mature or otherwise developmentally delayed in this process and need the parent, teacher, or other adult to stay more central to the monitoring of activities.

The developmental asset framework identifies six boundaries-and-expectations assets that address different contexts in which adolescents are involved and that stress the importance of adults who model positive and responsible behavior, of clear and consistent expectations from teachers and parents that help motivate young people to do well, and of positive peer influence. (See Table 8.)

Summary of Research Findings

Many research and evaluation reports examine the domains included in the asset category of boundaries and expectations. A large number of these pertain specifically to the influence of peers and the impact of family boundaries. Research on family boundaries is closely related to the literature on parenting style (see Chapter 1, on support). Parental monitoring is especially relevant—that is, how parents go about monitoring their children or adolescents and how that affects youth behaviors or outcomes. Parental monitoring is defined in many studies as knowing the whereabouts of young people, knowing what they are doing, and making sure that responsibilities are met (Kurdek & Fine, 1994).

Family Boundaries

Family boundaries have been shown to be directly or indirectly associated with:

- **Higher self-esteem** (Eccles et al., 1991);
- **Greater psychosocial competence and peer likability** (Kurdek & Fine, 1994; Steinberg et al., 1994);
- **Higher school achievement** (Astone & McLanahan, 1991; Christenson et al., 1992); **higher graduation rates** (Ensminger & Slusarcick, 1992) and **better school performance** (Dornbusch, Ritter, Leiderman, Roberts, & Fraleigh, 1987); and **greater adaptation to school** (Johnson, Shulman, & Collins, 1991); and
- **Decreased problem behaviors** (Barber, 1996; Galambos & Maggs, 1991); **reduced adolescent alcohol abuse** (Hawkins, Catalano, & Miller, 1992; Barnes & Farrell, 1992 [among African American adolescents]) or **reduced abuse of other substances** (Block, Block, &

Table 8. The Boundaries-and-Expectations Assets	
Family boundaries	Family has clear rules and consequences and monitors the young person's whereabouts.
School boundaries	School provides clear rules and consequences.
Neighborhood boundaries	Neighbors take responsibility for monitoring young people's behavior.
Adult role models	Parent(s) and other adults model positive, responsible behavior.
Positive peer influence	Young person's best friends model responsible behavior.
High expectations	Both parent(s) and teachers encourage the young person to do well.

Keyes, 1988; Flannery, Vazsonyi, Torquati, & Fridrich, 1994); **moderation of the effect of social influences on smoking** (Stacy, Sussman, Dent, Burton, & Flay, 1992); **decreased delinquency** (Patterson & Stouthamer-Loeber, 1984); **fewer self-regulation problems** (Kurdek & Fine, 1994); and **decreased early sexual behavior** (Miller, McCoy, Olson, & Wallace, 1986; Romer et al., 1994).

School Boundaries

A number of the studies pertaining to school boundaries are evaluations of in-school prevention or health-promotion programs or interventions (e.g., DeJong, 1987; Duryea & Okwumabua, 1988). Many of these studies have shown the programs or treatment protocols to have equivocal—or at best, weak—positive effects. The programs that have demonstrated success (i.e., those in which young people show evidence of decreased problem behaviors) are those that generally include "booster" treatments, in which young people are given additional exposures to the "treatment" or program over the course of time (Levental & Keeshan, 1993; Perry & Kelder, 1992).

Specifically, school boundaries are directly or indirectly associated with:

- **Higher academic orientation** (Rutter, 1983), **higher intrinsic motivation** (Eccles et al., 1991), and **increased achievement** (Lee & Bryk, 1989); and
- **Reduced frequency of drinking and drinking to excess** (Duryea & Okwumabua, 1988).

Neighborhood Boundaries

The effects of neighborhoods on adolescent development have been of increasing interest over the past several years to researchers, policy makers, and community leaders. Thinking about the role of neighborhoods has affected our own work in developing and revising the developmental asset framework. Some of the research reviewed here relates to a construct similar to what we consider to be neighborhood boundaries (i.e., something akin to neighbors being "on the lookout" for the welfare of all young people living in the area). In large part, however, studies that have examined neighborhood effects have looked at aspects of social disintegration (e.g., Brewster, 1994), poverty (e.g., Brooks-Gunn, Duncan, Klebanov, & Sealand, 1993; Duncan, 1994), the percentage of residents in "white-collar" occupations (e.g., Ensminger, Lamkin, & Jacobson, 1996), and access to appropriate or positive adult role models in the neighborhood. The presence of neighborhood boundaries is, nonetheless, directly or indirectly associated with:

- **Higher levels of achievement** (Bø, 1995); **lower levels of leaving school** (Brooks-Gunn, Duncan, et al., 1993) **or higher levels of high school graduation** (Ensminger et al., 1996);
- Decreased problem behaviors, including **decreased teenage births** (Brooks-Gunn, Duncan, et al., 1993); **decreased juvenile delinquency** (Sampson, 1997) and **decreased violent crime** (Sommers & Baskin, 1994); and improved health behaviors such as **the ability to evaluate the potential costs of early involvement in sexual activity** as well as **the use of contraception** (Brewster, 1994; Brewster, Billy, & Grady, 1993); and
- Improved adolescent outcomes such as **prosocial competence and involvement with conventional friends** (Elliott et al., 1996).

Adult Role Models

Much of the literature on the impact of role models on adolescent behavior pertains to the impact of adults who model negative behaviors (e.g., substance use, aggressive behaviors). Fewer studies pertain to the positive impact of adult role models (e.g., Brewster, 1994; Brewster et al., 1993). Still, adults who model positive behaviors are directly or indirectly associated with:

- **Higher levels of self-esteem and self-efficacy** (Whitbeck, 1987);
- **Decreased problem behaviors** (Brewster, 1994; Brewster et al., 1993); **decreased early sexual intercourse among females** (East, 1996); **reduced smoking** (Botvin, Botvin, Baker, Dusenbury, & Goldberg, 1992; Hops, Tildesley, Lichtenstein, Ary, & Sherman, 1990); **reduced alcohol use** (Chassin & Barrera, 1993; Hops et al., 1990; Leifman, Kühlhorn, Allebeck, Andréasson, & Romelsjö, 1995); **reduced use of marijuana and hard drugs** (Hops et al., 1990); **reduced impulsivity and aggressive behaviors** (Fry, 1988; Martin et al., 1994); **a decrease in other externalizing problems (e.g., conduct disorder)** (Brody, Stoneman, & Flor, 1996); and
- **Improved high school graduation rates** (Danziger & Farber, 1990 [young mothers with role models in the community or at school are more likely to stay in school]; Ensminger & Slusarcick, 1992); **positive school adjustment** (Ryan et al., 1994); **improved occupational aspirations and expectations** (Cook et al., 1996; Jackson & Meara, 1981); **higher achievement** (Achor & Morales, 1990); **increased involvement by females in competitive sports** (Brown, Frankel, & Fennell, 1989).

Peer Relationships

Peer norms and behaviors are known to have a strong influence on adolescents' behavior (e.g., Brown, 1990). Of the many studies concerned with the impact of peers on adolescent behavior, more of these have examined the influence of negative peer behavior than have looked at positive peer behavior. (Many studies have, however, examined the development of friendship and the developmental meaning or importance of peer relationships during adolescence.) Peer influence studies typically consider the impact on youth of peers who model specific types of behaviors (such as smoking); they aim to determine how observing certain peer activity or being around youth who engage in certain behaviors affects young people's initiation of similar behavior. One might easily surmise that youth who model positive behaviors (such as altruism) would be most likely to promote similarly positive behaviors among their peers. For the sake of clarity, however, and because there are so many studies directly pertaining to the influence of negative peer behavior, the research summarized here is separated into those reports of the impact of positive peer influence and negative peer influence.

Positive peer influence is associated with:

- **Development of social maturity** (Youniss & Haynie, 1992); and **increased altruism and perspective taking** (McGuire & Weisz, 1982);
- **Increased self-efficacy** (McFarlane et al., 1995); **increased self-competence** (Feiring & Lewis, 1991); and **increased self-esteem** (Coates, 1985; Eccles, Early, et al., 1997);
- **Higher academic achievement** (Chen & Stevenson, 1995; Hanson & Ginsburg, 1988); **higher math achievement** (Hanson & Ginsburg, 1988); **better grades** (Mounts & Steinberg, 1995); **increased school competence** (Cauce, 1986); and **higher educational aspirations** (Hallinan & Williams, 1990);
- **Increased involvement in sports** among females (Brown et al., 1989);
- **Increased self-assessed health behaviors** (Vilhjalmsson, 1994);
- **A buffering effect on depressive symptoms** (Herman-Stahl & Petersen, 1996; Windle, 1992); and **decreased stress** among males (Frey & Röthlisberger, 1996; Walker & Greene, 1987); and
- **Decreased alcohol use** (Perry et al., 1989).

Negative peer influence is associated with:

- **Increased problem behaviors** such as **increased smoking** (Aloise-Young, Graham, & Hansen, 1994; Bauman, Botvin, Botvin, & Baker, 1992; Botvin, Epstein, Schinke, & Diaz, 1994; Chassin, Presson, Sherman, Montello, & McGrew, 1986; Landrine, Richardson, Klonoff, & Flay, 1994 [among Caucasian youth]; Stanton & Silva, 1992; Urberg, Degirmencioglu, & Pilgrim, 1997; Urberg, Shyu, & Liang, 1990; Wang et al., 1995); **increased use of other substances** (Bailey & Hubbard, 1990; Coombs et al., 1991; Graham, Marks, & Hansen, 1991; Gutierres, Molof, & Ungerleider, 1994; Jessor & Jessor, 1975; Pruitt, Kingery, Mirzaee, Heuberger, & Hurley, 1991; Stattin, Gustafson, & Magnusson, 1989; Wagner, 1993; **increased early sexual behavior** (East, Felice, & Morgan, 1993 [among females]; Rodgers & Rowe, 1990; Romer et al., 1994; Treboux & Busch-Rossnagel, 1995 [among girls]); **increased antisocial behavior** (Dishion, Andrews, & Crosby, 1995);

- **Decreased school/academic adjustment** (Ryan et al., 1994) and **educational plans** (Cotterell, 1992); and
- **Lower self-esteem** (Cotterell, 1992; Ryan et al., 1994).

High Expectations

Fewer studies or program evaluations pertain to high expectations. Related constructs about parental expectations are more generally about parenting behaviors; high expectations may be thought of as a part of the behaviors associated with authoritative parenting. Our definition of high expectations, however, includes the expectations of teachers as well as parents. Indeed, most of the literature on high expectations examines the impact of teachers' expectations of their students for academic work. High expectations are associated most often with:

- **Positive academic performance** (Christenson et al., 1992); **academic achievement** (Achor & Morales, 1990; Chen & Stevenson, 1995; Reynolds & Gill, 1994; Rosenthal & Feldman, 1991); **greater effort** (Rosenthal & Feldman, 1991); **increased beliefs about ability to achieve in mathematics** (Chen & Stevenson, 1995; Dickens & Cornell, 1993 [especially among high-ability females]; Hanson & Ginsburg, 1988; Visser, 1987); **greater occupational aspirations and expectations** (Cook et al., 1996); **short-term improvement in grades and school attendance** among students in high-risk situations (Weinstein et al., 1991).

Variations in Findings

Research generally confirms that boundaries and expectations have a positive impact on adolescent development. Some studies suggest that certain factors (e.g., parents) may moderate the effect of boundaries and expectations on adolescent outcomes (e.g., Stacy et al., 1992). In other studies, boundaries and expectations have been found to be particularly salient for some groups of young people, such as males, certain ethnic groups, and youth in high-risk situations.

Gender

The relation of parenting behaviors (e.g., setting boundaries, monitoring children and youth) to adolescent outcomes is complex. This is clear in the many studies that have looked at variation by gender. Ensminger (1990) examined parental monitoring and boundary setting, finding that permissive family rules about curfews on school nights were associated with females having multiple problem behaviors (i.e., sexual activity, substance use, and assaulting others). Another study (Galambos & Maggs, 1991) demonstrated that firm parental controls, such as those exercised by authoritative parents, appeared to buffer females from engagement in problem behaviors when they were away from home and caring for themselves. Somewhat contrary to these findings, one study (Seydlitz, 1991) demonstrated that parental controls were more often likely to inhibit delinquency in males than in females; moreover, these controls were more effective in midadolescence for males and in later adolescence for females. Seydlitz (1991) expanded the idea of social control to include both direct and indirect controls. Direct controls are externally imposed restrictions and punishments, whereas indirect controls are internal psychological factors (e.g., not wanting to embarrass or hurt the parent through misbehavior). Seydlitz found that neither gender nor age alone was sufficient to understand the complexity of family controls and how they might inhibit delinquency.

Other studies of gender differences further illustrate the complex ways in which boundaries and expectations work for both females and males. For example, Whitbeck (1987) found (albeit in a relatively small sample) that parents' perceptions of their own efficacy as parents had a greater influence on self-efficacy among males and that parental behaviors more strongly affected the self-efficacy of females. Whitbeck concluded that parental modeling of self-efficacy may be a significant source of information about self-efficacy for males, whereas relationships with peers may be a more important source of such information for females. This and other research suggest that the relation of parenting behaviors such as boundary setting to adolescent behaviors may be moderated by a number of factors. The moderating factors may include age of the adolescent (early, mid-, or late adolescence), gender, type of controls or boundaries used, and aspects of the parent's personality such as self-perceptions of efficacy.

Gender differences are also evident with neighborhood boundaries. For example, Ensminger et al. (1996) examined the impact of neighborhood indicators (i.e., percentage of residents below poverty level, percentage in white-collar occupations, median income, median education) on the likelihood of school dropout and found no neighborhood effects for females as compared with males. This study suggests that neighborhoods may influence males more than they do females. (See similar findings in Chapter 1, on support.)

Race and ethnicity may interact with gender. For example, Achor and Morales (1990) examined a group of 100 Chicanas who had earned doctorates from institutions in the United States and who came from predominantly low-income, traditional families, families that are not always thought to be supportive of higher education. The researchers found that the high-achieving women were from families, regardless of income level, who held high expectations for educational attainment. In addition, the women had faculty role models and mentors, and they seemed to react to traditional barriers by treating them as challenges. They also rejected institutional messages that they were in some way unworthy.

Race and Ethnicity

A number of studies address the variation of boundaries and expectations as a function of ethnic group differences. For example, Steinberg et al. (1991) reported that the relation between authoritative parenting and school performance is greater among Caucasian and Hispanic adolescents than among their African American or Asian American counterparts. They found no ethnic differences related to other adolescent outcomes, however; that is, authoritative parenting appeared to have the same effect on psychosocial maturity, psychological distress, and behavior problems for African American, Asian American, Caucasian, and Hispanic youth.

In an interesting study examining ethnic differences and the effects of neighborhoods, Brooks-Gunn, Duncan, et al. (1993) found that the presence of affluent neighbors had a positive effect on childhood IQ, teenage births, and school dropout, even after the differences in the socioeconomic characteristics of the studied families were taken into account. They also found that the benefit of affluent neighbors was more pronounced for Caucasian adolescents than for African American adolescents.

In another study examining ethnic or cultural differences, Fry (1988) analyzed patterns of aggression among children in two Zapotec Indian communities that had different levels of adult violence. Fry found that children in the community with the higher level of adult violence engaged in more fighting compared with children in the community with the lower level of adult violence. Fry speculates that children learn "community-appropriate" patterns of aggression expression. While this study did not include a comparison to another ethnic-cultural group, there is no reason to think that these findings of socially learned aggression would not generalize to other cultures. For instance, a similar pattern of responses is evident in research that demonstrates that children who observe violence in their homes, or who are victims of violence, are more likely to be perpetrators of violence as adolescents or adults (e.g., Egeland, Jacobvitz, & Sroufe, 1988).

Studies of peer influence also reveal some interesting findings related to ethnic diversity. In general, smoking by peers has been found to be the best predictor of smoking among White adolescents. Peer smoking is a somewhat weaker predictor of smoking among Hispanic and Asian youth and has not been found to be a good predictor of smoking among African American youth (Landrine et al., 1994). Botvin et al. (1994) also examined predictors of smoking among a large sample of inner-city African American and Hispanic 7th graders. In contrast to the previous findings, they found that peers were critical social influences in the smoking process for youth of color. Botvin and colleagues hypothesized, however, that parents' positive attitudes toward adolescent smoking are also related to smoking patterns, and that low perceived social support from teachers predicted subjects' intention to smoke in the future.

Similarly, Coombs et al. (1991) found that substance users are more strongly influenced by peers than are youth who do not use substances, regardless of ethnic group differences. They suggest, however, that family factors underlie substance use among adolescents; an emotionally close parent-adolescent relationship will lessen the negative effects of peer influences.

In a cross-cultural examination of parental expectations, Rosenthal and Feldman (1991) compared first- and second-generation Chinese immigrant students and their Western peers in Australia and the United States. They found that among all three groups, a demanding but nonconflictual family environment was associated with high achievement and effort. These findings are consistent with others (e.g., Chen & Stevenson, 1989, 1995) that suggest that having parents, teachers, and peers who hold high standards or expectations contributes to academic success.

How Boundaries and Expectations Work

Family and School Boundaries

Children and youth who are raised in warm and nurturing family environments with consistent and realistic boundaries and expectations are more likely to internalize parental norms and standards (Baumrind, 1978) and later to exercise these boundaries and expectations as part of their own repertoire of behaviors in the myriad situations and contexts that face them throughout adolescence and into adulthood. Similarly, warm and supportive school environments with consistent boundaries and expectations help young people internalize educational norms and standards and may buffer the effects of negative peers (Kumpfer & Turner, 1990/1991).

The family that provides consistent boundaries is usually described as authoritative, with parents who are both responsive and demanding (Maccoby & Martin, 1983). In contrast, a family environment in which adolescents have been physically punished can lead to problems in both adolescence and later life. Strauss and Yodanis (1996) studied a nationally representative sample of American couples and concluded that having experienced any physical punishment during adolescence was associated with approving of violence against one's spouse, experiencing depression as an adult, and having high levels of marital conflict. Each of those elements in turn raised the probability of physically assaulting one's spouse. The most effective boundary setting parents can provide occurs within the context of a warm relationship in which parents do not hit their children.

Several researchers have suggested that the classification of parenting "style" is a complex one (e.g., Steinberg et al., 1991) and that sometimes a "higher degree of control may be an adaptive behavior on the part of a parent in response to higher levels of problem behavior in their child's peer group" (Mason, Cauce, Gonzales, & Hiraga, 1996, p. 2127). As such,

> when adolescents are part of a more positive peer group, the parenting environment is relatively forgiving. But, when their adolescent children are involved with problem peers the parenting challenge is considerable; underexerting or overexerting control is related to relatively elevated levels of problem behavior in their children. This challenge . . . is particularly salient for African Americans, who are over-represented in urban or inner city communities, where exposure to problem peers is greater and more difficult to avoid. (Mason et al., 1996, p. 2126)

Bulcroft, Carmody, and Bulcroft (1996) used a nationally representative sample of households with a child between ages 12 and 18 to show that the race, age, and gender of an adolescent also interact to affect the kinds of boundaries and independence parents grant. Hispanic parents maintain earlier curfews for both genders, at all ages, than Caucasian or African American parents. African American males of all ages are given more independence outside the home than are males of other races, but African American females' curfews stay relatively early even when they get older, as protection against increased sexual risk. The researchers concluded that Hispanic females in middle and late adolescence were among the most restricted youth, both inside and outside the home. Clearly, adolescents' experience of family boundaries may vary considerably across different contexts.

Sampson (1993) found that a lack of supervision by parents may be especially problematic for children growing up in environments with low community control, again suggesting the interaction of contexts and adolescent outcomes (e.g., Coley & Hoffman, 1996). In summary, research demonstrates that parental control and firm boundaries in the contexts in which a young person is engaged are especially important in managing her or his environment. The level of these boundaries and controls may need to be "adjusted" to fit the variability in context as well as the individual adolescent. In the same way that sensitive parenting is important in the early years, parental sensitivity to these environmental "requirements" is particularly important in predicting positive developmental outcomes for adolescents (e.g., Furstenberg, 1993); it may, indeed, be one defining characteristic of sensitive parenting during a young person's second decade.

Steinberg (1986) examined the importance of supervision or monitoring to adolescents' susceptibility to peer pressure in a study of the after-school experiences of more than 800 young adolescents (5th through 9th grades). He found that adolescents who were more removed from adult supervision were more susceptible to peer pressure and thus more likely to engage in antisocial activity. Steinberg also found, however, that authoritative parenting could buffer children from susceptibility to negative peer pressure in situations where parents were not present; authoritative parenting "carries over" or has an effect even in the parents' absence. By early adolescence, a young person likely has internalized the standards and limits set by the parents so as to exert her or his own boundaries in the form of self-control. Still, for adolescents whose parents monitor their whereabouts, involvement in risky behavior when parents are absent is decreased compared with young people whose parents do not monitor them (see, e.g., Richardson, Radziszewska, Dent, & Flay, 1993).

Researchers have noted that parental monitoring or boundary setting may not be a direct road to adolescent outcomes. Flannery et al. (1994) posit that parents' influence on adolescent outcomes may work through its effect on peer or other interpersonal variables (see also Chassin, Pillow, Curran, Molina, & Barrera, 1993). For example, family boundaries or parental monitoring indicate that a certain level of supervision and limit setting is present in the family life of an adolescent. Those boundaries inhibit the adolescent from getting involved with negative peer groups, which in turn lessens her or his chances of engaging in negative behaviors (such as antisocial behavior) (Patterson & Stouthamer-Loeber, 1984).

Although boundaries are important, the development of autonomy is equally important for adolescents. Autonomy seems to develop best, however, when adolescents are given gradually increasing opportunities to make decisions about their activities and responsibilities in environments that are both safe and emotionally supportive (Baumrind, 1971; Eccles et al., 1991; Maccoby, 1984; Ryan & Lynch, 1989). It is important that parents maintain connectedness with the adolescent during this period of increasing individuation. Even though the adolescent is spending more time away from direct parental supervision, there are many ways that parents maintain a monitoring function. For example, one study demonstrated that parents knowing their adolescent's friends was an important aspect of monitoring during adolescence (Feiring & Lewis, 1993).

The influence of parenting styles on adolescent development and outcomes also depends on the particular socialization dimension under study. For example, Herman et al. (1997) studied a diverse sample of more than 3,900 students, mostly ages 14 to 16. They concluded that parents' connectedness and involvement with adolescents were associated with better grades and educational expectations, but that parents' regulatory behaviors and degree of promoting psychological autonomy in their adolescents were associated with educational outcomes, with delinquency and substance use, and with psychological and physical symptoms of distress. Boundary setting or regulatory behavior seemed to have the strongest association with the prevention of delinquency and substance use.

Neighborhood Boundaries

Over the past several years, a growing body of research has suggested that the neighborhood or community context plays an important role in shaping developmental outcomes for children and adolescents. For example, one study describes how economic resources, adult supervision, and female role models in their neighborhoods influence young women's evaluations of the benefits and costs of sexual activity and affect the timing of their first sexual intercourse; young women with access to such supports have their first sexual intercourse at older ages than those without such supports (Brewster, 1994; Brewster et al., 1993).

In another study, Sommers and Baskin (1994) describe how neighborhood factors may influence whether females will initiate involvement in violent street crimes. The study, which examined some of the most severely distressed communities in New York City, describes how the stresses of poverty and the "increases in illegal opportunities combine with a weakening in the social control capabilities of neighborhood institutions" (p. 483). These females were from multiproblem families where the absence of conventional role models, social support, and material resources weakened the socialization functions of the family. They experienced detachment from such conventional institutions as school, marriage, and employment and by adulthood most were deeply entrenched in substance abuse and related deviant lifestyles. (p. 483)

Elliott et al. (1996) examined disadvantaged communities in Chicago and Denver. They found that the effects of a disadvantaged neighborhood on problem behaviors among youth may be moderated by informal control, which the researchers defined as a general respect for authority and whether neighbors would respond if they saw someone in trouble or breaking the law. Specifically, they report that the higher the level of informal control in a neighborhood, the higher the neighborhood rates of prosocial behavior and youth involvement with peers who are not engaged in problem behaviors, and the lower the rates of youth problem behaviors. Sampson (1997) noted that the effects of community social control probably do not occur directly, but rather operate through peers, school, and family. Neighborhoods with strong social controls provide influential norms of behavior for adults and youth, positive role models, and more effective networks between parents and their children's friends and parents. When neighbors are willing to get involved in boundary setting for youth, parents and adults at school are supported in their own disciplinary efforts, and youth experience a consistency of regulation that is less pronounced or even missing in more disorganized neighborhoods. The challenge for many neighborhoods is that social control, an important contributor to lowered adolescent delinquency, is weaker in neighborhoods with higher levels of poverty, ethnic diversity, and residential instability.

Adult Role Models

The process of social learning includes imitation and observational learning, or modeling. Modeling may be an important part of learning how to interact with peers. Children and adolescents also model adults' behavior, however. It is doubtful that individuals could ever develop their complex repertoires of social behaviors and skills without observing and modeling the behavior of adults (Bandura, 1977a). In an early study, Bandura, Ross, and Ross (1963) demonstrated that even very young children could develop aggressive behaviors by viewing adults who modeled those behaviors.

The development of imitation, although not well understood, begins early in life. Infants of just a few weeks of age have been shown to imitate the facial expressions and gestures of adults (e.g., Jacobson, 1979), and older babies will imitate more complicated actions. Although imitation declines in childhood, observational learning or modeling continues. Unlike imitation, observational learning generally involves a delay between when the behavior is observed by the child and when it is modeled.

Much of the literature pertaining specifically to adult role models examines the impact of adults modeling negative behaviors. The research suggests, however, that adolescents' expectations about their future lives, whether educational attainment, work, or family life, are influenced by adult role models—adults whom young people perceive as "like them" or whom they wish to "be like." Some research has shown that an adult role model can also be an older sibling of the adolescent (e.g., East, 1996). Büchel and Duncan (1998) showed the effects of positive role modeling in a study of German adolescents ages 12 to 14. Youth whose fathers actively participated in sports and who did volunteer work were more likely than other youth to be in a university-track program at school; the effects were particularly strong for sons and for adolescents in low-income families.

Positive Peer Influence

As mentioned earlier in this chapter, much of the literature on peer influence pertains to smoking or other substance use. A survey of approximately 1,000 middle and high school students found that about 20% said their friends pressured them against smoking marijuana, using alcohol, or having sex. Moreover, about 60% said their friends pressured them toward getting good grades, finishing high school, and excelling at something ("Peer Groups," 1996). A few studies suggest that peers have an indirect rather than direct influence on adolescent behaviors such as smoking. One study suggests that it is socialization that influences drug use: Frequent drug users use drugs in order to socialize with friends (Gutierres et al., 1994). Similarly, smoking may be used as a vehicle for entering a particular peer group (Aloise-Young et al., 1994), or drug use may even precede changes in affiliations with a particular peer group (Farell & Danish, 1993).

In general, having friends who approve of alcohol use, for example, or who model this and related behaviors is thought to be an important factor in the development of these behaviors (e.g., Jessor & Jessor, 1975; Stattin et al., 1989). Clinical observations also have suggested that drug use may be a way for adolescents to "self-medicate" in an attempt to cope with anxiety about social situations or with depressive affect or other negative feelings that may be associated with how adolescents perceive themselves in social situations (e.g., Gutierres et al., 1994).

The degree and kind of influence peers may have also depend on individual characteristics. For example, Vitaro, Tremblay, Kerr, Pagani, and Bukowski (1997), in a study of nearly 900 11- and 12-year-old males, found that delinquency at age 13 among youth who were either highly disruptive or conforming when they were 11 and 12 was not affected by the kinds of friends they had. At the same time, males who were moderately disruptive at ages 11 or 12 and who had friends who were aggressive and disturbing were more likely to become delinquent at age 13. In contrast, nonaggressive, nondisturbing friends seemed to provide some protection for moderately disruptive males—socially behaved peers helped moderately disruptive males from becoming even more disruptive, but had little impact on subsequent delinquency.

Generally, peer influence occurs when young people model behavior based on the behavior of a peer. Sometimes, however, modeling involves young people's perceptions of their peers' behaviors rather than the actual behaviors of others. These perceptions are not always accurate (e.g., Graham et al., 1991). Research has suggested that adolescents' perceptions of peer involvement in smoking, for example, are actually overestimations; adolescents choose to take up smoking because they perceive, however inaccurately, that their peers are smoking more than they actually are (e.g., Urberg et al., 1990). Similarly, adolescents have been found to overestimate the proportion of their peers engaging in sexual intercourse (Alan Guttmacher Institute, 1994). The effects of such inaccurate perceptions are considerable. For example, Romer et al. (1994) studied a sample of 300 African American youth ages 9 to 15 who lived in public housing communities. They reported that the more those young adolescents thought their friends had engaged in sexual intercourse, the greater their own involvement. Those peer perceptions were more strongly related than parental monitoring to levels of sexual intercourse. Moreover, the power of perceptions is suggested by the finding that condom use declined with age for all youth except for those who thought that most of their friends used condoms.

High Expectations

Having parents and teachers who expect them to do their best is important for adolescents. Much of the research about the importance of high expectations is related to the effects of teachers' expectations on academic outcomes. Parents' expectations have been studied mainly as part of parenting style.

The research consistently suggests that effective schools are characterized by, among other things, appropriately high levels of academic expectations (Cawelti, 1994; Rutter, 1983). Regardless of ability level, young people's scholastic achievement tends to be higher in classes where teachers have high expectations. (See also Chapter 6, on commitment to learning.)

High expectations are an important aspect of an authoritative parenting style (Maccoby & Martin, 1983), which is generally described as creating an at-

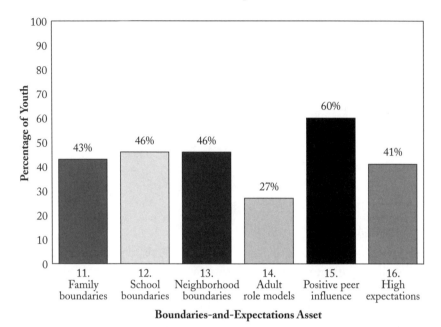

Figure 3 *Adolescents' experience of boundaries and expectations: percentage of 6th- to 12th-grade students who report experiencing each of the boundaries-and-expectations assets. From unpublished Search Institute data on youth in public and/or alternative schools who completed the institute's* Profiles of Student Life: Attitudes and Behaviors *survey during the 1996–97 school year; N = 99,462 students in 213 U.S. communities.*

mosphere of high expectations coupled with warmth and responsiveness. Parenting characterized by high expectations alone—without warmth and responsiveness—defines an authoritarian parenting style, which is not associated with the positive outcomes consistently found for authoritative parenting environments. (See Chapter 1, on support.)

Adolescents' Experience of Boundaries and Expectations

Although the majority of youth in our sample of almost 100,000 report that they experience positive peer influence, it is alarming to note that less than half of 6th–12th graders feel they have family boundaries, school boundaries, neighborhood boundaries, or high expectations from parents and teachers. Even more disturbing, three out of every four adolescents report that they do not have adults in their lives who model positive behaviors. (See Figure 3.)

As with other asset categories, 6th graders experience the highest proportions of the six boundaries-and-expectations assets. A particularly steep decline, from 82% to 49%, is reported for positive peer influence from 6th to 12th grade. This represents a decline of 40% over the age period; it is even more pronounced among males than females. Also noteworthy is that the percentage of youth who report having school boundaries drops sharply from 6th grade to 8th grade, from 70% to 50%. This decline of 20 percentage points over the middle school years suggests that, compared with elementary schools, middle schools and junior high schools do a much less successful job of articulating and reinforcing rules, norms, expectations, and standards. In four of the six assets in this category, females more frequently report the presence of boundaries and expectations in their lives.

What Is Missing from Our Definition of Boundaries and Expectations?

In general, the boundaries-and-expectations category of assets seems to represent the important sources of influence in adolescents' lives, cutting across the contexts in which they live. These assets reflect the overarching ways in which boundaries and expectations are described in the empirical literature. The family-boundaries asset, for example, includes adolescents' knowledge of family rules, parents' knowledge of their children's whereabouts, and the consequences for breaking those rules—all of which are reflected in the literature. Similarly consistent with the literature is our definition of school boundaries, which includes "getting into trouble" for breaking a rule; the literature suggests, however, that this definition might be improved if it clearly specified the presence of consequences.

Family and school boundaries are, of course, only one aspect of a family's or school's contribution to the healthy development of children and youth. Additional aspects of these important contexts are included in other asset categories (e.g., see Chapter 1, on support).

Consistent with the literature, our definition of neighborhood boundaries includes the presence of neighbors who tell parents if they observe the adolescent doing something wrong. Our definition does not, however, reference formal monitoring of children and youth (e.g., neighbors who are "on duty" at certain times) or neighborhood consequences, which also have been noted in the literature as an important aspect of safe neighborhoods for children and youth (e.g., Elliott et al., 1996). Moreover, the availability of economic or material resources in neighborhoods is not reflected in our measure of this domain. Research has shown that an impoverished neighborhood is less able to provide good boundaries for youth (e.g., Sampson, 1997).

Our measure of adult role models examines the presence of adults in the adolescent's life who model helping and prosocial behaviors. Adult role models may also be important as models of other types of positive behaviors and attitudes (e.g., valuing higher education). Our measure of positive peer influence assesses both the absence of peers who model negative behaviors and the presence of peers who model positive behaviors or attitudes (i.e., doing well in school).

We operationalize high expectations as parents and teachers who push the adolescent to be the best that he or she can be. Arguably, high expectations should also include parents and teachers who provide additional supports—such as activities that enhance learning—to enable the adolescent to be her or his best and who frame their expectations in an environment of warmth and responsiveness.

How Can Boundaries and Expectations Be Built?

Part of what adults must do to build the boundaries-and-expectations assets for adolescents is help adolescents begin to set their own boundaries and develop their own expectations. Adolescence is a developmental period in which the regulation of activities and responsibilities begins to be transferred from the parents and society to the child. This is a slow process that begins with parents co-regulating, with the adolescent, the adolescent's activities. The goal is that regulation should become an autonomous function by early adulthood (Maccoby, 1984). This does not mean that parents and teachers no longer set boundaries, monitor behavior, or hold high expectations for doing well. But it does mean that they recognize the adolescent's growing capabilities and need for increasing autonomy in this area.

Much of the information on how boundaries and expectations can be built in adolescence is in the literature on the prevention of adolescent problem behaviors. Although prevention programs specifically target the prevention of problem behaviors, their focus is on nurturing the development of adolescents' abilities to monitor their own behavior. Although some studies have suggested that prevention efforts are effective only when they begin in the early elementary years (Flannery et al., 1994), program evaluation reports have suggested that building self-esteem and self-efficacy is a technique that will enable adolescents to resist negative peer influence (e.g., Bandura, 1986, 1997; Coates, 1985). (See Chapter 8, on positive identity.) These prevention efforts enable the adolescent to assert her or his own boundaries when confronted with negative peer group influence. Increasing the ability of adolescents to resist social pressures is a major component of many prevention programs (Kirby et al., 1994; Silvestri & Flay, 1989; Stacy et al., 1992).

In general, teaching adolescents generic life skills may enable them to develop their abilities to monitor their own behaviors (Botvin et al., 1994), although

93

there is also some evidence that, to be effective, skill training must have a specific focus (e.g., substance abuse, sexual decision making). This suggests that generic life skills training should include the rehearsal of specific situations that the adolescent may encounter. The more general type of social skills training for young people has been shown to have more immediate effects on coping skills (e.g., Petersen, et al., 1997). Thus, the interpersonal domain may be the most appropriate target for prevention efforts geared to young adolescents. Targeting the interpersonal domain might include emphasis on problem solving with peers, making responsible choices, and developing strategies to deal effectively with peer pressure (Flannery et al., 1994). (See Chapter 7, on social competencies.)

Working directly with children and youth to increase their abilities to monitor themselves is one important way to build boundaries and expectations; another strategy is to improve parenting skills. Studies have shown that family management problems can be reduced through parent skills training and through family therapy (Baum & Forehand, 1981; Hawkins, Catalano, & Miller, 1992; Patterson, Chamberlain, & Reid, 1982). Parent skills training programs, for example, focus on teaching parents how to monitor their children's behavior. Studies also suggest the use of moderate amounts of contingent discipline (discipline that is a direct consequence of the child's behavior) and the consistent rewarding of prosocial behaviors (Hawkins, Catalano, & Miller, 1992; Patterson & Fleischman, 1979).

Another important technique to help build parental boundaries and expectations for youth is to encourage parents to engage other parents (i.e., parents of their adolescents' friends) in comonitoring the behavior of their children and youth (Romer et al., 1994). When neighbors are willing to be "on the lookout" and share the monitoring of neighborhood children and youth, they serve both to strengthen neighborhood boundaries and to help and support parents. In addition, neighbors must be willing to report behaviors they have observed to parents. The establishment of consistent neighborhood standards and rules should be developed through neighborhood discussion. School rules and standards should also be consistent and have appropriate consequences. Moreover, both school and neighborhood boundaries and expectations need to be shared with all youth and their families (e.g., through school newsletters, newspapers, and ongoing neighborhood dialogue).

Conclusion

Boundaries and expectations consist of the ways in which parents, schools, and neighborhoods keep their children and youth safe, teach the rules and regulations for behavior and the consequences for not following them, and encourage young people to do their best. Boundaries and expectations work best when there is substantial consistency across socializing contexts—although some degree of variability is inevitable. Boundaries and expectations are essential aspects of healthy development, but adults should keep in mind the developmental differences that occur between early and late adolescence. The boundaries and expectations required for the young adolescent are still provided by adults, whereas the older adolescent can be expected to be managing more of these functions autonomously.

Selected Readings

Brooks-Gunn, J., Duncan, G. J., Klebanov, P. K., & Sealand, N. (1993). Do neighborhoods influence child and adolescent development? *American Journal of Sociology, 99,* 353–395.

Brown, B. B. (1990). Peer groups and peer cultures. In S. S. Feldman & G. R. Elliott (Eds.), *At the threshold: The developing adolescent* (pp. 171–196). Cambridge, MA: Harvard University Press.

Elliott, D. S., Wilson, W. J., Huizinga, D., Sampson, R. J., Elliott, A., & Rankin, B. (1996). The effects of neighborhood disadvantage on adolescent development. *Journal of Research in Crime and Delinquency, 33,* 389–426.

Ensminger, M. E. (1990). Sexual activity and problem behaviors among Black, urban adolescents. *Child Development, 61,* 2032–2046.

Furstenberg, F. (1993). How families manage risk and opportunity in dangerous neighborhoods. In W. J. Wilson (Ed.), *Sociology and the public agenda* (pp. 231–258). Newbury Park, CA: Sage.

Maccoby, E. E. (1984). Middle childhood in the context of the family. In W. A. Collins (Ed.), *Development during middle childhood: The years from six to twelve* (pp. 184–239). Washington, DC: National Academy of Sciences Press.

Mason, C. A., Cauce, A. M., Gonzales, N., & Hiraga, Y. (1996). Neither too sweet nor too sour: Problem peers, maternal control, and problem behavior in African American adolescents. *Child Development, 67,* 2115–2130.

Rosenthal, D. A., & Feldman, S. S. (1991). The influence of perceived family and personal factors on self-reported school performance of Chinese and Western high school students. *Journal of Research on Adolescence, 1,* 135–154.

Sampson, R. (1993, April). *Community and neighborhood influences on adolescents.* Paper presented at the biennial meeting of the Society for Research in Child Development, New Orleans, LA.

Steinberg, L., Mounts, N. S., Lamborn, S. D., & Dornbusch, S. M. (1991). Authoritative parenting and adolescent adjustment across varied ecological niches. *Journal of Research on Adolescence, 1,* 19–36.

A healthy community offers a rich array of constructive, engaging opportunities and activities to all young people.

4

The Constructive-Use-of-Time Assets

As early as 1979, Bronfenbrenner suggested that healthy development must include a variety of constructive opportunities. Constructive use of time is the fourth asset category in the developmental asset framework, and it is the last category among the external assets. Whether offered through schools, community organizations, religious institutions, or for-profit centers, structured activities stimulate positive growth and also contribute to the development of other assets.

What Is Constructive Use of Time?

In 1992, the Carnegie Council on Adolescent Development (1992a) issued a report titled *A Matter of Time,* which highlighted the role of productive time use as a contributing factor in healthy adolescent development. Delineating the difference between structured time (e.g., involvement with 4-H or Girl Scouts) and unstructured time (e.g., "hanging out"), the report provided a "snapshot" of how much time young people have available outside school hours. The report posited, as have others before and since, that constructive deployment of "free" time was better for adolescents because it would (1) prevent involvement in risky behaviors during "free" or idle time, (2) encourage the development of other positive attributes, and (3) assist young people in developing positive social supports and skills (e.g., Barber & Eccles, 1997; Clark, 1988; Leffert, Saito, Blyth, & Kroenke, 1996).

97

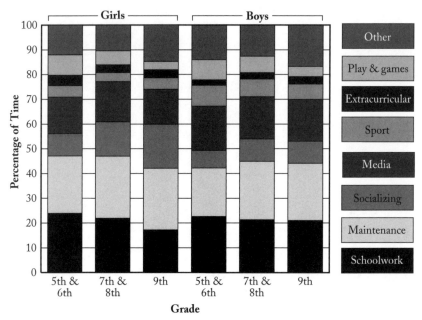

Figure 4 *Time allocation of preadolescents and young adolescents. From "Introduction: The Changing Life Space of Early Adolescence," by R. W. Larson and M. H. Richards, 1989,* Journal of Youth and Adolescence, 18, *p. 505. Copyright 1989 by Plenum Publishing. Reprinted with permission.*

Larson and colleagues (e.g., Csikszentmihalyi & Larson, 1984; Larson & Richards, 1989) have focused their research specifically on how adolescents spend their time. They describe how young people's "landscape" of activities or time use changes as they mature. For example, during childhood, free time is more focused on play, television, and home and family activities; during adolescence, free time includes more peer-related activities and more listening to music, as well as more time spent alone. (Figure 4 illustrates the difference in the time allocation of preadolescents and adolescents.) As Larson and Richards (1989) describe, involvement in play and games declines by more than half, whereas time spent in extracurricular activities stays about the same.

Constructive time use includes "leisure" time. Meeks and Mauldin (1990) suggest that leisure is both free or idle time and "freely chosen" time spent in activities. Leisure time does not necessarily mean time designated only for play, but instead an activity "where participation was engaged in for its own sake or for some intrinsic goal" (pp. 258–259).

The time outside school hours that young people spend in creative activities, youth programs, or religious institutions can be considered a time of informal education (contrasted with the formal education that makes up the major part of the school day) (Dubas & Snider, 1993; Leffert & Herring, 1998). Time spent in informal educational activities should not be considered a luxury. As Hechinger (1992) stated, without these activities

> large numbers of adolescents would fall into the traps of dangerous and harmful behavior. Thousands more would seek companionship, thrills, and power by joining youth gangs or would resort to fighting loneliness and depression by the use of alcohol and other drugs. (p. 191)

The constructive-use-of-time category comprises the domains of creative activities, youth programs, religious community, and time at home. (See Table 9.) It includes "free" or idle time, but in moderation. It is important that young people have unstructured time; it is equally important that most of this time be supervised. "Hanging out" with nothing special to do has been related to engagement in risky behaviors (Carnegie Council on Adolescent Development, 1992a).

Summary of Research Findings

Many studies and program evaluations have examined aspects of the constructive-use-of-time category. The authors of *A Matter of Time* (Carnegie Council on Adolescent Development, 1992a) suggest that constructive time use generally helps prevent adolescent engagement in risky behaviors, encourages other positive behaviors, and provides an arena of social support involving both nonparent adults (such as adult leaders of activities) and peers.

Creative Activities

Our review of the literature turned up little about time spent in creative activities, although a good deal is known about creativity and the creative process. As Weitz (1996) notes, in the report from the President's Committee on the Arts

Table 9. The Constructive-Use-of-Time Assets	
Creative activities	Young person spends three or more hours per week in lessons or practice in music, theater, or other arts.
Youth programs	Young person spends three or more hours per week in sports, clubs, or organizations at school and/or in the community.
Religious community	Young person spends one or more hours per week in activities in a religious institution.
Time at home	Young person is out with friends "with nothing special to do" two or fewer nights per week.

and Humanities, involvement in activities related to the arts and humanities enhances a range of learning styles, provides different ways of expressing knowledge, enhances academic performance, and deepens the development of creativity. Other studies have shown that involvement in creative activities is associated with:

- **Higher self-esteem** (Reynolds, 1995);
- **Increased creativity, intrinsic motivation, and long-term retention** (Conti, Amabile, & Pollak, 1995); and
- **Higher achievement** (Baum, Renzulli, & Hébert, 1995 [creativity may serve as an intervention or remediation for underachievement]; Bergin, 1992 [creativity may influence school achievement; reciprocally, school achievement may influence further involvement in such activities]).

Youth Programs

Structured youth programs are "transitional" activities in that they have similar "demand characteristics" as later adult roles (Kleiber, Larson, & Csikszentmihalyi, 1986). Although adolescents do not usually have the experiences connected with the demands and responsibilities of adult life (aside from employment, for many youth), structured activities may present them with important challenges and activities that require mental effort. Such activities offer youth leisure time within a "context of effort and demand" (p. 175). Larson (1994) also suggests that extracurricular activities help to integrate adolescents into the social world by providing a connection to the community and to prosocial values. These activities play an important part in the lives of resilient youth, especially when they involve cooperation with others (Werner, 1994).

Most of the studies and program evaluations reviewed pertaining to this asset category specifically concern youth programs, including sports, recreation, camps, mentoring, and drop-in centers. Involvement in youth programs is associated with:

- **Increased self-esteem** (Hudkins, 1995; Iso-Ahola & Hatfield, 1986); **increased popularity** (Braddock, Royster, Winfield, & Hawkins, 1991); **increased sense of personal control** (Duke, Johnson, & Nowicki, 1977); and **enhanced identity development** (Shaw, Kleiber, & Caldwell, 1995);
- **Better development of life skills** (Dubas & Snider, 1993) such as **better-developed leadership skills and speaking in public** (Heinsohn & Cantrell, 1986); **better-developed decision-making**

skills (Orr & Gobeli, 1986); and **increased dependability and job responsibility** (Brown, 1982);

- **Greater communication in the family** (Abbott, Sutton, Jackson, & Logan, 1976);
- **Fewer psychosocial problems such as loneliness, shyness, and hopelessness** among youth who participate in exercise programs (Page & Tucker, 1994);
- **Increased involvement in constructive activities in young adulthood** (Lindsay, 1984);
- **Decreased involvement in risky behaviors such as drug use** (Collingwood, Sunderlin, & Kohl, 1994; Jenkins, 1996; Richardson et al., 1989; Shilts, 1991; Zill, Nord, & Loomis, 1995); and **decreased juvenile delinquency** through the deterring influence of sports and adult role models (National School Safety Center, 1989);
- **Improved developmental outcomes** for poor African American youth (Jarrett, 1995); **improved achievement** for rural youth (Lee, 1984); and **improved aspirations for academic or college preparatory programs in high school, a desire to complete high school and attend college,** among 8th-grade African American males (Braddock et al., 1991; Hawkins, Royster, & Braddock, 1992);
- **Increased academic achievement** (Hanks & Eckland, 1976; Posner & Vandell, 1994); **increased grade-point average** among 11th graders (Barber & Eccles, 1997); **increased likelihood of college attendance** (Barber & Eccles, 1997; Oden, 1995); **improved selection of colleges and career choices** (Rockwell, Stohler, & Rudman, 1981); and **improved protection of students at risk of dropping out of school** (Mahoney & Cairns, 1997; Zill et al., 1995); and
- **increased safety** for inner-city youth (Halpern, 1992 [structured programs give inner-city youth a safe place to go, often one of the few safe places in their lives]).

Competitive sports are only one aspect of youth programs, and, by and large, sports programs are associated with positive outcomes, as noted earlier. For example, structured sports activities have been shown to help diminish or protect youth from engagement in substance use.

While sports experiences can be positive for young people, involvement in competitive sports is not always positive. For example, the Robbers Cave experiment, a classic study from the child development literature, showed that intense competition can have negative effects (Sherif, Harvey, White, Hood, & Sherif, 1961). In this field study, two groups of boys attending a summer camp were kept in separate cabins and in some separate activities. In addition, they were pitted against one another through competitive activities, such as tug-of-war and baseball. The intensity of competition resulted in animosity between the two groups that was resolved only when they were required to work together to solve a problem. When a pipeline carrying water to the camp was cut and a truck carrying food for an overnight trip ran into a ditch, the groups had to cooperate to tow the truck out of the ditch.

The relation of highly competitive sports and problem behaviors is complex. Highly competitive sports involvement has been associated with:

- **Increased problem behavior in the form of alcohol use** (Jerry-Szpak & Brown, 1994); and **increased use of other substances** (e.g., Collingwood, Reynolds, Kohl, Smith, & Sloan, 1991); but also
- **Decreased rates of smoking** among males (Waldron, Lye, & Brandon, 1991; Zill et al., 1995).

The contradictory set of findings, which suggest that sports participation may influence either an increase or a decrease in adolescent substance use, may be related to the intensity and stress of competition. If the competition is intense, substance use may actually increase, perhaps as a result of stress or, as with steroid use, because of the belief that some substances will enhance performance. This has been shown repeatedly, for example, among female gymnasts, who face grueling practice and performance demands that often result in increased incidence of eating disorders and substance use. Whether competitive sports are positive often depends on how they are managed by the adults leading them (Danish, Petitpas, & Hale, 1990). Adults must keep the competitive aspect in perspective, remembering that it is only one part of the young person's development, and must be alert to the development of behavioral problems or overt symptoms related to psychological problems (e.g., substance use, eating disorders).

Religious Community

Congregations (churches, temples, synagogues, mosques, etc.) are places where young people may be bound together by a shared perspective and similar values. They also provide young people with the opportunity to be a part of an intergenerational community, which may not be possible in other settings. (See also Chapter 6, on positive values.) Time spent involved in congregations is associated with:

- **Positive adaptation** among a group of immigrant adolescents (Bankston & Zhou, 1995); **increased sense of well-being** (Donahue & Benson, 1995; Moore & Glei, 1995); **increased self-esteem**

(Thomas & Carver, 1990); and **increased life satisfaction** (Hong & Giannakopoulos, 1994);

- Decreased problem behaviors including **decreased alcohol use** (Burkett, 1977; Cochran, Wood, & Arneklev, 1994; Donahue & Benson, 1995; Kandel, 1980; Rohrbaugh & Jessor, 1975); **decreased alcohol dependence** (Clapper, Buka, Goldfield, Lipsitt, & Tsuang, 1995); **decreased marijuana use** (Kandel, 1980); **decreased use of other drugs** (Adlaf & Smart, 1985); **decreased delinquency** (Mulvey, Arthur, & Reppucci, 1997, Thomas & Carver, 1990); and **decreased early sexual activity** (Jensen, Newell, & Holman, 1990; Zelnik, Kantner, & Ford, 1981); and
- **Lower levels of depression** (Wright, Frost, & Wisecarver, 1993).

Time at Home

Young people need structured programs, but they also need time at home. Garbarino (1995) suggests that some young people from relatively affluent families are being overprogrammed:

> One source of social toxicity for children lies in the increasing demands for premature maturity. . . . When affluent parents see their children as an investment, the result is often greater and greater pressure on the children to yield dividends as measured by admission to competitive schools and display of precocious talents. In addition, those parents are so immersed in the monetarized economy that they can't afford to spend much time with their children or don't think they are expert enough to fine-tune their children's behavior and development, so they throw money at the problem instead. (p. 110)

Not all adolescents are overprogrammed. Young people who do not come from affluent homes may not have enough structured activities in their lives. Yet in addition to programs and activities outside the home, all children and youth will benefit from time spent at home with their parents, at least when they do not live in abusive or neglectful home environments. Studies of time spent with family have found that it is associated with:

- **Decreased use of alcohol and other drugs** (Donnermeyer & Park, 1995 [among young people who spend more free time with their family]; Shilts, 1991);
- Decreased problem behaviors including **decreased antisocial be-**

havior among males (Cochran & Bø, 1989); and **decreased delinquency and court adjudication** (Zitzow, 1990);

- **Decreased modeling of peers' delinquent behaviors,** counteracting the negative effects of peers on delinquency (Warr, 1993) (see also Chapter 3, on boundaries and expectations); and
- **Improved emotional state of early adolescents** (7th–9th graders, but not preadolescents [5th and 6th graders]) (Larson, 1997).

Variations in Findings

Although the research generally suggests the positive impact of time spent in creative activities, youth programs, religious activities or communities, and at home, studies are not entirely consistent. For example, as mentioned earlier, competitive sports have also been shown to be related to increased levels of the use of alcohol (Jerry-Szpak & Brown, 1994) and other substances (e.g., Collingwood et al., 1991). In addition, the impact of time use may differ for certain groups of young people.

Gender

Researchers have found that males and females use their time in differing ways. In a study of adolescents in Australia (Garton & Pratt, 1991), gender was the strongest predictor of participation in youth activities; males participated more in sports activities and females more in activities labeled "vocational" (such as going to the library, visiting museums, and playing musical instruments). Other studies have also pointed to gender differences along more stereotypical male-female lines (for example, females spending more time in meal preparation and males spending more time in sports) in terms of how children and youth choose to participate in activities (e.g., Mauldin & Meeks, 1990).

Females and males not only tend to prefer differing activities, their experiences of activities also differ. One study (Shaw et al., 1995) has described the importance of sports participation in the psychological maturity and identity development of young women. The authors suggest that the challenge of sports and other physical activities may be particularly important for young women, who—in contrast to young men—typically have socialization experiences that "encourage caring, fitting in, and concern for others rather than strength and independence" (p. 260). Sports may allow girls and young women more opportunities to explore alternative, or less "traditional," role options in the process of developing a sense of identity. Conversely, traditional male gender roles may be reinforced when adolescent males participate in sports, which may limit or narrow, rather than expand, their opportunities for identity development.

Although not specifically intended to examine gender differences, a longitudinal study by King, Elder, and Whitbeck (1997) found that adolescent females living in rural areas were more involved in religious youth activities than males were. They also noted that the young people who were growing up on farms were more involved in religious youth activities than their rural nonfarm counterparts. Moreover, although church attendance declined during early adolescence, the overall proportion of adolescents involved in religious youth activities increased over the course of adolescence.

Race, Ethnicity, and Cultural Differences

Time spent in sports activities or other youth programs may promote positive developmental outcomes for young people of color. For example, Hawkins, Royster, and Braddock (1992) and Braddock et al. (1991) demonstrated that sports participation enhanced the academic aspirations of 8th-grade African American males, strengthening their intention to enroll in academic or college preparatory programs in high school, to complete high school, and to attend college. Their findings are similar for African American females, although in some respects they may be more strongly influenced by intramural than by interscholastic participation. African American females who participate in sports may feel less socially isolated in the school environment, and their participation in sports may also encourage teachers to give more attention to nurturing females' physical and academic abilities. Hawkins and colleagues also found that African American young adolescents often derive social status advantages (as defined by popularity and a sense of importance) from participation in sports. This enhanced social status occurs regardless of their family socioeconomic status or standardized test scores.

Other research has examined the effect of activities on African American youth. In studying factors associated with academic success among rural African American adolescents, Lee (1984) suggested that academic success was linked to both curricular and extracurricular school activities. Although Lee's sample size was small, the author suggested that school programs should encourage the maximum participation of African American students in both academic and after-school activities.

Constructive time at home was the focus of a study of Ojibway adolescents (Zitzow, 1990). The study demonstrated that young people who spend time in family activities—such as cleaning up, recreational fishing, or eating together—exhibit less delinquency as compared with youth who do not spend time in family activities. This finding is consistent with data pertaining to other cultural groups (e.g., Cochran & Bø, 1989; Zitzow, 1990).

Cross-cultural differences in how adolescents use their time were found by

Fuligni and Stevenson (1995) in a study of more than 500 11th-grade students in Minneapolis, Minnesota, Taiwan, and Japan. Typically, Japanese students are described as overburdened with schoolwork, leaving them little time for the extracurricular activities that are thought to be a central part of healthy adolescent development in Western cultures. Researchers found, however, that students in all three countries participated in sports and other extracurricular activities. And while the American students spent more time in extracurricular activities, all three groups spent similar amounts of time alone.

Socioeconomic Status

Other research (e.g., Zill et al., 1995) has shown the positive impact of involvement in extracurricular activities for vulnerable groups of young people (such as adolescents at risk of dropping out of school). For example, although they focused on younger children (3rd graders), Posner and Vandell (1994) demonstrated the importance of structured programs for children living in poverty because such programs provided exposure to more learning opportunities than children from low-income families may have in other types of after-school care. Structured activities also provided rich social experiences, including more involvement with adults and peers than children in less-structured care arrangements may have. The authors concluded that formal or structured programs may alleviate some of the negative effects of poverty.

Significantly, however, structured youth programs are less available to urban children who are poor. The National Commission on Children (1991) reported that 74% of urban children who were not poor were involved in organized sports, compared with only 49% of urban children who were poor. Differences in nonurban areas also were found (although less pronounced than differences among urban children): 88% of children who were not poor were involved in organized sports, compared with 74% of children who were poor. This pattern was seen across types of activities (e.g., scouting, club activities, religious activities, involvement in special classes). In addition, Dean and Yost (1991) observed that religious youth programs tend to be directed toward, or at least attract, young adolescents and that regardless of faith tradition, they do not reach older adolescents and adolescents who are at risk.

How Constructive Use of Time Works

Cairns and colleagues (Cairns & Cairns, 1994; Mahoney & Cairns, 1997) have suggested that constructive use of time is important for healthy adolescent development because it provides support from "a network of influences. . . . Development is a holistic process involving biological, psychological and social-environmental influences that become fused" (Mahoney & Cairns, 1997, p. 241). Any factor alone (such as involvement in extracurricular activities) is important only in terms of its relation to other aspects of the adolescent's life.

Creative Activities, Youth Programs, and Religious Community

Various researchers have suggested that involvement in creative activities and youth programs contributes to adolescent identity development (e.g., Barber & Eccles, 1997). Involvement in these types of activities is important not only because it occupies idle time, keeping adolescents from "hanging out" at malls or getting into trouble (see Chapter 7, on positive identity). Time spent in creative activities, youth programs, and religious programs is also important because it helps develop skills, creates challenges, and provides fulfilling experiences (Zill et al., 1995). Youth programs also put young people in contact with caring, non-family adults (see Chapter 1, on support), including adults who may serve as mentors or role models.

In addition, youth programs and groups also are an important means for empowering youth (Dubas & Snider, 1993). If adult leaders are knowledgeable and well trained, they will allow their youth members to make or assist in decisions about activities and establish a partnership of shared responsibility between the youth and the adults. This will "minimize the message that adolescent behavior is inevitably a problem or that young people cannot make important positive contributions" (Price et al., 1990, p. 15). Youth programs and youth groups are also important components of adolescents' lives because they provide a sense of belonging, develop skills through real-world experiences, enhance a sense of self-worth, and develop reliable relationships with group members and their adult leaders (Dubas & Snider, 1993; Hamburg, 1990).

Researchers who reviewed about 150 studies of adventure programs such as Outward Bound reported that the positive effects observed—ranging from improved self-concept to improved problem-solving skills, leadership skills, and independence—also seemed to last for months without fading, unlike more typical educational intervention programs (Viadero, 1997). The researchers attributed the impact of such programs to the immediate consequences that result from decisions in outdoor programs, the removal of young people from their typical surroundings (forcing them to adapt to new situations and to draw positively on inner resources and on peers), the way those programs help young people accomplish difficult tasks, and the frequency of feedback that youth get from caring adults in the programs.

Mahoney and Cairns (1997) examined the effects of extracurricular activities on school dropout. Predicting that the impact of extracurricular activities was relative to the constraints of the rest of the adolescent's life, they anticipated

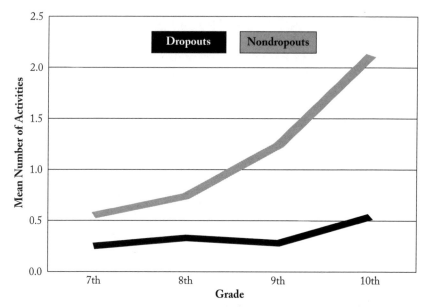

Figure 5 *Mean number of extracurricular activities participated in as a function of dropout status and grade. From "Do Extracurricular Activities Protect Against Early School Dropout?," by J. L. Mahoney and R. B. Cairns, 1997, Developmental Psychology, 33, p. 247. Copyright 1997 by the American Psychological Association. Reprinted with permission.*

that the least competent adolescents would benefit most from extracurricular involvement. "In contrast, highly competent children—as judged by social-academic performance in school—are already firmly embedded in the system and the values that it represents. For these students, extracurricular activities may be redundant in terms of school involvement" (p. 242).

For young people who are at risk of dropping out in particular, Mahoney and Cairns suggest that participation in extracurricular activities may provide "an opportunity to create a positive and voluntary connection to the educational institutions" (p. 248). Unlike the programs in which these students are usually involved (i.e., remedial education or school dropout prevention programs), extracurricular activities and programs focus on promoting positive development. Mahoney and Cairns argue that alternative programs for students at risk may inadvertently serve as catalysts in the formation of deviant peer groups. In contrast, extracurricular activities can "provide a gateway into the conventional social networks, while, simultaneously, promoting individual interests, achievements, and goals" (p. 248). They found that young people who dropped out of school participated in significantly fewer extracurricular activities at all grades, including the years prior to dropping out of school. (See Figure 5.)

Werner (1994) found that interest in hobbies or extracurricular activities provided solace to young people "when things fell apart in their home lives" (p. 135). But most of all, Werner found that self-esteem and self-efficacy are built through the supportive relationships found in those activities; this demonstrates one of the ways in which constructive time use can affect the development of other assets, in this case, enhancing the development of identity in adolescence. Other studies have suggested that young people develop supportive and positive relationships when they are involved in structured activities (e.g., Baum et al. 1995). For example, Shilts (1991) found that young people who did not use substances tended to be highly involved in extracurricular activities and to spend more time with their families and less time with peers. Those findings, consistent with the theoretical literature (e.g., Jessor & Jessor, 1977; Johnston, Bachman, & O'Malley, 1980), suggest that young people who spend time in activities are not spending time associating with drug-using peers.

Another contribution of youth programs is simply that they provide a safe place for children and youth to go (Halpern, 1992); particularly for inner-city youth, "even a small measure of security can mean a lot" (p. 229). One study of the Urban Youth Network (Halpern, 1992), which operates in eight of the most disadvantaged neighborhoods in Chicago, demonstrated that participation in structured activities would generalize to other settings or enhance the likelihood of participation in the future. For example, children who participated in activities spent part of their time doing homework with help or instruction from youth workers and were less likely to withdraw from other academic tasks. In addition, youth programs may offer structure and predictability, something that can be in short supply for young people growing up in high-risk situations.

Sports or exercise programs may benefit young people in part because of how physical activity affects the biochemical mechanisms in the brain (Page & Tucker, 1994). Regular physical exercise has been linked to increased levels of brain norepinephrine and serotonin (Ransford, 1982), which have been shown to promote feelings of well-being. Most sports and exercise programs in which adolescents are involved are group activities; over time, adolescents may learn to associate their feelings of well-being with exercise and group activities (Page & Tucker, 1994).

Time at Home

In today's culture, when adolescents spend time at home, they are not necessarily with their parents. One of the hallmarks of adolescent development is the decrease in parental supervision; because the majority of parents are in the work force, many adolescents may spend considerable time at home alone in the after-school hours. In addition, adolescents spend progressively more time in the company of their peers with little or no supervision, or with a different kind of supervision than typically existed during childhood.

Although this increased autonomy is developmentally appropriate for adolescents, it provides the possibility of increased exposure to experimentation in health-compromising behaviors (Crockett & Petersen, 1993). Some youth are more likely to socialize with problematic or deviant peers, increasing their exposure to avenues for misconduct (Crockett & Petersen, 1993; Patterson & Stouthamer–Loeber, 1984). Steinberg (1986) found, however, that adolescents who spent time alone in the after-school hours did better if they had contact with their parents, or supervision "in absentia" (such as through phone calls), and if they had rules and procedures that they followed when their parents were not present.

Smith (1992) demonstrated that what adolescents did when spending time with parents or on homework may be much more important in promoting academic achievement than the actual amount of time they spent with their parents or doing homework. Warr (1993) found, however, that the quantity of time that adolescents spent with their parents might moderate the effects of peer influence (which could, at times, be negative). It may be that when peer influence is negative, the quantity of time spent with parents affects behavior simply because it reduces the amount of time spent with peers.

Time at home, of course, may also be spent in solitary activities. Larson (1997) found that although adolescents may initially feel lonely or depressed during their time alone, they may subsequently feel more positive about solitary time, which may allow them to recharge their batteries, so to speak. Larson and Csikszentmihalyi (1980) found that adolescents were more cheerful and involved following a two-hour time period when they had been alone. Time alone may be time in which young people reprocess the events of their day in the safety of their homes, surrounded by familiar things.

Larson (1997) also found that a moderate amount of solitude was more important to adolescents than to preadolescents. Adolescents had more choices over their activities and also reported a greater desire to be alone, compared with young people in late childhood. Larson suggests that adolescents' ability to make choices about solitude may be related to the positive effect on emotional state that solitude seems to have. Larson points out, however, that the findings are not necessarily congruent with the experiences of depressed adolescents or adolescents with other behavioral or emotional problems. Spending large amounts of time alone is highly correlated with depression (e.g., Merrick, 1992). Although adolescents may benefit from a moderate amount of time spent alone, excessive solitary time may inadvertently provide adolescents with time to ruminate, which may contribute to depressive affect (Nolen-Hoeksema, Morrow, & Fredrickson, 1993).

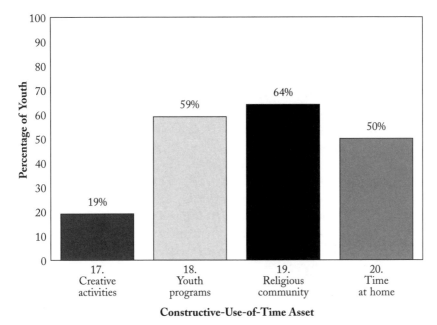

Figure 6 *Adolescents' experience of constructive use of time: percentage of 6th- to 12th-grade students who report experiencing each of the constructive-use-of-time assets. From unpublished Search Institute data on youth in public and/or alternative schools who completed the institute's* Profiles of Student Life: Attitudes and Behaviors *survey during the 1996–97 school year; N = 99,462 students in 213 U.S. communities.*

Adolescents' Experience of Constructive Use of Time

Our data show that only slightly more than half of youth report that they participate in youth programs. (See Figure 6.) Given the competitive and selective nature of some interscholastic extracurricular activities, low participation of youth in sports would not be surprising. These data suggest, however, that nearly half of youth do not participate in clubs, scouting programs, or other organized after-school activities either. Moreover, only about one in five report that they spend time in creative activities. Similar to Search Institute's findings on developmental assets, Mahoney and Cairns (1997) have noted that more than half of the females in their sample and two thirds of the males were involved in only one activity, or none at all. In addition, and perhaps even more troubling, only half of youth in our sample report that they spend time at home (defined as going out with friends "with nothing special to do" two or fewer nights a week).

Our data show gender differences in the constructive-use-of-time assets. Females report that they spend more time in creative activities, in religious community, and at home, compared with males. Males reported that they spend slightly more time in youth programs, which may be a result of greater availability of athletic teams for males than for females.

In general, youth report a decline between the 6th and 12th grades in the time they spend in activities that make up the constructive-use-of-time assets. Reports of time spent in youth programs rise slightly between the 7th and 9th grades, but in the 10th through 12th grades fall to the same levels reported by 6th graders. Time spent in creative activities and in religious programs and time at home all decline over the course of adolescence, the latter two assets by 25 percentage points between 6th and 12th grades. Our data showing declines in time spent participating in religious programs parallel those of other research; regardless of faith tradition, studies show a higher involvement of younger adolescents than older adolescents in religious youth programs (e.g., Dean & Yost, 1991; Leffert & Herring, 1998; Roehlkepartain & Scales, 1995).

What Is Missing from Our Definition of Constructive Use of Time?

Together, the four constructive-use-of-time assets represent the primary activities and contexts in which adolescents spend their time—situations in which adolescents can practice new skills, develop their sense of competence, establish and maintain positive peer networks, and form mentor or role-model relationships with nonfamily adults. These activities and contexts reflect some of the important aspects of "constructive use of time" discussed in the research literature.

Our measures of a set number of hours (i.e., three or more hours in lessons or practice in music, theater, or other arts; three or more hours per week in sports, clubs, or organizations at school and/or in the community; one or more hours per week in activities in a religious institution; and being out with friends "with nothing special to do" two or fewer nights per week) may seem somewhat arbitrary, however. It may be that "three or more hours" is sufficient for many young people; it may be a great deal for some youth, and perhaps not enough to counteract negative environments for other groups of young people. The breadth or distribution of the assets across the contexts of creative activities, youth programs, religious activities, and time at home also does not reflect the fact that some young people may not be "well rounded"—they may spend a great deal of time in music or sports activities, for example, and no time, or very little, in other activities. Can we really say that a young person who spends 15 hours per week in music-related activities (e.g., individual lessons, group music practice, and individual practice) is not sufficiently engaged in constructive use of time? Our measures do not capture positive individual differences that may come with certain personality types or interests.

In addition, our definition of time spent in religious activities or communities pertains to quantity of time. It does not measure a young person's spiritual beliefs. Indeed, young people may be attending religious activities for purely social reasons having nothing to do with their religious beliefs per se. They may attend because their parents make them, or because they see their friends there (see Leffert & Herring, 1998). Participation in religious activities is constructive in the same way that participation in other nonschool youth programs is constructive, independent of a young person's religious beliefs.

Much of the research pertaining to the relation between religion and adolescent behavior has examined the impact of belief systems, not strictly the amount of time spent in religious-based activities (e.g., Wallace & Williams, 1997) (see Chapter 6, on positive values). In addition, the research generally shows that the importance that adolescents attach to religion is a more critical influence than their attendance is. Although one could infer that an adolescent who has strong religious beliefs translates those beliefs into participation in religious activities, one cannot necessarily infer the converse. As previously mentioned, an adolescent could attend activities sponsored by a religious organization simply for social reasons. Consequently, while our measurement of religious activities and community may show a relation to promoting healthy behaviors and protecting against unhealthy or risky behaviors, it is not necessarily a result of belief systems or religiosity.

How Can Constructive Use of Time Be Built?

Effective programs are more likely to both attract and retain the involvement of youth in constructively using their time. Based on a compilation of the work of several researchers (Quinn, 1994; Saito & Blyth, 1993; Schorr & Schorr, 1988), Leffert et al. (1996) summarized the characteristics of effective programs:

1. They offer a broad spectrum of services and opportunities that are tailored to the needs and interests of adolescents. These services and opportunities must recognize, value, and respond to adolescents' diverse backgrounds and experiences and make intentional efforts to extend services to underserved populations.
2. They collaborate with other programs and reach out to families, schools, and other community partners in youth development.
3. They provide a supportive atmosphere for young people and encourage caring relationships with staff and constructive relationships with peers. It is important that adolescents feel respected and empowered and that they can trust the adult staff.

4. They employ committed youth workers who advocate for and with youth.
5. They are easy to access and use, and offer a continuity of services.

Not only is a broad range of activities and opportunities important. The characteristics of the people who work with youth in these settings are equally important. McLaughlin, Irby, and Langman (1994) described the attributes of "wizards," the people who successfully guide young people in youth organizations:

> They see genuine potential in their youth. They focus on youth, putting youth at the center of programs. They have a belief in their own abilities to make a difference. They feel they are giving back something they owe to a community or society. And in everything they do with their organizations, they are unyieldingly authentic. (pp. 95–96)

Participation barriers (such as financial or transportation obstacles) also must be addressed. For example, a Search Institute study (Saito, Benson, Blyth, & Sharma, 1995) found that the top four barriers keeping youth from participating in activities were lack of interesting programs, transportation problems, lack of knowledge about programs, and cost. In addition, the mobility or dislocation experienced primarily by low-income families and families of color added to the perceived barriers.

In *Within Our Reach* (1988), Schorr and Schorr described how many health, education, and family support programs prevent negative outcomes for children who grow up in high-risk settings. The programs described were sufficiently intense and flexible, and they attempted to meet the needs of the people they served, rather than being constrained by traditional bureaucratic boundaries (Werner, 1994). Effective programs must pay attention to young people's developmental needs and to the developmental differences among youth (such as the difference between middle school and high school students). Describing how a tumbling team organized in Chicago's crime-ridden Cabrini-Green public housing community became for its members a refuge from gangs, drugs, and death at an early age, Irby and McLaughlin (1990) noted a key developmental attribute of successful programs for youth: "[The tumbling team] also is an organization that stresses the *positive* aspects and interests of youth" (p. 37, italics in original).

Conclusion

A young person's involvement in positive and constructive activities, both structured and unstructured, is an essential component of healthy development.

Whether offered in schools, community organizations, or religious organizations, constructive activities contribute to positive growth and development and promote the development of other assets. When young people spend time in such activities, they have the opportunity to develop and master skills, interact and develop relationships with peers, and have important relationships with adults other than their parents or guardians.

Much of the literature reviewed here also underscores the importance of well-trained leaders and sensitivity to the developmental needs of the group targeted by a particular activity. The literature overall forms a solid base of support for the domain of constructive use of time and its impact on youth outcomes.

Selected Readings

Bronfenbrenner, U. (1979). *The ecology of human development: Experiments by nature and design.* Cambridge, MA: Harvard University Press.

Cairns, R. B., & Cairns, B. D. (1994). *Lifelines and risks: Pathways of youth in our time.* Cambridge: Cambridge University Press.

Csikszentmihalyi, M., & Larson, R. (1984). *Being adolescent: Conflict and growth in the teenage years.* New York: Basic Books.

Dubas, J. S., & Snider, B. A. (1993). The role of community-based youth groups in enhancing learning and achievement through nonformal education. In R. M. Lerner (Ed.), *Early adolescence: Perspectives on research, policy, and intervention* (pp. 159–174). Hillsdale, NJ: Lawrence Erlbaum.

Larson, R. W. (1997). The emergence of solitude as a constructive domain of experience in early adolescence. *Child Development, 68,* 80–93.

McLaughlin, M. W., Irby, M. A., & Langman, J. (1994). *Urban sanctuaries: Neighborhood organizations in the lives and futures of inner-city youth.* San Francisco: Jossey-Bass.

Price, R. H., Cioci, M., Penner, W., & Trautlein, B. (1990). *School and community support programs that enhance adolescent health and education* (Carnegie Council on Adolescent Development, Working Papers). Washington, DC: Carnegie Council on Adolescent Development.

Quinn, J. (1994). *A matter of time:* An overview of themes from the Carnegie Report. *Voice of Youth Advocates, 17,* 192–196.

Werner, E. E. (1994). *Overcoming the odds. Journal of Developmental and Behavioral Pediatrics, 15,* 131–136.

The Internal Assets

A young person's commitment to learning is strongly influenced by relationships with family, peers, and others, as well as by the school environment.

5

The Commitment-to-Learning Assets

What Is Commitment to Learning?

Commitment to learning has been defined in various ways. Hay (1993) defined the study of achievement motivation simply as "understanding goal-oriented activities" (p. 16). Huang and Waxman (1995) added complexity to the definition in stating that achievement motivation is "the extent to which students feel the intrinsic desire to succeed and earn good grades" (p. 211). An even more comprehensive picture was drawn by Schunk (1995), who wrote that academic "self-regulation" includes motivational processes such as setting performance goals, holding positive beliefs about ability, valuing learning, and being proud of one's efforts.

This last definition hints strongly at the richness of the commitment-to-learning concept, suggesting that it is a combination of personal beliefs, values, and skills. However, those definitions do not capture fully the role of family, peer, and other relationships in affecting young people's commitment to learning; the influence of the school environment on those beliefs, values, and skills; or the impact on commitment to learning of individual differences in pubertal development, gender, ethnicity, or socioeconomic status. The research we review, however, demonstrates the powerful effects of all those relationships and contexts on young people's orientation to learning and to school.

Among the terms that reflect one or more of the dimensions of commitment to learning are effective schools, schoolwork, studying, positive school experiences, liking school, school engagement, bonding to school, commitment to classwork, intellectual development, formal and informal learning, mastery goals (learning for its own sake), evaluation goals (learning mainly to get good grades), school success, educational aspirations, and commitment to school. (Table 10 shows the specific assets in the commitment-to-learning category.)

Commitment to Learning in and out of School

Why is commitment to learning so important for adolescent development? Positive adjustment to and engagement with school pervasively influences social, psychological, and behavioral outcomes among adolescents. Of course, commitment to school and commitment to learning are not the same thing. Indeed, Mark Twain advised young people not to let their schooling get in the way of their education!

Learning from one's experience, learning about values and beliefs, learning about one's spirituality, learning how to get along with difficult people, acquiring specific job skills or skills that enable one to have pleasure doing a hobby, learning how to manage money—all are examples of learning that could occur in school, but that perhaps primarily occurs outside of school. Even more broadly, the desire to learn new things, pleasure in doing so, and knowing how to go about learning new ideas or skills together constitute a "commitment to learning" that is deeper and more lifelong than simply pursuing success in school.

Why, then, in our conceptualization and measurement of youth assets do we emphasize the school-related aspects of commitment to learning? Young people's orientation to school has such a comprehensive impact on them that it is the principal focus of the assets. Besides home, school is where most adolescents spend the majority of their waking hours for most of the year. Young people are changing physically, intellectually, emotionally, socially, and spiritually. Their awareness of those aspects of self is becoming pronounced; school—the crucible in which they experience numerous relationships with adults and peers and numerous opportunities for success or failure—can broadly and

Table 10. The Commitment-to-Learning Assets	
Achievement motivation	Young person is motivated to do well in school.
School engagement	Young person is actively engaged in learning.
Homework	Young person reports doing at least one hour of homework every school day.
Bonding to school	Young person cares about her or his school.
Reading for pleasure	Young person reads for pleasure three or more hours per week.

deeply affect most areas of functioning. Youth evaluate themselves alongside their peers and in terms of the expectations they perceive from parents and others, including teachers. Young people's school experiences can affect their sense of their bodies and looks, their conclusions about how smart or slow they are, and their understanding of their social skills and implied social status.

For example, Kasen, Cohen, and Brook (1998) followed a mostly White, socio-economically diverse sample of more than 450 1- to 10-year-olds until they were ages 9 to 18. They reported that, independent of age, gender, IQ, socioeconomic status, childhood conduct problems, or the proportion of deviant or achieving friends in adolescence, school-related variables had significant positive effects. Those youth with higher academic achievement had less risk of dropping out of school, having a personality disorder, or committing a crime. Those with higher academic aspirations also had less risk of school dropout and of committing and being convicted of a crime, as well as less alcohol use. Finally, those who experienced school settings in which teachers tried hard to make the work interesting and in which students were given a lot of responsibility had less risk of involvement in an adolescent pregnancy or of committing or being convicted of a crime.

Our focus on the school aspects of commitment to learning, however, should not obscure one central point: Young people's commitment to learning at school can only become deep enough for genuine success if schools, family, and community are working together to support the total development of young people, including their health and social development. Only when all the important players in young people's lives are involved in "connecting the dots" (Lawson & Briar-Lawson, 1997) can commitment to learning truly flourish.

Summary of Research Findings

Achievement Motivation

Not surprisingly, achievement motivation—the desire to do well in school—has been linked to numerous positive outcomes related to academic achievement, including better attitudes toward school, greater effort at schoolwork, and higher grades and test scores. More surprising, perhaps, is that higher achievement motivation also has been associated with better mental health, communication skills, and lower levels of risky behavior. Achievement motivation has been associated, directly or indirectly, with:

- **Increased high school completion, increased enrollment in college, increased reading and math achievement test scores, and higher grades** (Brooks-Gunn, Guo, & Furstenberg, 1993 [mother's educational aspirations affecting outcomes for children of teen mothers]; Hahn, Leavitt, & Aaron, 1994; Jessor et al., 1995; Paulson, Coombs, & Richardson, 1990; Wentzel, 1993a; Wilson-Sadberry, Winfield, & Royster, 1991 [increased postsecondary plans]);

- **Increased positive perceptions of school and of teachers** (Entwistle, Kozeki, & Tait, 1989; Jessor et al., 1995);
- **Less sexual intercourse, less childbearing** (Gibson & Kempf, 1990 [among 12- to 15-year-old Hispanic females but not among 16- to 18-year-olds]; Hahn et al., 1994);
- **Less drug use** (Hawkins, Catalano, & Miller, 1992; Resnick et al., 1997);
- **Increased school effort** (Goodenow, 1992); and
- **Increased goal setting, positive expectancies for success, personal control, managing of stress and anxiety, and effective communication skills** (Hay, 1993 [especially if also have positive self-perceptions about physical attractiveness, social acceptance, and scholastic competence (as conceptualized by Harter, 1982)]).

School Engagement and Bonding to School

Similar to achievement motivation, school engagement and bonding (or the feeling of connectedness to school) have been related to positive school outcomes, and to both better mental health and lower levels of risky behaviors. School engagement and bonding have been associated, directly or indirectly, with:

- **Lessened drug use** (McGee, 1992 [especially for middle-class youth]; Paulson et al., 1990); and **lessened chance of being solicited to sell crack cocaine** (Weinfurt & Bush, 1995);
- **Less nonmarital childbearing by age 19** among both White and Black females (Plotnick & Butler, 1991);
- **Greater use of "deep" or "transformational" study techniques,** especially in the higher grades (Ainley, 1993 [only among average-ability youth, not highest-ability]; Connell, Halpern Felsher, Clifford, Crichlow, & Usinger, 1995; Paulson et al., 1990; Pryor, 1994; Wentzel, 1991);
- **Higher academic self-concept, more time spent on homework, and increased college attendance** (Marsh, 1991);
- **Better attendance** (Connell, Halpern Felsher, et al., 1995);
- **Greater feelings of support,** both at school (Connell, Halpern Felsher, et al., 1995) and at home (Connell et al., 1994); and
- **More positive perception of number of personal strengths** among males (Williams & McGee, 1991).

Contrary findings related to the effects of bonding or connectedness with school also have been reported:

- Relationship with school **not related to overall life satisfaction** (Leung & Leung, 1992 [Hong Kong Chinese adolescents]).

Homework

Few studies have looked at the effects of time spent on homework, but most of those have found a positive relationship between time spent on homework and school success. Time spent on homework has been associated with better mental health and lower drug use; it also has been associated, directly or indirectly, with:

- **Higher achievement test scores, grades, or both** (Corno, 1996 [for middle and high school youth, not elementary]; Keith et al., 1986; Leone & Richards, 1989; Thomas et al., 1993);
- **Improved scientific literacy** (Reynolds, 1991);
- **Greater completion and accuracy of homework** (Miller & Kelley, 1991 [if accuracy in homework was required]);
- **Lessened conduct problems** (Hagborg, 1991); and
- **Lessened chance of marijuana use** (Smith, 1992).

Contrary findings related to the effects of time spent on homework also have been reported; for example:

- Time on homework is **not related to achievement**, either in year 1 or year 3 (Smith, 1990, 1992), or to **educational aspirations** (Hagborg, 1991).
- Time on homework is associated with **greater external locus of control** (Hagborg, 1991).

Reading for Pleasure

Of the commitment-to-learning assets, the least well represented in the literature is reading for pleasure. Nevertheless, the amount of time spent reading has been associated, directly or indirectly, with:

- **Increased time on homework** (Lee, Winfield, & Wilson, 1991); **increased reading achievement** (Lee et al., 1991; Smith, 1990); and **increased overall academic achievement** (Smith, 1990).

Variations in Findings

A variety of personal and contextual variables have been shown to affect young people's commitment to learning.

Gender

Despite the well-documented gaps between adolescent females and males in math and science achievement (Eccles, 1997), females overall have more positive attitudes toward and achievement in school. Females seem to be more engaged and interested in school than males (Lee & Smith, 1993). A study of a diverse sample of more than 1,000 7th graders followed through 8th grade (Roeser & Eccles, 1998) also found that females generally and African Americans of both genders valued education significantly more than did males generally and White adolescents of both genders. Moreover, even though educational values of both genders and all racial groups declined between the 7th and the 8th grade, males' educational values declined more substantially than did those of females. Even among youth considered to be "at risk" of school failure, middle school females who are at risk still have more positive attitudes toward school than middle school males who are at risk (Browne & Rife, 1991). Females spend more time on homework than do males in middle school, although by the 9th grade, they appear to spend less (Leone & Richards, 1989). Females also read for pleasure more than do males (Moffitt & Wartella, 1992).

Females also may experience more negative impacts of gender stereotyping on commitment-to-learning dimensions than males do. Fundamentally, because females begin puberty earlier on average than do males, if they experience that transition at the same time they are making the transition from elementary to middle school or junior high school, they seem to suffer more than do males, particularly in their self-esteem (Simmons & Blyth, 1987). Elements of the typical 7th grade, compared with the typical 6th grade, and of how math and science are taught, also may cause a gender-linked difference in interest in subjects like math and science. Math and science become more drill and practice oriented, students work alone more, and competition is emphasized more in 7th and 8th grade than in 6th grade, causing both females and males to lose interest in those subjects, but females more dramatically (Eccles, 1997).

Gender-linked socialization also may exert a toll on commitment to learning. For example, the social element of school as reflected in one's sense of membership or belonging in the school has a stronger relationship with school success for females than it does for males (Goodenow, 1992). The findings of a study of more than 300 students in the 4th, 6th, and 8th grades suggest how this may negatively affect females and serve as one mechanism for their divergence from males in early adolescence in math and science achievement. Juvonen and Murdock (1995) found that "smart and diligent" students are the most popular among peers in the 4th grade, but the least popular students by the 8th grade. If females tend to be more engaged, do more homework, and get better grades overall than males, their popularity may decrease as they move into early adolescence. Given how important group membership and belonging is to females, they may lose interest in doing well, particularly in those subjects where success seems more connected to loss of popularity. If these feelings also interact with differential parent expectations for females' and males' success in various subjects, these gender-linked expectations and perceptions about popularity together may constitute a powerful disincentive to success.

The difference in females' and males' beliefs about their competency is crucial; research shows that students who are more confident about their academic success are more interested in their schoolwork and more convinced of the usefulness of their education (Berndt & Miller, 1990). Yet even if gender differences in expectations and competency beliefs become more pronounced in middle school, it is clear that they are formed far earlier. For example, a study of 1st through 6th graders reported that differences in females' and males' competency beliefs appear as early as the 1st grade: Even at that young age, males feel more confident in sports and math, and females feel more confident about music and reading (Wigfield & Eccles, 1994b).

Young people scored as more "feminine" on measures of gender role orientation have lower achievement motivation than those who are scored as more "masculine" or "androgynous." Males also seem to be less vulnerable to academic failure than females; one study found that 2nd- through 5th-grade females did less well on a task than males did after being told they had done poorly on a previous task (Pomerantz & Ruble, 1997). Moreover, achievement motivation has less of a relationship to self-image for females as they make the transition from 6th to 7th grade; for males, just the opposite occurs: As they move from the 6th to the 7th grade, self-image is more associated with achievement motivation than it was in the 6th grade (Elmen, 1991).

Socioeconomic Status

Socioeconomic status (SES) and ethnicity are related both to levels of achievement and to the different pathways students take to academic success. Because they also correlate with each other, their separate effects are often difficult to untangle. Achievement has been shown to be "strongly associated" with SES and "moderately" related to minority status (Lee & Smith, 1993). When researchers look at the relative impact of SES compared to other variables, however, the role of SES diminishes. For example, a study of an ethnically and socioeconomically diverse sample of Australian adolescents found that parents' educational aspirations for their children were three times more important than SES in affecting the adolescents' own educational aspirations (Marjoribanks, 1996). In the United States, a large study of African American high school seniors from mostly low-income families, followed for four years, reported that the effect of having plans for postsecondary education was three times stronger than the effect of SES on actual enrollment in college or other postsecondary education (Wilson-Sadberry et al., 1991). In a unique study that followed for 20 years the children born to 250 poor, Black teen mothers, Brooks-Gunn, Guo, and Furstenberg (1993) found that if the teen mother had high educational aspirations for herself during her child's first year of life, the child's chances of dropping out of high school 15 to 20 years later were significantly reduced. Clearly, lower SES by itself does exert a negative influence on achievement, yet by itself it also does not doom young people to academic failure.

Race and Ethnicity

Some racial and ethnic differences in commitment to learning have been reported. For example, Goodenow (1992) reported that sense of school belonging had a stronger relationship with school success for Hispanic middle school students than for African American students. She reasoned that because of historical discrimination practices, African American students cannot afford the luxury of their school success being linked to whether they are respected or liked. Stanton-Salazar (1997) observed that many students of color face a difficult task that White students typically do not face, that of learning to function successfully in different, nonoverlapping worlds with different and sometimes conflicting languages, cultures, and norms. He argued that young people of a racial minority learn best to operate within the "culture of power" (p. 25) that schools represent when they have strong family and community supports both for succeeding in the high-status world and for maintaining their unique cultural identities and connections.

Ogbu and Simons (1994) hypothesized that student status as either a voluntary or an involuntary minority would matter in their beliefs about and behaviors toward school. Chinese Americans in this study of 5th through 12th graders were considered to be in the United States voluntarily, African Americans were considered mostly involuntary minorities, and Mexican Americans were considered to be a mixed group, although more voluntary than involuntary. Voluntary minorities studied more, attended classes more, did more homework, and felt greater parent and community pressures to do well and greater pride in their school achievements. Involuntary minorities were less likely to believe in the United States as a land of opportunity, more likely to believe that Whites don't think minority students are smart, and more likely to report more stigmatization by friends for doing well in school (although the majority of all groups reported that friends supported school success).

African Americans in particular were more likely to believe that experience, common sense, and street knowledge were as or more important to "making it" than school success. Overall, African American students seemed to question the value of school more than Chinese Americans or Mexican Americans. Mexican Americans also had a mixed pattern of beliefs; many were unclear about whether they were preparing for success in the United States or for their return to Mexico. The message about the value of schooling seemed to be more ambiguous for those students than for the Chinese Americans.

Muskal and Chairez (1990) also investigated the impact of different immigration patterns on achievement. They interviewed high-achieving Hispanic high school students, and found different pathways to success depending on whether students came from "immigrant" families (having parents who were not born in the United States and having peers who spoke primarily Spanish) or "autonomous" families (living in middle- to upper-income neighborhoods of mixed ethnicity, regardless of parents' birthplaces). Immigrant students benefited more from school programs and teacher mentoring, whereas autonomous students benefited most from parental monitoring and both community and peer pressure to succeed in school. Fuligni (1997) studied an ethnically diverse sample of more than 1,000 8th and 10th graders, and found consistent differences between foreign-born recent immigrants and native students across ethnic backgrounds: Adolescents from immigrant families valued academic success more and had higher educational aspirations, and believed their parents held similar values and hopes for their achievement. The immigrant adolescents studied more and did more homework, and reported both more encouragement to do well from their friends and more studying together with their friends. The strong common support for education shared by the students, their friends, and their parents was a more significant explanation for their receiving higher grades in English and math than was socioeconomic background.

Another study found that Asian American middle school students spent significantly more time on homework, attended school more often, had higher achievement motivation and parent involvement, and watched less television than did White students. Asian American students also spent less time developing friendships than White students (Huang & Waxman, 1995). Similar to Asian American parents, White and Hispanic American parents have been reported to have a greater influence than African American parents on their adolescent children's academic success. Moreover, for White students, parents and peers often converge in supporting school achievement, whereas for African

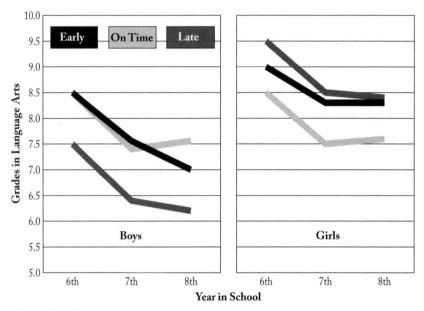

Figure 7   *Pubertal timing-by-gender interaction on grades in language arts across 6th, 7th, and 8th grades. From "The Effects of Pubertal Development on Achievement during Adolescence," by J. S. Dubas, J. A. Graber, and A. C. Petersen, 1991,* American Journal of Education, *99, p. 453. Copyright 1991 by The University of Chicago. Reprinted with permission.*

American students, parental support for school success often is countered by peers' lack of support or even hostility to success (Steinberg et al., 1992). The theory has been advanced that Black students may avoid academic success in order to avoid "acting white" (e.g., Kunjufu, 1988), but Ogbu and Simons (1994) reported a more subtle dynamic at work. Acting White, to the African American students in their sample, had more to do with dress and language than with school success; school success itself was not necessarily a reason for peer ostracism.

Pubertal Timing

Studies have found that the timing of puberty makes a difference in commitment to learning. In middle school, males who mature early, ahead of their peers, get better grades than boys who mature on time or later than their peers. For females, it is the late maturers who are so advantaged (Dubas, Graber, & Petersen, 1991). As shown in Figure 7, Dubas et al. found that early-maturing males in 6th and 7th grades, and on-time maturers in the 8th grade, had the highest grades in language arts; the late-maturing males received the lowest grades. In contrast, late-maturing females received the highest grades in language arts, followed by early-maturing females and, finally, females maturing on time. The researchers found a similar pattern in literature and social studies grades.

Early-maturing males look and sound more like men, and so may be more self-confident and socially competent with both peers and teachers. Such social competence is critical in school success. Late-maturing females may be less exposed to the social and sexual pressures that early physical development can bring and may be better able to maintain close and supportive friendships with same-sex peers. For both genders, being relatively free of sexual pressures creates a climate in which time can be devoted to schoolwork and homework and in which the social support of teachers and peers can facilitate attention to school success. By 12th grade, no GPA effects of pubertal timing are observed in either females or males, but it is the on-time developers of both genders who have the highest achievement motivation. The effect of pubertal timing may be different in 12th grade than in 6th through 8th grades because by 12th grade, nearly all young people have begun puberty and most have largely completed that transition. Early and late developers no longer stand out as much, because mature development is now normative: Most young people have now developed in significant ways physically, socially, emotionally, and cognitively. As Dubas et al. (1991) noted, "It is the unique experience of being different from one's peers that is associated with achievement differences" (p. 455).

Age and Grade

The research suggests that children in elementary school are more engaged in school than are middle school students (Wigfield & Eccles, 1994b) and that 6th graders are more involved and motivated than students in higher grades (Huang & Waxman, 1995). Although self-esteem does not seem to drop from 1st through 6th grade, students' beliefs in their competencies in reading, math, sports, and social abilities decline: Younger children have greater confidence in their specific abilities, if not in their overall sense of worth (Wigfield & Eccles, 1994b). Across the 5th through the 9th grade, some changes in time spent on homework are also evident, but only among average or low-achieving students. Among those groups, time spent on homework declines, but among high-achieving students, time spent on homework remains fairly stable from 5th through 9th grade (Leone & Richards, 1989). Teacher support is important at all ages, but the association between teacher support and motivation seems to weaken across 6th through 8th grade (Goodenow, 1992).

Elmen (1991) has concluded that there is a curvilinear relationship of age with social concerns about achievement. Anxiety about the social consequences of academic success, conformity to peer pressure not to work hard for school success, and gender role ideology about achieving at school are most intense during early adolescence and then drop in high school to the lower intensity levels more characteristic of the elementary school years. During early adolescence, self-consciousness increases, the stability of the self-image weakens somewhat, and young adolescents' concern with peer acceptance rises. All those age- and grade-related changes have an impact on achievement motivation, particularly as experienced through gender.

Longitudinal research has shown that higher levels of commitment-to-learning dimensions in the 7th through 9th grades are related to lower levels of problem behavior three years later in 10th through 12th grades. An important conclusion from this work is that the positive effect on later outcomes of having early protective factors—such as expectancies for success and a positive orientation to school—outweighs the negative effect of also having early risk factors. Having just a little protection was not dramatically helpful, but for students who had high levels of protective factors, even added risk factors in their lives only minimally increased the chance of later problem behavior (Jessor et al., 1995). In short, these specific assets may be more powerful than risks, if young people have assets at high levels.

School Environment

Aspects of the school environment have been linked to young people's levels of the dimensions that make up commitment to learning. For many students, the transition from 6th grade to 7th grade in a different school brings a marked decline in their sense of academic, sports, and social competence, as well as in their belief that it is useful to do well in subjects such as reading and math. After following nearly 2,000 young adolescents over this transition, Wigfield and Eccles (1994b) concluded that after the sharp declines in competency beliefs in all those areas, belief in sports and social competence did recover somewhat by the end of 7th grade, but belief in reading and math competence did not. For many children, then, these researchers concluded that the transition to 7th grade becomes a divide from which they never fully recover academically.

Those researchers observed that young people's perceptions that academics were less useful and important in the 7th grade than they had been in the 6th might be a strategy for trying to buttress self-esteem, which also declined in 7th grade. Even though average self-esteem levels recovered somewhat by the end of 7th grade, they were still lower than they had been in the 6th grade.

Teacher attributes have an impact as well. When young adolescents move from having confident and supportive teachers in the 6th grade to having 7th-grade teachers who feel less confident and seem less supportive, they have lower expectancies for success in math and feel it is more difficult than do children

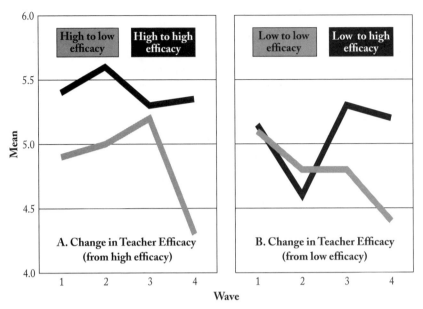

Figure 8 *Changes in low-achieving students' expectations of their performance as a function of changes in the efficacy of their teachers. From "User-Friendly Science and Mathematics: Can It Interest Girls and Minorities in Breaking Through the Middle School Wall?" by J. Eccles, 1997. In D. Johnson (Ed.),* Minorities and Girls in School: Effects on Achievement and Performance, *p. 85. Thousand Oaks, CA: Sage. Copyright 1997 by Sage Publications, Inc. Reprinted with permission.*

who avoid that change in their teachers' attributes. That impact is strongest among students who already are low achievers (Eccles & Midgely, 1990).

Those effects are especially striking in reverse: Young adolescents who move from less confident and supportive teachers to more confident and supportive ones report increases in their interest in math. Again, that effect is the strongest for low-achieving students (see Figure 8). Eccles and colleagues (Eccles, 1997; Midgely, Feldlaufer, & Eccles, 1989) measured young people's expectations and beliefs about their performance, twice in 6th grade and twice in 7th grade. The young people made a school transition between the second time of measurement (Wave 2, Graphs A and B) and the third time of measurement (Wave 3, Graphs A and B). All of the youth represented in the figure were low-achieving students, and, as shown in Graph A, when they went from a high-efficacy (more confident of being able to teach everyone in the class) to a low-efficacy teacher (less confident, and more certain that there were some groups of students who would never learn math), their confidence in their abilities for math dropped. But when low-achieving young people went from a high-efficacy to another high-efficacy teacher, they continued to be confident in their math abilities. Graph B in Figure 8 shows that young people who went to a high-efficacy teacher in 7th grade after having had a low-efficacy teacher in 6th grade increased in confidence. But confidence continued to go down if young people went from a low-efficacy teacher to another low-efficacy teacher. The researchers concluded that declines in motivation and expectancies for success were "not a general consequence of early adolescence" (Eccles & Midgely, 1990, p. 146), but resulted rather from young adolescents' developmental needs not meshing with their schools' organization or teachers' practices.

As a further example, those researchers found that students who felt more constrained in their classroom decision making in 7th grade than in 6th grade also reported greater declines in their interest in math. Unfortunately, many students may experience that contextual lack of support in middle or junior high. Eccles and Midgely (1990) reported that, compared with what 6th-grade teachers thought about 6th graders, 7th-grade teachers thought 7th graders were less trustworthy and needed more controlling. For their part, students saw 7th-grade teachers as less supportive, less fair, and more controlling, as well as perceiving that teachers' practices focused more on social comparisons, from grading practices to tracking.

Tracking is the practice of separating students into different curriculum paths or tracks on the basis of previously demonstrated or even predicted ability. Research shows that when young adolescents' school environments emphasize such comparisons, students focus on performance goals rather than individual mastery goals; yet performance orientations, ironically, are associated with lower actual performance. For example, in Roeser and Eccles's (1998) study of 7th graders followed through the 8th grade, students who perceived their school as emphasizing competition and the different treatment of students based on their abilities decreased in the value they placed on education, and their self-esteem and actual achievement declined as well. In contrast, students who perceived their schools as emphasizing effort and individual improvement increased their feelings of educational value, their own academic competence, and their actual achievement from 7th to 8th grade.

Other research also has shown that the practice of tracking has a depressing effect on school engagement and expectations (see review in Wheelock, 1992). Berends (1995) studied more than 25,000 10th graders, with follow-up two years later. Students in the general and vocational tracks felt less bonding to their schools, had lower expectations that they would attend college, and had more discipline problems than did students in college prep tracks. General and vocational track students also were more likely to drop out. Although the differences between the two groups in Berends's study were fairly small (e.g., college prep students had an average school engagement score 11% to 17% of a standard deviation higher than students in a lower track), the patterns were consistent: Over their high school years, students in the lower tracks became more disadvantaged in their bonding to school. This finding is very similar to what Eccles and Midgely (1990) reported: Underachieving students suffered the most if going from supportive 6th-grade teachers to less supportive 7th-grade teachers, and gained the most if their 7th-grade teachers were more supportive than their 6th-grade teachers had been. In the next section, we will see that this pattern of the "rich getting richer" extends to the influence of the family as well, with the students who most need family support—low achievers—typically getting the least.

School reforms that try to change those patterns do make a difference. Studying a national sample of nearly 9,000 8th graders, Lee and Smith (1993) found that schools that employed team teaching, less departmentalization of subjects, and less tracking had "somewhat" higher average levels of engagement and achievement. In addition, in those restructuring schools there were "somewhat" smaller gaps in engagement and achievement among students of different races and family incomes. Although the differences were small, they were consistent and meaningful both in raising students' achievement (regardless of prior achievement levels) and in contributing to greater equity in achievement among diverse students. Schools that had fewer 8th-grade students were engaged in more restructuring activities, leading the researchers to argue that schools organized as grades K–8, rather than grades 6–8 or 7–9, may be better environments for young adolescents because young adolescents seem to do better if "their age group is not isolated" (p. 180).

How Commitment to Learning Works

Increasing student achievement generally and reducing achievement disparities among students of different races and income levels is an enormous challenge. Half of students say they are bored or "just get by" much of the time in school (Cross, 1990; Steinberg, Brown, & Dornbusch, 1996). Students are interested in their leisure pursuits far more than in schooling, spend only about 6½ hours per week on homework (Leone & Richards, 1989), and generally use poor study methods when they do study (Jones, Slate, Blake, & Holifield, 1992). Their hours of reading for pleasure drop in middle school, as do their positive attitudes toward reading (Ley, Schaer, & Dismukes, 1994) and their beliefs both in their competencies in reading and math and in the usefulness of those subjects (Wigfield & Eccles, 1994b). Leone and Richards (1989) have concluded that students spend "relatively little time on schoolwork" and "do not appear to exert much effort when they do study" (p. 545).

The lack of engagement and interest is especially troubling because students who are more engaged consistently achieve better grades and test scores. Engaged students use deeper study strategies (Ainley, 1993 [e.g., linking ideas, looking for evidence, trying to identify main ideas]). Further, students who are engaged in learning because they like it (task or mastery orientations), and not just because they want to get good grades (evaluation, ability, or performance orientations), also use more elaborate learning strategies than those who learn primarily to get good grades. They tend to stick with challenging tasks longer and end up earning higher grades (Nolen & Haladyna, 1990; Urdan & Maehr, 1995; Wentzel, 1993a). Students who learn mostly to get good grades tend, like disengaged students, to rely most on memorization and other superficial study techniques.

Students do best when they, their parents, and their teachers focus on the intrinsic rewards of learning more than on the extrinsic rewards of getting high scores or grades. The evidence clearly suggests that a focus on grades and on doing better than others in school can be a particularly powerful negative influence at the middle school level, depressing a young person's self-esteem, interest in school, and academic achievement.

We have seen how some aspects of culture and context affect the dimensions of commitment to learning, but what is the general relationship of these variables to school success and other positive youth outcomes? How is it that some youth believe in their abilities to do schoolwork well, value schoolwork, are interested in it, and put effort into doing it?

Effect of Family

The kind of home environment in which young people grow up significantly affects their commitment to learning. A study of 9th graders, for example, found that the home literacy environment in a child's early years was strongly related in the 9th grade to whether he or she had a positive attitude toward reading. Children who were read to, especially by more than one person, used a library, had restrictions on television watching, and had book collections in the home (both their own and their parents') had better attitudes about the value of reading (Kubis, 1994).

When parents are involved with their children's schooling (one of the support assets), commitment to learning also improves (see Chapter 1, on support). Finn (1993) found that parents' direct involvement in talking with their child about school—but not their involvement with school personnel or activities at school—significantly explained the differing academic performance levels of successful versus unsuccessful 8th graders who were at risk of school failure.

Similarly, Leone and Richards used the Experience Sampling Method (young people report what they are doing and feeling when electronically beeped or paged) to understand what adolescents are doing and with whom at different times of the day; they found that average and above-average students were more likely to do homework with their parents. Lee (1984) found that rural, Black 8th through 12th graders had higher math and reading achievement scores if parents both encouraged them in their education and exerted tight control within the context of a close-knit family life.

Parental monitoring and involvement also have been found to increase the time that young people spend on homework. Young people whose parents ask them about what is going on in school, and whose parents know where the youth is and what he or she is doing, spend more time on their homework; that in turn predicts higher achievement (Keith et al., 1986). In a diverse Australian sample, Marjoribanks (1996) also found that parents' aspirations for their children's education were three times more influential than family SES in explaining adolescents' own educational aspirations. Parents' expectations are even more influential than young people's own previous performance in affecting young people's attitudes about math achievement (Elmen, 1991). Moreover, 6th-grade students at risk of school failure are more likely to view their parents as less demanding and as having more casual expectations for performance than are more successful students (Brown & Rife, 1991).

More broadly, Connell, Halpern Felsher, et al. (1995) followed a sample of mostly poor, urban African American 7th through 9th graders for three years and reported that greater school engagement was predicted by higher levels of perceived adult support at home. Students who felt supported (i.e., who felt they had psychological resources devoted to them) subsequently felt more competent, more connected to others at school, and, among males, that they had more autonomy. These dynamics are similar to those other researchers have reported. Steinberg et al. (1991) found that an authoritative parenting environment (warm and democratic, but firm) facilitates academic success in part by helping adolescents develop a sense of autonomy and a healthy psychological orientation to work. In turn, those feelings contribute to more positive attitudes toward school and more positive competency beliefs.

Family communication styles   Reviewing the relevant research, Elmen (1991) concluded that family communication styles also were important influences. Families in which children were involved in family decision making and in which their opinions were sought seemed to develop higher self-esteem and to have lower self-consciousness and a more confident assessment of their own abilities, all of which in turn contributed to competence beyond the family.

Unfortunately, the causal sequence described here can work against a young person, too. Young people who are unsupported at home feel less engaged at school, but youth who are disengaged at school also, in turn, receive less support from families. Connell et al. (1994) reported that low family support indirectly caused low engagement. Low family support seemed to lower self-perceptions of competence, connectedness, and autonomy, but low school engagement seemed to directly cause low family support.

Ryan et al. (1994) found that, among suburban middle school students, those who felt more secure with parents and teachers and most able to access their help in dealing with school and emotional concerns had more positive attitudes about school (particularly their sense of control, autonomy, and engagement at school) and higher levels of motivation.

Redundancy   The study by Ryan et al. (1994) showed that redundancy in experiencing assets is important for positive youth development. The moderate correlations among parent and teacher support variables led the researchers to conclude that young people who feel secure and supported by parents are more likely to have better relations with teachers, too. Parents who have positive attitudes about school may influence their child's teachers to have positive attitudes toward the child, and this in turn may increase parents' sense of bonding to the school. One study of 9th graders showed the importance of such relationships: The greater parents' bonding to the school, the greater their young adolescents' bonding and subsequently, the higher their grades (Pryor, 1994).

Attitudes toward school have important effects on nonschool outcomes as well. Plotnick and Butler (1991) studied a national sample of more than 1,000 14- to 15-year-olds until they reached age 19. For both White and Black teenagers, the only variable that significantly reduced their odds of being teenage parents was having positive attitudes toward school. In fact, for every increase of one standard deviation in their positive attitudes toward school, their chance of being a teenage parent was reduced by 24%.

Effect of Other Social Contexts

Ryan et al. (1994) have noted that the results of their and others' research underscore "how much schooling is an interpersonal as well as a cognitive enterprise" (p. 244). This body of research demonstrates how other assets, working together, contribute to building the commitment-to-learning assets. Students who feel secure and supported at home, whose peers support their pursuit of academic success, and whose teachers relate to them in caring and supportive ways clearly are more likely to believe they are capable of doing well at school, to be engaged in schoolwork, and to value what they learn at school, all of which tend to lead to better grades and test scores. Sometimes the pathways are direct, and sometimes they are more indirect. For example, several studies have shown that involvement in extracurricular activities (and for African American adolescents especially, sports involvement) is associated with higher grades (Finn, 1993; Hawkins, Royster, & Braddock, 1992; Lee, 1984; National Center for Education Statistics, 1995). The explanation offered for those findings is that participation in school activities both reflects and generates commitment and attachment to school in general.

Further, peer and community variables can be significant contributors to commitment to learning. Connell, Halpern Felsher, et al. (1995) reported that, for males but not females, neighborhood indicators of risk (such as crime and income data) were correlated with grades and school attendance three years later. Moreover, males who had a higher percentage of middle-class families in their neighborhoods were significantly more likely to stay in school. Ogbu and Simons (1994) also reported that Chinese American students were more likely than African American or Mexican American students to say that parents and the community expected them to get As and were proud of their school achievements; those Chinese American students, in turn, had more achievement motivation and earned better grades.

Similarly, Jessor et al.'s (1995) longitudinal study of 7th through 9th graders found that problem behaviors decreased when friends modeled conventional behavior and when youth perceived greater controls and regulation from adults in their environment. Those peer and community supports probably serve to reinforce young people's understanding that adherence to certain norms and expectations is a requirement for social acceptance. Ryan et al. (1994) also have reported that middle school students who try to emulate adults have higher self-esteem and school engagement, whereas those who try to emulate friends have lower levels, suggesting that identification with adults promotes internalization of adult values. Further, peer group membership exerts a strong influence on effort among young adolescents in particular. Juvonen and Murdock (1995) reported that, compared with 4th or 6th graders, 8th-grade students were more likely to attribute their failures to lack of effort and less likely to attribute their success to effort. Because students who work hard and succeed are increasingly judged as less popular as they move through the grades of school, 8th graders wanted to maintain their popularity by minimizing the degree to which peers thought they tried hard. An interesting finding, however, is that they were more likely to tell teachers they did well because they studied hard.

Goodenow (1992, 1993a, 1993b) has shown that a student's sense of belonging, of psychological membership at school, is strongly correlated with motivation; the effect of school belonging is "strikingly" more predictive of success than the value that friends attach to schoolwork. Young people who feel liked, valued, and respected by other students and by teachers have higher expectations for success and express greater value for and interest in their schoolwork. All those orientations lead to academic success, which increases peer and teacher acceptance and respect, and these in a reciprocal fashion further strengthen the orientations that lead to success: "As students feel themselves to be full and valued members of the school, they are willing to put forth more effort, and to commit themselves more fully to the purposes of the school" (Goodenow, 1992, 15). (In an analysis of the National Education Longitudinal Study [NELS] of 8th graders, Finn [1993] found that school belonging did not differentiate outcomes among successful and unsuccessful students who were at risk, but the NELS measures may not have been adequate to measure the construct as Goodenow conceptualized it.) Arhar and Kromrey (1993) studied nearly 5,000 7th graders in 24 racially and socioeconomically diverse middle schools; they concluded that low SES schools (those in which 25–55% of the students received free or reduced-price lunches) need to offer particularly strong social support to students. The effects of interdisciplinary team teaching on increasing students' sense of bonding to school were significant in low SES schools; they were a relatively unimportant influence on student bonding in higher SES schools. In a study of 24 racially and socioeconomically diverse elementary schools, Shaps, Battistich, and Solomon (1997) also reported that students' sense of the classroom as a community where they belonged had a strong positive effect on student trust in and respect for teachers, cooperative behavior in helping others learn, conflict resolution skills, concern for others, and altruistic behavior. Specific teacher practices such as promoting cooperation, being warm and supportive, emphasizing intrinsic rather than extrinsic motivation, and drawing students out for deeper thinking and discussion all contributed to the students' sense of classroom community and, thus, to the positive outcomes.

Other researchers also have found that feeling secure in one's social skills and social acceptance is important to commitment to learning. Taylor's (1991) review of research on school success among disadvantaged African American children concluded that social competence was a key protective factor; youth who felt socially competent had higher levels of self-esteem and self-efficacy, which in turn strengthened commitment to schooling and motivation for learning. Wentzel (1991) studied middle school youth and found that those who are seen by peers and teachers as socially responsible got higher grades. Young adolescents who shared, cooperated with others, helped others, trusted their classmates, and solved interpersonal problems without getting upset had in those indicators of social competence a "powerful predictor of academic performance" (p. 1077). Control of emotions and behavioral outbursts in general (behavioral restraint) may be especially important for male students to be perceived by peers and teachers as socially responsible (Finn, 1993; Wentzel & Feldman, 1993). Moreover, if students try to do well both in their academic tasks and in being socially responsible, they get higher grades than if they pursue academic goals alone (Wentzel, 1993a).

Teachers' perceptions of students' socially responsible behavior are vital to the interplay of these dynamics, but Wentzel (1991) found that teachers were more likely to see students' disruptive behavior than their cooperative or helping behavior. Some students then may be misjudged as being less socially responsible than they really are; that mistaken judgment is likely in turn to affect their engagement, motivation, and academic performance. Socially responsible behavior may be more private. This research suggests that teachers and other adults must be more dedicated and their observations more acute to ensure that they are seeing the whole student—the more private prosocial behavior as well as the more public disruptive behavior.

Adolescents' Experience of Commitment to Learning

The assets that make up the commitment-to-learning category (see Figure 9) show varied trends when we compare younger to older adolescents. A common trend, however, is a sharp decrease over the middle school years with a partial recovery over the high school years. Adolescents' reports of reading for pleasure, for example, start out low (33% of 6th graders read for pleasure), decline throughout middle school, and then are essentially stable. Slight majorities of 6th- through 12th-grade youth report high levels of achievement motivation and bonding to school, but reports of both these assets decrease markedly during middle school and then rise only slightly or stabilize in the high school years at lower levels than in middle school. Finally, reports of school engagement drop slightly over middle school but then recover to slightly higher levels among 12th graders. The asset of homework is the only exception to the drop over middle school. Reports of homework start at 43% for 6th graders, rise slightly between 6th and 12th grade, and return to 42% for 12th graders.

The research suggests that it would be wrong to attribute these middle school declines in commitment to learning to normal developmental processes: The declines are not inevitable; they are likely to come about because of a mismatch between young adolescents' needs and the schools' organization and curriculum practices.

Also notable is that females are more likely than males to have all of the commitment-to-learning assets: Percentages for females are generally 10–15 points higher than those of males. The only asset a majority of females do not have

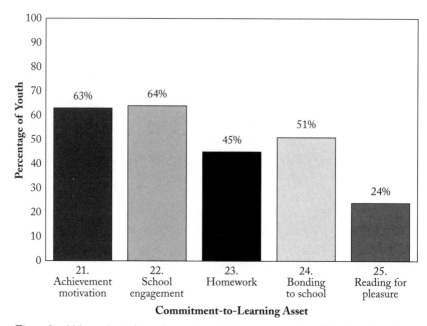

Figure 9 *Adolescents' experience of commitment to learning: percentage of 6th- to 12th-grade students who report experiencing each of the commitment-to-learning assets. From unpublished Search Institute data on youth in public and/or alternative schools who completed the institute's* Profiles of Student Life: Attitudes and Behaviors *survey during the 1996–97 school year;* N = 99,462 *students in 213 U.S. communities.*

is reading for pleasure. In contrast, a majority of 6th- through 12th-grade males have only two of the five commitment-to-learning assets (achievement motivation and school engagement). This gender-based distribution of commitment-to-learning assets is consistent with the data we have already reviewed.

What Is Missing from Our Definition of Commitment to Learning?

Our review of the literature has shown how students' orientations to learning matter: Students with a desire to master a subject or task tend to do better than students who learn mostly because they are striving for good grades. The question might then be asked, does our measure of achievement motivation really measure performance motivation? Would a better measure, that is, one that better predicted ultimate outcomes such as grades, be a measure of motivation to achieve individual satisfaction or mastery?

Moreover, although it is undeniably important for youth to be committed to learning through their school experiences, the importance of learning outside of school is underrepresented in our framework. How important to positive youth development are other kinds of achievement motivation and engagement than doing well at school? How about becoming a top athlete, musician, gardener, camp counselor, and so forth? A lifelong orientation to learning is based on the pursuit of individual interests and talents. The one indicator we include of out-of-school learning, reading for pleasure, does not measure well all that is involved in developing such an orientation. Watching others, practicing body movements, building things, and listening are all ways to learn. Many activities— Internet sleuthing, watching educational videos, visiting museums, observing debates, practicing musical or athletic or craft skills—can help promote a commitment to learning based on interests, but they are not covered by our current measures.

We have seen in this review that another key dimension of commitment to learning is the expectancy of adolescents that they will succeed. We do not measure expectancy of success. As Wigfield and Eccles (1994b) have reported, motivation is context based. Students are not equally motivated by all subjects or all tasks all the time. Like self-esteem, which Harter (1990a) and others (Demo, 1985) have shown to be multidimensional, motivation is not a unitary concept. Our measures of commitment to learning are incomplete in not assessing differences in motivation across particular contexts.

Another important issue in our commitment-to-learning dimensions is reflected in the pattern of gender differences. Although there is no reason to suspect that these patterns are inaccurately measured, the overall impression left is that commitment to learning as we measure it is a concept that perhaps unfairly favors females. Are there aspects of a more broadly defined "commitment to learning" that would favor males and thus provide a more complete picture? For example, would the addition of measuring different contexts for motivation and different measures of engagement with learning create more equitable and accurate gender distribution for the commitment-to-learning asset category?

Finally, a purely time-based measure of homework may not provide a full picture in a society in which homework practices vary across thousands of school districts and evolve over generations. What if many teachers allow homework to be done at school? If teachers don't typically assign much homework, how fair or differentiating is the use of a measure of hours of homework done per week? And, as Miller and Kelley (1991) point out, hours of poorly done, inaccurate homework would hardly be predicted to have the same value as the same time spent doing homework accurately. We might ask how our measure of time spent on homework would be improved if we could somehow add an indicator of how accurate students' completed homework was.

How Can Commitment to Learning Be Built?

Elmen (1991) has perhaps best captured the complexity of the research we have reviewed in this chapter in concluding that "the issue of adolescent achievement motivation encompasses more than school grades, achievement motivation, or fear of success alone. It is the mutual influence of all these played out in a growing and changing individual who is involved in a unique set of social relationships" (p. 145). Attempts to have an impact on young people's achievement that are too narrowly targeted may be ineffective at best and harmful at worst. Public debate that turns on "either-or" solutions to educational issues inevitably leads practitioners and policy makers in a too-narrow direction that is likely to fail.

The research consistently shows, for example, that schools that nurture positive relationships among students and among students and teachers are more likely to realize the payoff of more engaged students achieving at higher levels. Schools that focus mainly on performance goals such as higher test scores without also nurturing both that positive social climate and a love of learning for its own sake may well see short-term "results." The research suggests, however, that the more lasting effect will be students whose pursuit of grades and test scores interferes with their developing more effective learning strategies and, ultimately, with getting the higher-level performance they desire.

It is not unreasonable to suspect that young people who experience the support asset of a positive school climate will also have higher percentages of commitment-to-learning assets. In fact, in Search Institute's sample of nearly 100,000 6th through 12th graders studied in the 1996–97 school year, a caring school climate had a correlation of .40 with school engagement and .35 with bonding to school, among the strongest relationships of assets with each other. The more adolescents felt their school had a caring climate, the more they cared about their school, the more interested they were in their schoolwork, and the harder they tried. Moreover, the asset that correlated most with the outcomes of grades was not achievement motivation or hours of homework done per week, but school engagement ($r = .33$, with higher engagement predicting higher grades) (Scales, Benson, et al., 1998).

This chapter has reviewed research that shows how important individual differences and social contexts are for adolescents to be engaged. Parents' attitudes and behaviors directly affect young people's perceptions of their own abilities, their expectations for success, and the importance they attach to school success. Peers, teachers, and the community all have either complementing or contradicting influences on young people's sense that they are included and accepted, believed to be capable, and valued for what they do at school.

The effects of all these dynamics are both profound and circular. Success or failure breeds confirmation of the attitudes, values, and expectancies held before; for underachieving students, the effect may be further disengagement and lack of support both at home and at school. That is a particularly strong and vicious circle to break, again underscoring the reason why so many narrow, incremental "reforms" in education have had limited impact on achievement. Research has shown that successful schools:

- Offer adolescents safe places;
- Adopt and make familiar to everyone a core set of values;
- Consistently involve parents and family members;
- Foster positive relationships among youth and between adults and youth;
- Compete for and engage students' minds and keep them interested;
- Allow students to explore issues and ideas related to gender and ethnic differences;
- Provide authentic instruction for all students;
- Ask young people to think and communicate in depth about meaningful topics;
- Stimulate discussions about educational and personal futures;
- Develop connections among different parts of young people's lives;
- Connect the school day with after-school time; and
- Encourage and enable students to make a contribution to the school and community (Scales, 1996).

Among the specific educational practices that have been shown to foster those goals are minimizing the tracking of students and the strict departmentalization of subjects (Lee & Smith, 1993); providing students with challenging work accompanied by plentiful teacher feedback (Thomas et al., 1993); using interdisciplinary teaching teams that organize teaching around themes more than separate subjects (Arhar & Kromrey, 1993); using more cooperative learning (learning activities done in groups) and less individual student work in isolation (Perlmutter, Behrend, Kuo, & Muller, 1989); building intimacy in relationships through smaller teacher-student ratios, teacher-based guidance or advising programs, and similar actions (Felner et al., 1997); and using "micro" practices such as "cognitive modeling," in which teachers or peers explain their own thoughts and reasons for actions as they do them (Schunk, 1995).

Research suggests that "authentic instruction" seems to be particularly important for engaging students who are less connected to school. Authentic instruction involves three major processes. First, students are asked not just to repeat information, but to "construct" new knowledge by synthesizing, interpreting, posing alternative solutions, or other complex thinking. Second, teachers engage students in "disciplined inquiry." Instead of just skimming the surface of a subject, students go deep into the subject matter so that they are exposed to the subject's central ideas or theories. Finally, the teacher helps students use the subject matter and study methods they have learned to address problems or issues that have a value beyond the school—that is, that are connected to the real world—and students communicate about what they have learned to an audience beyond the teacher and the school (Newmann & Wehlage, 1995). An example of a practice that achieves all three of those processes is service-learning in the schools.

We have seen that underachieving and disengaged students are especially at risk of becoming more disadvantaged as their school careers progress. Fine, Weis, and Powell (1997) contended that, apart from specific practices that encourage positive school experiences for all children, inequities in achievement among different racial and socioeconomic groups of youth can only be overcome if schools are persistent in building a greater sense of community, demonstrating a commitment to "a creative analysis of difference, power, and privilege" (p. 249), and investing in democratic practices with youth, such as greater youth participation in school decision making. These practices also create an authentic environment in which youth of color can believe that their success is both possible and desired by teachers and other school staff. Gregory (1995) has observed that an experience of even a small success can help turn around an underachieving student; if that success is perceived by the student to be "authentic . . . she can trust what she is experiencing" (p. 147). Experiencing genuineness, honesty, and consistency by being both challenged and nurtured helps young people feel that success is authentic and can be believed. That kind of success can affect young people's sense of expectancy for success in the future; the cycle of expectancy, ability attributions and competency beliefs, motivation, and effort may then be altered for the good. In contrast, Thomas et al. (1993) reported on an example of inauthentic success: Giving high school biology students extra credit to compensate for their low performance and help them raise their grades resulted not in better performance but in worse achievement test scores.

The research suggests that a great challenge lies in reversing an apparently all-too-common middle school slump in achievement motivation, school engagement, and bonding to school. Search Institute's own data show that 6th graders are significantly higher on all those variables than 8th graders, and on two of the three, higher than 12th graders. Our data are cross-sectional; we cannot be sure that the drop occurs to individual children as they get older, but the research we have reviewed in this chapter does support the interpretation that the middle school years are typically a time of lowered interest, motivation, and effort in school. Yet the research also shows that this drop is not inevitable and that it is more likely a result of ineffective school organization and curriculum practices than it is an inherent part of growing up.

The Role of Parents, Peers, and Community

The interest parents show, the help and encouragement they offer, their expectations for success, and the capability they communicate to their children all have profound effects on children's readiness not only to learn but to work at learning. In addition, the complementary positive pressure of "community" expectations is also important for many students: When friends and neighbors expect success, value schoolwork and its connection to future life success, and show pride in young people's school accomplishments, then what happens at school becomes a more important part of young people's lives. Repeatedly, the research suggests the separate and additive importance of parental, peer, and community expectations for school success and support for the choices necessary to achieve success (e.g., choosing friends with similar values, devoting time to doing homework). Those expectations and supports are often more important than socioeconomic influences in explaining school success. Regardless of whether they live in poverty or in crime-ridden neighborhoods, youth whose parents, friends, and neighbors provide those positive expectations and supports can succeed in learning.

Parents especially need to know that their continued involvement with their child's schooling is critical throughout middle and high school. Parent education should stress that talking about what goes on in school, reading at home and talking about what family members read, monitoring homework time, and expressing a general interest in school—as well as having regard for their child's accomplishments in learning—all are probably more important than attending meetings at school, which many employed parents simply cannot do.

Parents and other adults in young people's lives also could take a more active role in talking with young people about the role of education in preparing them for the jobs and careers they want. The National Education Longitudinal Study of 1988 (National Center for Education Statistics, 1990) showed that only one third to one half of 8th graders said their parents or school counselors ever had such conversations with them. Yet having these discussions is part of expressing and reinforcing parent and community norms and expectations about the value of education.

A neighborhood's or community's commitment to learning can be less direct, too. Financial and volunteer support for after-school programs supports learning; young people who are involved in extracurricular activities increase their connectedness and bonding to school, which enhances their school success. Even the degree to which community members have "collective efficacy"— a common willingness to intervene, for example, if they see adolescents skipping school—can support learning. Sampson et al. (1997) found that the higher the self-reported collective action neighborhoods took on youth skipping school, the lower the juvenile delinquency and crime rates. That collective behavior clearly expresses norms about where youth should be during the day— at school—and thereby supports broader expectations of the community that youth should be committed to learning. A good description of how families, schools, and communities can work together in these mutually supportive roles is found in Lawson and Briar-Lawson's (1997) portrayal of "the family-supportive community school model" of educational reform.

Ultimately, everyone in the community can play a role in communicating these messages, even employers of young people. At one McDonald's restaurant in Middleton, Wisconsin, for example, students who are part-time McDonald's employees can elect to be in the "McStudy" program and be paid at their normal hourly rate for an hour of studying before or after their regular working hours. They can't talk on the phone, they can't eat, and they have to be where they can be seen by the manager—they really have to study ("McStudy Program," 1997). This may be a small step, but nonetheless it illustrates that developing young people's commitment to learning isn't just the responsibility of the schools and of parents; it's the responsibility of the entire community.

Conclusion

Young people's commitment to learning, as defined by their achievement motivation, engagement with and bonding to school, amount of time spent on homework, and amount of reading for pleasure they do, is shaped first and foremost by their parents' child-rearing styles. Also influential are parents' attitudes about school and expectations for their children's school performance and the kind of literacy environment they create in the home. Supportive, authoritative parents who show interest in their children's schoolwork, talk with teachers, express standards for achieving at school, and ensure that children are exposed to plentiful and varied intellectual stimulation in the home are laying the foundation for a strong commitment to learning to develop. Youth whose friends and neighbors also model and reinforce those attitudes, expectations, and behaviors; whose teachers are perceived to be caring and challenging; and whose school organization and curriculum maximize learning for its own sake more than learning for the sake of getting good grades, are indeed more likely to attain good grades and achieve better overall success in school.

They also are more likely to enjoy a host of other positive outcomes associated with a strong commitment to learning.

Selected Readings

Brooks-Gunn, J., Duncan, G. J., Klebanov, P. K., & Sealand, N. (1993). Do neighborhoods influence child and adolescent development? *American Journal of Sociology, 99,* 353–395.

Connell, J. P., Halpern Felsher, B. L., Clifford, E., Crichlow, W., & Usinger, P. (1995). Hanging in there: Behavioral, psychological, and contextual factors affecting whether African American adolescents stay in high school. Special Issue: Creating supportive communities for adolescent development: Challenges to scholars. *Journal of Adolescent Research, 10,* 41–63.

Elmen, J. (1991). Achievement orientation in early adolescence: Developmental patterns and social correlates. *Journal of Early Adolescence, 10,* 125–151.

Goodenow, C. (1992, April). *School motivation, engagement, and sense of belonging among urban adolescent students.* Paper presented at the annual meeting of the American Educational Research Association, San Francisco, CA. Ann Arbor, MI: Society for the Psychological Study of Social Issues.

Keith, T. Z., Reimers, T. M., Fehrmann, P. G., Pottebaum, S. M., & Aubey, L. W. (1986). Parental involvement, homework, and TV time: Direct and indirect effects on high school achievement. *Journal of Educational Psychology, 78,* 373–380.

Ogbu, J. U., & Simons, H. D. (1994). *Cultural models of school achievement: A quantitative test of Ogbu's theory. Cultural models of literacy: A comparative study. Project 12.* Washington, DC: Office of Educational Research and Improvement. (ERIC Document Reproduction Service No. ED 376 515)

Roeser, R. W., & Eccles, J. S. (1998). Adolescents' perceptions of middle school: Relation to longitudinal changes in academic and psychological adjustment. *Journal of Research on Adolescence, 8,* 123–158.

Ryan, R. M., Stiller, J. D., & Lynch, J. H. (1994). Representations of relationships to teachers, parents, and friends as predictors of academic motivation and self-esteem. *Journal of Early Adolescence, 14,* 226–249.

Steinberg, L., Lamborn, S. D., Dornbusch, S. M., & Darling, N. (1992). Impact of parenting practices on adolescent achievement: Authoritative parenting, school involvement, and encouragement to succeed. *Child Development, 63,* 1266–1281.

Wigfield, A., & Eccles, J. S. (1994a). Children's competence beliefs, achievement values, and general self-esteem: Change across elementary and middle school. *Journal of Early Adolescence, 14,* 107–138.

Positive values become deep
commitments that guide how
young people think and act.

6

The Positive-Values Assets

What Are Positive Values?

The dictionary defines *values* as the "social principles, goals, or standards held or accepted by an individual, class, or society" (Neufeldt, 1988, p. 1474). Values are the guideposts individuals internalize to create a framework for their thinking and their behavior. Stated somewhat differently, a value, such as caring, should be understood as a "context that creates possibilities" (Chaskin & Rauner, 1995, p. 673). Some values may be understood by some people as absolute prohibitions or commandments that may not be violated under any circumstances (e.g., killing another person), whereas that same value or other values may be understood by others as more general guidelines whose inviolability ebbs and flows under different circumstances (e.g., killing another is morally repugnant but necessarily acceptable in self-defense or in war). Ultimately, values become internally deep commitments that consistently guide how one thinks and behaves.

Search Institute calls the values assets "positive values" for several reasons. First, some values an individual might hold could be considered by many, if not most, people as quite negative. For example, white supremacists hold a certain value about race that goes beyond pride in one's own heritage to include hatred and violence toward other races, a value that could hardly be called positive. Second, although not "universal" in a strict sense, the positive values we identify seem to be held by a majority of Americans. Positive values, then, signify widely shared beliefs that, when put into action, have benefits for both individuals and society.

For adolescents, who are gaining a sense of their emerging identities, exploring and developing values—that is, seeking to understand the commitments they hold dear—constitute a crucial part of their development. In contrast to younger children, whose levels of cognitive maturity are considerably less well developed, most adolescents can appreciate not only the basic distinction between what they or others consider right and wrong, but also exceptions, inconsistencies, and conflicts among competing values. Adolescents' broadening exposure to others and their more varied social worlds puts them face-to-face with value dilemmas that younger children usually do not experience. Moreover, adolescents' more complex cognitive skills, and their richer emotional reactions to the twists and turns of their own and others' attitudes and behaviors, make the experience of defining a consistent set of personal values a particularly challenging aspect of adolescent development.

Values can powerfully affect behavior. For example, one large study of young adolescents found that the belief that it would be "against my values to have sex while I am a teenager" was a better predictor of young people's intentions to have intercourse than either their fear of consequences or their beliefs about what parents and peers would think of them (Donahue, 1987). The challenge for promoting youth development, of course, is that in the increasingly diverse United States of the late 1990s, there is neither a single accepted value system nor any "widely acknowledged authority positioned to influence or advocate today's values definitively" (Alban Institute, 1997, p. 5). So concerned are Americans about values that a *U.S. News and World Report* survey of 1,000 adults found that teaching children values and discipline was the issue identified as most important in education today, outranking even keeping drugs away from schools and far outranking raising student achievement standards ("Hot Issues," 1997).

Given the pluralism of values in our society, defining a list of so-called universal values is difficult. Any list leaves out arguably important values and includes values with which some, or even many, people might disagree. Several efforts are under way that seek to identify and promote shared values. For example, Character Counts!, a nonpartisan alliance of educational and human-service organizations, convened educators, youth leaders, and ethicists to deliberate the content and purpose of "character education." In what has become known as the Aspen Declaration, the group identified six "pillars of character"—trustworthiness, respect, responsibility, fairness, caring, and citizenship—that have become the basis for their efforts (National Commission on Civic Renewal, 1998).

Another organization exploring shared values is the Institute for Global

Ethics, which surveyed participants in the State of the World Forum's annual meeting in 1996. The 272 participants from more than 40 countries (most highly educated) were asked to indicate the single most important from a list of 15 values. The values selected were compassion (21%), responsibility (16%), truth (16%), reverence for life (12%), freedom (9%), self-respect (8%), and fairness (6%) (Kidder & Loges, 1997).

Although different, Search Institute's framework of positive values for youth overlaps with each of these lists of values. It includes six values that appear to have "universal currency, affirmed by nearly all citizens regardless of age, income, or race or ethnicity" (Benson, 1997, p. 48). More generally, the six values we identify as assets include both prosocial values (caring, and equality and social justice) and values of personal character (integrity, honesty, responsibility, and restraint [refraining from early, unprotected sexual intercourse and use of alcohol and other drugs]). (See Table 11.)

Summary of Research Findings

An important limitation of this review is that there are relatively few quantitative studies of the effects of values on adolescents. For example, one review (Chase-Lansdale, Wakschlage, & Brooks-Gunn, 1995) has noted that the value of caring is "not a top priority" in psychological research or as a "way of thinking about youth" (p. 515) among researchers. The same could be said of most of the other values in this asset category, except for restraint.

Another difficulty in summarizing the research on positive values is that studies frequently report the impact not of values per se but of behaviors that researchers take to be reflections of corresponding values. Yet it may be incorrect to assume that a given behavior implies the existence of a similar underlying value.

For example, a number of studies show that especially for adolescent males,

Table 11. The Positive-Values Assets	
Caring	Young person places high value on helping other people.
Equality and social justice	Young person places high value on promoting equality and reducing hunger and poverty.
Integrity	Young person acts on convictions and stands up for her or his beliefs.
Honesty	Young person "tells the truth even when it is not easy."
Responsibility	Young person accepts and takes personal responsibility.
Restraint	Young person believes it is important not to be sexually active or to use alcohol or other drugs.

higher levels of behavioral and emotional restraint or self-control are associated with a variety of positive outcomes, including less marijuana or other drug use (Block et al., 1988; D'Angelo et al., 1995; Farrel & Danish, 1993); less adult alcohol use (Clapper et al., 1995); better grades (D'Angelo et al., 1995; Feldman & Wentzel, 1990); fewer sexual partners and less depression (D'Angelo et al., 1995); less delinquency (Feldman & Weinberger, 1994); and better peer acceptance and peer relations (D'Angelo et al., 1995; Feldman & Wentzel, 1990).

Adolescents who act with self-control or restraint may believe it is important to use restraint, but it does not necessarily follow that youth with lower levels of behavioral restraint do not have this value. An adolescent might believe it is important to postpone sexual intercourse and to say no to alcohol and other drugs, but also believe even more strongly that saying yes to sex or drugs will bring her or him a desired goal, such as a love relationship, peer acceptance, greater gender-role stability, or other outcomes they desire. Although the research findings on the benefits of youth behavioral restraint are impressive, they do not directly address the effects of adolescents' valuing restraint.

A final caveat in reviewing this body of work is that many, perhaps even most, of the studies we discuss here (except those concerning restraint) are small samples of fewer than 100 children or youth. The cumulative effect of consistency in the findings across many such small studies is reassuring and gives us confidence in drawing some conclusions about the operation and effects of values in young people's lives. Nonetheless, the results of any single study with such a relatively small sample size should be viewed with caution. This is not to say that the studies are not valuable, however. A number of these small studies are longitudinal, following the same group of children or youth for several years or longer. Because such studies are a distinct minority of all studies dealing with youth, their data are particularly enlightening in suggesting how values develop over time.

Keeping those considerations in mind, a moderate amount of research shows that the values we include in this category are linked with better mental health, more effective social skills, lessened risky behavior, and greater academic performance. The positive values we measure have been associated, directly or indirectly, with:

- **Higher levels of prosocial behavior** (Eisenberg, Miller, Shell, McNalley, & Shea, 1991; Estrada, 1995; Ford, Wentzel, Wood, Stevens, & Siesfeld, 1989; Krevans & Gibbs, 1996; Roberts & Strayer, 1996);
- **Better means-end problem-solving skills** (Lamborn, Fischer, & Pipp, 1994); **better formal reasoning skills** (Darmody, 1991); and

higher conflict resolution skills (Solomon, Battistich, & Watson, 1993);

- **Greater overall well-being** for Black youth (Moore & Glei, 1995); **higher self-esteem** (Johnson, 1993; Solomon et al., 1993); and **more hopefulness** (Johnson, 1993);

- **Greater belief in male responsibility to prevent pregnancy** (Pleck, Sonenstein, & Ku, 1993); **less intention to have sexual intercourse, less actual sexual intercourse, and greater use of condoms or other contraception** (Donahue, 1987; Ford & Norris, 1993; Gibson & Kempf, 1990; Kirby et al., 1994);

- **Less affiliation with deviant friends** (Whitbeck, Simons, Conger, & Lorenz, 1989); **less likelihood of being solicited to sell crack cocaine** (Weinfurt & Bush, 1995); and **less drug use** (Barnea, Teichman, & Rahav, 1992; Wills et al., 1996);

- **Greater competence** among Black 9th-grade males (Call, Mortimer, & Shanahan, 1995 [helpfulness at home]); and **greater competence** among 9th-grade females (Call et al., 1995 [helpfulness at work]); and

- **Higher grades and math and reading scores** (Hanson & Ginsburg, 1988; Rosenthal & Feldman, 1991; Wentzel, 1991); and **higher perceived scholastic competence, less worry about school** (Johnson, 1993).

Some contrary findings also have been reported about the effects of positive values on youth: Helpfulness at home has been associated with a negative effect on competence for White 9th-grade males (Call et al., 1995), and more responsibility for chores at home has been associated with poorer perceptions by parents of how 5- to 18-year-old youth are performing at school (Taylor et al., 1992).

Variations in Findings

Gender

Research on the effect of context on adolescents' values sheds light mostly on gender differences and to a lesser degree on age differences. The data are limited regarding variations in impact by race or ethnicity, socioeconomic status, or other cultural factors.

Females consistently are found to have higher levels of prosocial and personal character values. In reviewing research from the mid-1970s to the early 1990s, Beutel and Marini (1995) concluded that females consistently showed more compassion (defined as concern and responsibility for others) than did males and attached a greater importance to finding meaning and purpose in life. Those gender differences also appeared to be stable across social classes and were not explained by females being more religious or having more social supports than males. Similarly, females generally are found to have greater empathy and emotional insight (Roberts & Strayer, 1996) and better role-taking skills (Eisenberg, Carlo, Murphy, & Van Court, 1995) than males do. They appear to be better able to identify problems as having a social or moral component (Bear, 1989) and score higher on general tests of moral reasoning—findings that appear consistent across both race and social class (Silberman & Snarey, 1993). When asked how they would respond in various morally ambiguous situations, females tend to make more socially responsible choices than do males (Ford et al., 1989). One study (Kelly & Worell, 1978) found that, when given the opportunity to cheat by giving themselves a higher score than they deserved in order to obtain class credit, female college students cheated significantly less than male college students (16% versus 24%, respectively). In a study of Finnish youth, Keltikangas-Järvinen and Lindeman (1997) also reported that among 11- to 17-year-olds, males accepted immoral acts (lying, theft, and fighting) more than females.

Caring, empathy, honesty, responsibility, and restraint seem consistent with some traditional notions of female gender roles. Because adolescent males often are found to be more sex-role stereotyped than females (Morrison, McLeod, Morrison, Anderson, & O'Connor, 1997), it is not surprising that males in Search Institute's studies say they have fewer of those values than females report having (see Search Institute data later in this chapter). On a related note, Massad (1981) studied 300 White, upper-middle-class 8th and 11th graders and reported that males did seem to have a more limited range of sex-role behavior available: The higher the males' scores on measures of "masculinity," the higher their self-esteem and their acceptance by peers. In contrast, females could score high either on "femininity" or "masculinity" and still have high self-esteem; their acceptance by peers was highest if they had a balanced role orientation, especially if their scores on both "masculinity" and "femininity" were high.

A national study of more than 1,000 sexually experienced 15- to 19-year-old males found that adherence to a traditional dominant-culture masculine ideology (e.g., encouraging the hiding of feelings, emphasizing the importance of always appearing strong, valuing sexual conquests) was associated with less sexual restraint, less caring, and less belief in male responsibility to prevent pregnancy (Pleck et al., 1993). At the same time, positive values such as caring, responsibility, and restraint are consistent with masculine role conceptualizations in some cultures, such as Hispanic and Native American cultures.

Some studies have reported no consistent or significant gender differences on values (Daniels, D'Andrea, & Heck, 1995; Estrada, 1995; Whitbeck et al., 1989). For example, reviewing studies of infants through elementary school–age children, Shaklee (1983) concluded that females and males were not typically different in their expressing caring for others, and that their play was less sex typed when alone or with strangers than with children they knew. Those results led Shaklee to observe that gender-linked behavior was a function of the "importance of social definitions of behavioral appropriateness" (p. 275). This suggests that the values underlying such behaviors also might not be as sex linked as traditional stereotypes would suggest.

Moreover, other studies suggest that even if youth hold positive gender-stereotyped values, these values do not necessarily lead to more positive behavioral outcomes for either gender. For example, Bear (1989) found females were more able to identify social and moral problems than boys, but that did not lead them to reason at high moral levels when deciding whether they would copy software if it was unclear that copying was forbidden. Similarly, Ford et al. (1989) found that females made more socially responsible choices when confronted with hypothetical dilemmas, but that gender differences disappeared if adolescents thought they could make an irresponsible choice and not get punished. In the absence of negative consequences, females were just as likely to make a socially irresponsible choice. Eisenberg et al.'s (1995) small study of 28 children who were followed for 15 years sheds light on why this may have occurred: Females had more positive emotions about values and more negative emotions about the possible consequences of their choices. In short, females' behavior may be more deeply affected than males' behavior by the values they hold.

In addition, Roberts and Strayer (1996) reported that while females scored higher on empathy, empathy predicted their prosocial behavior less strongly than it did males' prosocial behavior. Perhaps high levels of empathy are so unusual among adolescent males that the capacity for empathy and the values of caring that underlie it exert a more powerful influence than among females, whose caring norms already tend to be high.

Finally, in a study of gender differences in moral reasoning, Daniels et al. (1995) found that when presented with moral dilemmas, females and males were equally likely to offer spontaneous solutions based on care frameworks (desire for fairness and concern for feelings) or justice frameworks (desire for appropriate or deserved consequences): Females were not more likely to offer care-based solutions. In fact, when prompted about whether there were other ways of solving the dilemma and finally asked what the best solution would be, both females and males overwhelmingly chose care-based solutions.

Race and Ethnicity

The Daniels et al. (1995) study also shows the importance of cultural context. The researchers attributed the similarity of male and female moral reasoning styles among the native Hawaiian young people they studied in part to the "Aloha spirit" that Hawaiians learn as children. Both females and males are taught the importance of being kind, being agreeable and patient, and seeking harmony with others and with one's environment. Under such circumstances, it is not surprising that both used a framework of caring more than one of justice to resolve moral dilemmas.

In other examples of culture's impact, Moore and Glei (1995) reported that African American adolescents in their study scored higher on a measure of overall well-being, in part because they believed more than White youth did in the importance of working to overcome social inequalities. Call et al. (1995) studied a large sample of diverse 9th graders, including Black, White, Hispanic, and Asian youth, and concluded that the youth of color perceived more opportunities to be helpful at work than did White adolescents, and that African American males' competence improved when they had responsibilities such as chores at home, whereas White males' competence declined with increasing chores. Rosenthal and Feldman (1991) studied Chinese and White high school students living in both the United States and Australia, and concluded that the Chinese students' greater restraint and industriousness were responsible for their getting higher grades. Finally, Ford and Norris (1993) studied the effects of acculturation on the sexual behavior of a small sample of urban Hispanic youth (70% of Mexican heritage and 30% of Puerto Rican heritage). They reported that high acculturation away from Spanish-speaking culture and toward English-speaking culture was associated with a greater likelihood of sexual intercourse for young women (as well as a greater reported use of condoms) and a greater variety of sexual behaviors (and a higher number of non-Hispanic partners) for youth of both genders.

Age

The most common age-related data on values in the research literature pertain to changes in young people's moral reasoning. Those studies reflect changes not necessarily in fundamental values per se, but in the capacity of adolescents to better perceive the needs of others as they grow older, as well as to recognize both general principles for making moral decisions and occasions when exceptions are warranted. For example, Lamborn et al. (1994) studied White, middle-class, 9- to 20-year-olds; they reported that at ages 9 to 12, children could reason from their understanding of either honesty or kindness to understand that "constructive criticism" was a form of caring. They could not explain until ages 13 to 15, however, how honesty and kindness might work together to make social lying acceptable (i.e., that it was generally kinder to someone to critique them honestly than to lie, but that in some circumstances, it was kinder to be less honest). Those young adolescents also could not explain how three abstractions—honesty, kindness, and jealousy—operated to create "jealous truth" (telling the truth in an intentionally hurtful way), a reasoning skill not observed by Lamborn et al. (1994) until ages 16 to 20. The researchers interpreted the results to mean that a value is not one concept that people learn at a certain age, but rather "several related concepts that differ greatly in complexity" (p. 504).

Similarly, the heightened capacity older youth have for abstract reasoning affects the level of their values as reported in research. Roberts and Strayer (1996), for example, found in a sample of 5-, 9-, and 13-year-olds that increasing age was associated with increasing levels of empathy, but that this association was not direct. As the youth got older, they better understood what others might be experiencing and became better able to take another's perspective; it is this increased understanding that seems directly related to caring about another. The ability to think more broadly also means that as youth mature, they use more of their own values as guideposts for decisions. For example, Nucci and Turiel (1993) studied a sample of Christian and Jewish youth ages 10 to 16 and reported that as age increased, children's positions on moral issues were determined less by the word of God as they understood it than by their own values of social justice and fairness. Rather than religion providing children with the basis of their morality, the researchers concluded that the children held "a distinct moral position based on justice and welfare criteria from which they apprehend the word of God" (p. 1483). Finally, in a study by Graham, Weiner, and Benesh-Weiner (1995) of 3rd- to 8th-grade African American males, older males were more likely to recognize a controllable misconduct as one that others would be more angry about. Those older males admitted that they would be dishonest and give more false excuses about voluntarily doing something wrong than about transgressing in ways they felt they could not help for some reason. In other words, they may have considered the value of honesty to be important as an ideal, but it clearly would be situational rather than absolute in practice. The progression of ideas about values is not always linear, however. Among Finnish youth, Keltikangas-Järvinen and Lindeman (1997) showed that acceptance of various kinds of lying, theft, and fighting was greatest among mid-adolescents of about age 14, but least among 11- and 17-year-olds. The researchers suggested that the findings reflected a desire to conform to friends' expectations, which peaks around puberty.

Gender roles also interact with age to influence values. Studying a statewide sample of Michigan 5th through 8th graders, Nelson and Keith (1990) reported that among both females and males, older adolescents had less traditional gender-role beliefs than did younger children. This is consistent with other research that has disputed the theory of "gender intensification" during early adolescence—that is, that each gender becomes more firmly committed to what is expected of them as young men and women during this stage. McNeill and Petersen's (1985) review of the research concluded that there was little evidence for a general gender intensification during early adolescence: Females do not become more traditionally feminine and males more traditionally masculine in their beliefs. The research suggests that the gender differences reported in some values probably emerge much earlier in childhood and are relatively stable. If anything, there may be more developmental movement away from than toward traditional gender-role beliefs as youth mature.

Other Variables

In a small but provocative study of 14- and 15-year-olds, Miller (1991) reported that behaviorally disordered adolescents, compared with nondisordered youth, were observed helping, sharing, and cooperating more in the classroom. The helpful youth rated themselves, however, as doing less—as being less helpful than they really were. For some youth, self-perceptions of not living up to an ideal value, such as caring, led them to believe they really were uncaring, when their behavior demonstrated the opposite. This study suggests the importance of adults' helping youth to identify and understand their values and the ways in which they put those values into practice in everyday life.

Finally, Graham et al. (1995) compared the excuses that aggressive and non-aggressive males gave for bad behavior. Aggressive males were less likely to be dishonest about their responsibility for bad behavior—more likely to simply say they had chosen to do something bad. The researchers concluded that dishonesty in such situations was socially motivated and that aggressive males were less concerned with managing negative social reactions than were nonaggressive males. The best lesson to draw from this research is not that those aggressive youth placed a higher importance on the value of honesty, but that their relatively poorer personal management and social skills led them to behave "honestly" (a conventional value), and yet, ironically, in a manner that showed how they devalued other social conventions (in which most youth would make excuses or be dishonest).

How Positive Values Work

Perhaps the two most consistent findings in the research are the close association between prosocial values and prosocial behavior, and the critical role of parents and family in influencing children's values. A review of the literature by the American Psychological Association (1997) concluded that even children as young as 21 months can demonstrate empathy. Although at that age empathy clearly is not a cognitively internalized value, children's imitation of caring sounds and gestures in response to others is an important foundation for the eventual construction of internally motivated caring values and behaviors. Other reviews (e.g., Chase-Lansdale et al., 1995) also have demonstrated that early emotional closeness to parents, along with parenting styles during adolescence that promote relationships within the family where youth are both close and differentiated from parents, is a strong predictor of caring values and behaviors. Perspective taking or seeing things from another's point of view seems to be an important component of caring, probably through enhancing empathy. Studies have found perspective taking, empathy, and caring to be related to the mother's emotional communication, nurturance, and warmth (Eisenberg & McNally, 1993; Kasser et al., 1995; Kelly & Worrell, 1978 [especially for females]) and to parents' use of non–power-assertive methods of discipline (Krevans & Gibbs, 1996 [especially using statements of disappointment as a corrective for undesired behavior]).

Parental Modeling

McDevitt, Lennon, and Kopriva (1991) studied a diverse sample of 12- to 18-year-olds and found that while adolescents perceived their mothers as promoting prosocial actions more than fathers, both parents' modeling of prosocial behavior affected children's prosocial reasoning. Two behaviors that both parents used effectively were not being "callous" toward or rejecting the child and simply but consistently asking the child to be kind and responsible. Walker and Taylor (1991) looked at the influence of parenting on moral development among children in grades 1, 4, 7, and 10 who were followed for two years. The researchers concluded that although parents' levels of moral reasoning were not associated with children's levels, parenting style was: Children had more principled moral development frameworks if parents in an observed family discussion task used supportive, Socratic styles—asking questions, asking the child's opinion, and paraphrasing the child's comments, but not lecturing or challenging.

One mechanism by which values may affect behavior was suggested by Whitbeck et al.'s (1989) small study of White, rural and small-town families with 7th graders. Adolescents who more strongly identified with their parents valued achieving affluence and success and being altruistic more than did 7th graders who identified less with their parents. Parents' explicit endorsement of altruism did not have a direct effect on adolescents' values, but rather was associated with adolescents choosing less deviant friends. Parents' values may work in part by influencing their adolescents' peer group affiliations and the friend-ships they form.

Values may also operate as symbolic representations of significant others in young people's lives whom they do not wish to disappoint. Because identifi-cation with parents is associated with internalizing parental values, children who hold those values have, in Sigmund Freud's terms, a superego watching over their actions even when parents are not around, an internal voice ready to state its approval or disapproval of contemplated behavior. Even an anticipated transgression would provoke guilt and other related feelings, making the trans-gression less likely. Simple worrying about getting caught and punished enters the picture as well. Indeed, when Ford et al. (1989) studied the conditions under which 14- to 19-year-olds would make responsible or irresponsible choices in various situations, they concluded that worries about getting caught did operate if adolescents feared negative consequences; if not, self-interest and peer ap-proval took over as governing dynamics, especially among males. The researchers concluded that "adolescent social responsibility is largely a function of processes such as anticipated guilt, empathetic concern, and fear of negative sanctions" (p. 421).

Religious Influence

Religion is an obvious possible source and reinforcer of adolescents' values. Benson, Masters, and Larson (1997) warn in their review of the literature, how-ever, that although the weight of the research evidence is for the positive effects of religion on developmental outcomes, most of the studies have been correla-tional, not longitudinal. Thus, cause and effect cannot be firmly established. Moreover, most studies of adolescents and religion have looked at White stu-dents already connected to schools and/or congregations. Adolescents of color and disconnected, disaffected youth are rarely represented in the research.

Despite those limitations, research studies do consistently show that how important an adolescent's religion is to her or him has a significant effect on attitudes and behaviors. Attendance at religious services is generally a less im-portant contributor to those attitudes and behaviors. For example, Benson and Donahue (1989) reanalyzed the data from roughly 50,000 high school seniors in each of several Monitoring the Future studies in the late 1970s and mid-1980s (widely respected University of Michigan studies on risky behavior among youth, especially alcohol and other drug use). They found that the importance of religion was the second most significant predictor (after the number of nights spent out having fun) of young people's alcohol and other drug use and of school truancy. Lorch and Hughes (1985) also reported that religion's importance to youth was a more important predictor of their alcohol and other drug use than was attendance at religious services or whether their denomination was more fundamentalist or liberal in orientation. (See also Werner & Smith, 1992.)

In a review of the research, Benson, Donahue, and Erickson (1989) concluded that adolescents for whom religion was an important life influence were consistently less likely to engage in sexual intercourse or use drugs, somewhat less likely to engage in delinquent behavior, and consistently more likely to be altruistic in their attitudes and behavior than youth for whom religion was not important. More recently, Resnick et al. (1997) reached similar conclusions in their study of 12,000 U.S. adolescents. Juhasz and Sonnenshein-Schneider (1987) found that, for 13- to 19-year-olds, the more religious adolescents were, the more important they considered the opinions of their parents, friends, and religious authorities to be about whether to have sexual intercourse. One study has further reported that adolescents' future intended involvement in religion has an independent protective effect on risky behavior. Litchfield, Thomas, and Li (1997) found that among more than 550 Mormon adolescents, their intent to go on a mission, get married in a temple, and be active in the church had predictive significance over and above their current religiosity for lower consumption of beer, cigarettes, or pornography.

Benson et al. (1989) reported that studies tended to show a decline in religiousness as adolescents aged from 10 to 18 years, but that females, Hispanic males, and African Americans of both genders tended to stay higher in their religiousness. Juhasz and Sonnenshein-Schneider (1987) reported a similar trend in their data: Females generally and Hispanic males as a group were more influenced by external sources of morality in their sexual decision making. Although the strength of influence exerted by parents, peers, and religious authorities declined for males as they aged, that influence remained high for females. King et al. (1997) reported a contrary finding, however. In their study of 365 White, rural 7th through 10th graders, females were not more religious than males. Nonetheless, even though both increased their involvement with church youth groups over time, females were consistently involved at higher levels. This study also compared farm youth and nonfarm rural youth, finding that youth who lived on farms were more religious and more involved in church youth group activities, and expressed a stronger commitment to religious values than did nonfarm youth.

Finally, Donahue and Benson (1995) analyzed data from more than 34,000 6th through 12th graders and reported that the importance of religion had moderate positive correlations (mid-.20s) with altruistic values and behaviors, as well as negative correlations with risky behaviors such as alcohol and other drug use and early sexual intercourse. Perhaps more important, they reported that the impact of religiousness was much stronger on influencing positive outcomes (increasing altruistic attitudes and behavior) than on influencing negative outcomes (avoiding risky behavior). They speculated that religion exerts its influence because of its socialization pressure to avoid health-compromising behavior and to engage in prosocial behavior such as caring for or serving others: "These messages are essentially constant across religious communities in the United States, regardless of theological perspective" (p. 156).

Benson et al. (1997) showed, however, that not all religious approaches had those effects. Faith with an accepting and liberating message appeared to be associated with less antisocial behavior and more prosocial behavior among youth, whereas faith that had a controlling and rigid orientation seemed to be associated with young people's antisocial behavior. Benson et al. (1989) added another dimension to how religion may exert its influence on values. Their review of research concluded that religion exerted its greatest influence on attitudes and behaviors where its voice was different from the society at large. That may be why the influence of religion on delinquency is lower than it is on early sexual intercourse or alcohol use. Few mixed messages are given to young people about delinquent behavior, whereas many conflicting messages about sexuality and alcohol exist in our society. That explanation may only be partially valid, however. As Donahue and Benson (1995) showed, religion had its greatest impact in their study not on various risky behaviors but on altruism, an outcome that would seem to have a high degree of societal desirability and consensus.

Values and Student Achievement

Wentzel's (1993b) study on the relationship between student achievement and classroom behavior showed another path by which values may operate. She found that both prosocial and antisocial behavior were independent predictors of grades, test scores, and teacher preferences for different students. Middle school youth who behaved prosocially (who were caring, responsible, and restrained) both gave academic assistance to and received it from their classmates, showed greater interest in their classwork, and were involved in more social exchanges with their teachers. Those patterns led to greater academic success, which in turn reinforced their values to be socially responsible.

In a related study, Hanson and Ginsburg (1988) followed 30,000 sophomores from the national High School and Beyond study for two years and reported that "values" had a significant impact on later achievement, in part by affecting student effort. What they called values, however, we have conceptually placed under different headings. Those values (and our related assets) included parents' educational expectations for their children and peers' values about education (both part of our boundaries-and-expectations assets), students' feelings of control over their futures (part of our positive-identity assets), parents' concern for the child's well-being (part of support), and, for Black youth, young people's values about the importance of religion (closest to our constructive-use-of-time assets). Together, those "values" were twice as important as family socioeconomic status in explaining current student performance and 50% stronger than SES in predicting two-year changes in academic performance.

Wentzel's work and other studies (see Chapter 5, on commitment to learning) suggest that at the least, our values of caring, responsibility, and restraint are entwined with the educational "values" defined by Hanson and Ginsburg and that by affecting student classroom social behaviors, these values are partially responsible for the academic effects those researchers reported. Even the values of honesty and integrity may play a similarly indirect role in affecting educational and other outcomes. Wentzel (1991) reported that 12- to 13-year-olds who trusted their peers were more likely to be socially responsible in their own behavior (more caring and restrained); this led to better grades. Similarly, Weinfurt and Bush (1995) followed nearly 4,000 Black, urban 6th and 7th graders for one year and reported that children who were perceived by their peers as untrustworthy in year 1 were more likely to be solicited to sell crack cocaine by year 2.

The value of restraint is well represented in the research, although most of the studies focus on behaviors, not the effects of valuing restraint. Donahue (1987) did report that teenagers' belief that it was against their values to have sex while a teenager was strongly related to their behavioral intention to postpone sexual intercourse. However, the related belief of some adults that telling teenagers to adopt the value of "just saying no" would be an effective deterrent to sexual intercourse has yet to be supported by any of the studies that have tested this assumption. One study (Miller, Norton, Fan, & Christopherson, 1998) found that among a sample largely composed of Mormon youth, abstinence values in year 1 were related to lower intentions to have sex in year 2 and to less likelihood of sexual intercourse in year 3. Among the several hundred 10th- and 11th-grade students in year 3, however, just 7% had ever had sexual intercourse. Among U.S. 10th and 11th graders, nearly 50% have had sexual intercourse (Kann et al., 1998), which suggests the Miller et al. sample is highly suspect in terms of how broadly the findings can be generalized. In contrast, a more complex, developmentally sophisticated reinforcement of values against having unprotected sex has been shown to be effective.

In the most thorough study of its kind, Kirby et al. (1994) reviewed dozens of studies on the impact of various kinds of sexuality education and AIDS education programs on rates of adolescent sexual intercourse and contraceptive behavior. They reported that studies showed that comprehensive sexuality education that included information on contraception "consistently" either delayed the onset of sexual intercourse, had no effect, or increased the use of contraceptives. The successful curricula had several distinguishing features, including a narrow focus on sexual risk reduction, a social learning or social influence focus with practice of necessary skills for remaining either abstinent or protected, and "reinforcement of individual values and group norms against unprotected sex that are age and experience appropriate" (pp. 358–359). "Age and experience appropriate" meant more of a "just say no" prohibition for younger youth, but for older youth meant a gradual and respectful acknowledgment of their increasing responsibility for their decisions, and the increasing opportunities they had for making sexual choices consistent with their emerging personal value system. Because all of the successful programs used values in this way, and none of the ineffective ones did, the researchers concluded that this kind of focus on the value of restraint was an especially important characteristic of successful sexuality education programs.

Adolescents' Experience of Positive Values

The research shows that values are potentially important influences on adolescent behaviors. But to what extent do youth actually hold positive values? Our data show that reports of integrity, responsibility, and honesty decline over the middle school years before rising significantly in the high school years. Reports of caring, equality, and social justice decline and then plateau in the high school years; reports of restraint progressively decline, with the largest drops between the 7th and 8th grades, and 8th and 9th grades. Females' reports of all the values are at least 10 percentage points higher than males'; indeed, restraint is the only value that less than half of females report having. Only a minority of males report having the prosocial values (caring, and equality and social justice) and restraint, and a slight majority of males report having integrity, honesty, and responsibility. (See Figure 10.)

Having greater levels of these positive-values assets may be one reason why females are found to be less likely to engage in binge drinking or to use marijuana or other drugs (except for current cigarette use, where only Black females seem to have lower use rates than males [Kann et al., 1998]); have early sexual intercourse (Kann et al., 1998; Haffner, 1995; "Sexual Behavior," 1992); cheat less (Kelly & Worell, 1978); and be more likely to be helpful, both at home (Call et al., 1995) and in community volunteering (Benson, 1997).

What Is Missing from Our Definition of Positive Values?

Probably the most noteworthy limitation of our set of positive values is simply that the list is not more comprehensive. Many other values exist that are poten-

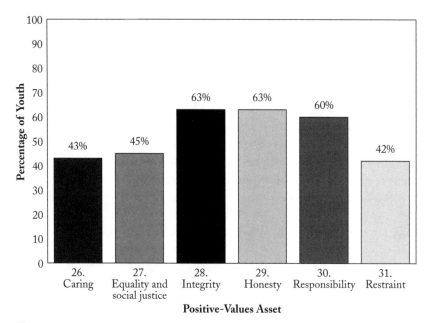

Figure 10   *Adolescents' experience of positive values: percentage of 6th- to 12th-grade students who report experiencing each of the positive-values assets. From unpublished Search Institute data on youth in public and/or alternative schools who completed the institute's* Profiles of Student Life: Attitudes and Behaviors *survey during the 1996–97 school year;* N = *99,462 6th–12th graders in 213 U.S. communities.*

tially important in young people's lives and that many adults would wish young people to have. Examples of additional important values that we do not measure include loyalty, spirituality, interdependence, persistence, effort or hard work, conscientiousness, kindness, agreement, patience, harmony, cultural identification, and family solidarity. Some of these additional values may be particularly important to some cultures, such as harmony for Native American youth.

   In addition, we do not adequately measure important domains such as young people's gender-role beliefs, some of which may evolve into values. We do ask young people if they think it is important for "everyone" to have equal rights and opportunities, but that single item masks a great deal of potential personal ambivalence and uncertainty by lumping together gender-role beliefs with beliefs about race and ethnicity, disability, socioeconomic status, language, sexual orientation, and religious diversities. Among 6th through 12th graders in our large sample, only 45% agreed with the value of equality; this conceivably could be even lower if more specific items were addressed. In short, we are missing a great deal of information about young people's emerging personal belief systems.

   In describing the other asset categories, we have identified a small number of assets that, in general, adequately represent the essence of each category. Given the sheer number of positive values that different people might consider to be most crucial, the category of positive values may not have captured the "most important values." How adequately our measurements reflect the lessons of the research is difficult to judge.

A related problem in dealing with our "short list" of values is that important values are implied in other asset categories, but not explicitly identified as values. For example, several of the commitment-to-learning assets (e.g., achievement motivation, school engagement, bonding to school) may reflect an underlying value young people have developed about the importance of education, working hard, and trying one's best in all things. How much do variations in young people's underlying, implied "values" contribute to the variations we see in young people's achievement motivation, school engagement, or bonding to school?

A similar question arises about young people's participation in religious organizations. Constructively occupied time offers a positive impact in its own right (see Chapter 4), but how much of the positive effect we see attributed to connection with religious organizations has to do instead with belief in the particular values taught by that faith community, values that pertain to matters ranging from how one behaves in the family to how one resolves conflicts or works for social justice? Because most, if not all, of our 40 assets build either on the values we explicitly include in each asset category or on other implicit ones, or both, we cannot accurately state how much the six explicit "positive values" influence adolescents; we can state with certainty only that the influence is more than we are measuring.

Finally, a problem we introduced at the beginning of this chapter is that young people can hold a value but still behave in a way contrary to it. Particularly during adolescence, as young people intensively explore who they are, what they believe in, and what they stand for, inconsistencies among values, and between values and related behaviors, are hardly surprising. At the most mundane of levels, young people may love their parents and feel it is important to have their love and admiration, but reject and ridicule them when they're with their peers because it is also important to show they're not too close to or dependent on their parents. A young person might believe in general that nonviolent resolution is the best way to handle conflicts, and yet agree to fight someone after school because the value of appearing strong and unafraid is, at least at that moment, more important. Or a boy or girl might believe that drinking at unsupervised parties can only lead to trouble, but do so anyway because he or she believes it is even more important not to be ostracized for abstaining. In short, researchers have not established a direct relationship between what young people believe and what they do. This suggests that we should be cautious in ascribing simple behavioral effects to values.

How Can Positive Values Be Built?

Young people's values are shaped by the people and institutions they interact with most: family, friends, school, and neighborhood, as well as any religious affiliations. As the research reviewed in this chapter and in the chapter on support (Chapter 1) has shown, early supportive parenting and multiple relationships with caring adults build a foundation for later success by promoting positive personal beliefs, capacities, and identification with adults. Values are both directly molded and indirectly encouraged in this process. For example, if a child grows up believing she is academically competent and that her parents feel it is important for her to take math, she will be more likely to place a higher value on math, more likely to take math, and more likely to do well in it. More broadly, a child experiencing parental warmth with firmness and high expectations may develop a belief in his capacity to persevere even when things get difficult. Together, that value and that personal belief may constitute much of what is called "resilience."

Programs and practices that echo these kinds of early family dynamics can affect young people's values. For example, a study of kindergartners followed through the 4th grade looked at the effects of the well-known Child Development Program that works with teachers to help them promote the prosocial values of fairness, kindness, and social responsibility in students (Battistich, Solomon, Watson, Solomon, & Schaps, 1989). The researchers found that children in the program, in contrast to children not in the program, were significantly more considerate of others' needs and had more interpersonal sensitivity. Moreover, those differences increased from kindergarten to the 4th grade.

Social Environment

Young people's values also are responsive to the wider social environment. For example, in the American Council on Education's annual survey of about 350,000 incoming college freshmen (reported in Bronner, 1998), the proportion who say that developing a meaningful philosophy of life is essential has dropped from 83% in 1968 to 41% in 1998, while the proportion who say it is essential to be well off financially has risen from 41% in 1968 to 75% in 1998. Also, commitment to promoting racial understanding is an essential value for only 32% of first-year students in 1998, compared with its high, in 1992, of 42%. Broader social trends in the economy, the rising costs of college, and the ebbs and flows of race relations clearly have had an effect on such responses across different eras.

Character Education Programs

A plethora of character education programs has been developed to build values among children and youth. These programs—variously called character education, values education, or moral education programs—use lessons, rewards, and symbolic gestures (uniforms, "honesty month," etc.) to try to instill values such as fairness, honesty, industriousness, loyalty, obedience to rules and authority, diligence, and patriotism. Damon and Gregory (1997) reported that by 1996, there were at least 150 separate character education centers around the country. Despite the enthusiasm in many quarters for the character education approach, they reported that there had been very little evaluation of its effects: "The most that we know . . . [is that] although they seem benign and well-intentioned, there is little evidence that they are actually having effects on youth conduct" (p. 120). Kohn (1997) criticized the character education movement both for being ineffective educationally (viewing teaching, for example, as "a matter of telling and compelling," p. 7) and for being based on an underlying politically and socially conservative ideology with which many school officials and parents would disagree if it were made obvious: "Character education nowadays, is, for the most part, a collection of exhortations and extrinsic inducements designed to make children work harder and do what they are told. . . . The point is to drill students in specific behaviors rather than to engage them in deep, critical reflection about certain ways of being" (p. 1).

The Role of Community

In contrast, Damon and Colby (1996) criticize moral education for being too much based in schools rather than taken on as a community-wide enterprise that includes the school as one important institutional player. In their view, schools have focused too much on "reflection" about morals and not enough on moral "habits" or deep reflexes. Moral behavior, for Damon and Colby, depends on "something beyond moral beliefs per se. . . . It depends on how and to what extent the individual's moral concerns are important to their sense of themselves as people" (p. 36). They believe that to help young people integrate moral habit, emotion, and reflection, communities must make explicit what often is either implicit or absent; a community "youth charter" expresses a "coherent moral voice" (p. 34) among teachers, parents, neighbors, clergy, youth workers, and other residents about what is expected of young people. According to Damon and Gregory (1997), such a youth charter (which may be written, but is more effective as a shared understanding and common practice among adults and youth) needs to go beyond telling young people what not to do. They add to Kohn's (1997) criticism of character education the observation that the emphasis of today's character education too often is "exclusively on bad behavior and how to deter, define, or repair it" (p. 122), whereas what young people need is to be exposed to values, moral ideas, and models they find positively inspiring. A youth charter that emerges from town meetings, positive media coverage, and working committees of parents, community leaders, and neighbors provides clear and consistent expectations from the important people in young people's lives about how they are expected to live, how they can connect the moral messages they hear with the choices they have to make every day, and how adults in the community can help young people become productive and responsible citizens.

Adult support The importance of adults' providing support for the development of values was underscored in Lamborn et al.'s (1994) study of 9- to 20-year-olds. The researchers examined how complexly children and youth could think about abstractions derived from the values of honesty and kindness (such as "constructive criticism" or "social white lies"). They found clear age-stage differences in reasoning: Older youth reasoned more complexly than younger children. Familiarity with the content also mattered. Study participants who did not have the chance to practice this kind of complex reasoning ended up scoring one or two steps below their age expectations.

This is consistent with other research that has found that adolescents use higher moral development reasoning when considering nonsexual dilemmas (with which they are more familiar) than sexual ones (which are, in contrast, relatively infrequent in most adolescents' lives) (Delamater & MacCorquodale, 1978). In addition perhaps to their heightened emotional tension when dealing with sexual dilemmas, adolescents' relative lack of experience with sexual situations causes them to revert to a lower level of reasoning. Similarly, Kirby et al. (1994) reported that practicing refusal skills and effective communication (behaviors that reinforce values to avoid unprotected sex) was a critical component of effective sexuality education programs.

Not just any practice will do, however. Examining how children and their parents reasoned on different moral dilemmas, Walker and Taylor (1991) reported that the best predictor of a child's moral development growth over the two years of the study was whether a family chose not to discuss a hypothetical moral dilemma provided by the researchers, but picked instead a real dilemma that had been experienced and suggested by the 1st, 4th, 7th, and 10th graders in the study. In support of this finding, the researchers noted that the "moral education paradigm" had shifted over the past 20 years, from providing students with hypothetical or imaginary problems to solve to involving them in the "resolution of real moral and political problems through student self-governance and community building" (p. 280).

Service-learning programs   It is in part educators' recognition of the power of this newer paradigm that has led to the expansion of service-learning programs in middle and high schools. Research has consistently shown that those programs, which integrate community service into core academic courses and help students to speak and write thoughtfully about those experiences, can have positive effects on values, attitudes, and behaviors related to caring and social responsibility (Scales & Blyth, 1997).

For example, a study of a diverse sample of more than 1,000 6th through 8th graders found that service-learning students, compared with control students, maintained their sense of concern for others' social welfare; in contrast, control students' concern for others dropped over the school year. In addition, if students had more than 30 hours of service-learning, they were more likely to increase their sense that they could be effective in helping others—that is, to believe that their helping actions would make a difference (Scales, Blyth, et al., 1998).

Engaging youth   Finally, a study of helping, sharing, and cooperating behavior among behaviorally disturbed young adolescents (Miller, 1991) underscored a simple element in effective values development: asking children to exhibit the behavior dictated by the underlying value. In that study, teachers of behaviorally disturbed students were more likely than other teachers to explicitly ask their students to take the perspective of other students. The results also showed that those students engaged in more prosocial behaviors than their peers who were not asked.

Similarly, McDevitt et al. (1991) found that 12- to 18-year-olds scored higher on prosocial reasoning if their parents had a history of asking them to be kind and responsible. Uncountable early influences and complex environmental factors from childhood through adolescence affect the development of young people's values. Nevertheless, asking youth to be a certain kind of person or act a certain way may have an impact as well. Just as many people, young or old, volunteer time or contribute money because they are asked to do so, young people who are asked to tell the truth, help others, promote equality, give money, and so forth may comply. By telling youth, in effect, that we think they are the kind of people who are honest, helpful, or interested in social justice, adults perhaps set in motion a desirable self-fulfilling prophecy: Young people try to live up to the positive image we have of them.

"Asking youth" is something everyone in a community can do—parents, teachers, neighbors. Communities collectively ask youth to behave in certain ways through community standards and norms. Asking young people to think about and habitually to live out the values that adults in their community concur are important is the essence of a youth charter. The impact a clear youth charter can have on the development of healthier communities could be substantial. Yet, paradoxically, the connection between the values communities wish youth to hold and how healthy those communities are is not often made, as Stone (1997) noted in an account of interviews that researchers from the Chapin Hall Center for Children conducted with participants in five well-known comprehensive community-based initiatives. One of our positive values, caring, is both a value most adults wish to teach young people and a value that, even if unspoken, has driven the emergence and success of nearly all community initiatives: caring about children and youth, caring about the environment, caring about safety, caring about neighborhoods, and so forth. The connection between caring as an element essential to successful youth development and as an element essential for successful community development was obvious to the Chapin Hall researchers, but was articulated by only one or two interviewees. As adults go about the critical job of helping young people develop positive values, we should not lose sight of the link between values as assets in youth development and the role of those same values as assets in community development.

Conclusion

Adolescents' values are molded by everything they are and do. Although almost every experience has an impact on values development, two strategies emerge as crucial in helping build positive values in young people. First, adults need to ask young people explicitly to behave in ways that reflect the underlying values adults wish youth would develop. Second, adults in different parts of young people's lives—school, family, congregation, neighborhood—need to be consistent in their collective expression of an explicit set of value expectations for youth. Youth will be exposed to a tremendous variety of values. They will experience many nuances of meaning as values get tested in everyday life. Adult explicitness and consensus about values may be decisive factors in whether and how readily young people adopt as their own the kinds of values we measure. Although the number of research studies on the effects of values is relatively small, the potential positive effects of adolescents holding the values we measure are clear. When adults in young people's lives hold similar positive values, make these values explicit, and intentionally seek to promote them, they provide a solid guiding influence that helps youth navigate through their social worlds and internalize positive values.

Selected Readings

Chase-Lansdale, P. L., Wakschlag, L. S., & Brooks Gunn, J. (1995). A psychological perspective on the development of caring in children and youth: The role of the family. *Journal of Adolescence, 18*, 515–556.

Damon, W., & Gregory, A. (1997). The youth charter: Towards the formation of adolescent moral identity. *Journal of Moral Education, 26*, 117–130.

Donahue, M. J., & Benson, P. L. (1995). Religion and the well-being of adolescents. *Journal of Social Issues, 51*, 145–160.

Kohn, A. (1997). How not to teach values: A critical look at character education. *Phi Delta Kappan, 78*, 428–439.

Lamborn, S. D., Fischer, K. W., & Pipp, S. (1994). Constructive criticism and social lies: A developmental sequence for understanding honesty and kindness in social interactions. *Developmental Psychology, 30*, 495–508.

McDevitt, T. M., Lennon, R., & Kopriva, R. J. (1991). Adolescents' perceptions of mothers' and fathers' prosocial actions and empathic responses. *Youth and Society, 22*, 387–409.

Walker, L. J., & Taylor, J. H. (1991). Family interactions and the development of moral reasoning. *Child Development, 62*, 264–283.

Social competencies are the skills
young people need to confront new
situations, face hard decisions, and
interact effectively with others.

7

The Social-Competencies Assets

What Are Social Competencies?

Social competence involves the personal skills that children and adolescents use to deal with the many choices, challenges, and opportunities they face. A difficult concept to define, it generally refers to adaptive functioning, in which the individual may call on both personal and environmental resources (e.g., being able to use one's knowledge about social situations to decide on an action, being able to ask for help) to achieve a certain outcome (Peterson & Leigh, 1990; Waters & Sroufe, 1983). Young people who are socially competent "often possess sound judgment and the ability to manage circumstances to benefit themselves and others in social situations" (Peterson & Leigh, 1990, p. 100). Social competence develops within the social contexts that the individual relates to and with (Lerner, 1987), but socially competent adolescents "are neither passive recipients nor passive reactors to stimuli but are both active and reactive agents to their developmental and environmental circumstances" (Peterson & Leigh, 1990, p. 100).

Five social competencies make up the third category of the internal assets. They are planning and decision making, interpersonal competence, cultural competence, resistance skills, and peaceful conflict resolution. (See Table 12.)

Unlike the framework of developmental assets, the model generally used to explain youth behavior operates primarily from a deficit perspective. Our literature review was affected by this prevailing view. Little research emerged that specifically addressed how peaceful conflict resolution works or how it might vary as a function of individual or contextual differences. For example, a study might describe the impact of child or adolescent aggression on peer acceptance. If aggression toward peers results in peer rejection, we then make the inference that the inverse operation applies—that peaceful conflict resolution may result in a positive outcome. This may be likely, but it is not necessarily the case. We have made every attempt to find and review literature pertaining to the positive aspects of this construct, but in some cases, this was not possible.

Summary of Research Findings

Our literature review identified studies relating to the broad topic of social competence as well as to how social competence generally is related to de-creased problem behaviors such as substance use (e.g., Caplan et al., 1992). So-cial competence, as it is often described in the social development literature, is not always differentiated into separate dimensions of competence. That litera-ture does, however, suggest the overall importance of social competence in terms of healthy development. One of the few studies to disentangle the differ-ent components of competence, conceptually and empirically, was Masten et al.'s (1995) 11-year longitudinal study of children and adolescents. The results showed that competence in middle childhood was made up of three separate dimensions: academic achievement, conduct, and peer social success. The same three dimensions operated in late adolescence, supplemented by job competence and romantic competence, two dimensions that were linked to young people's recent academic and social success.

Planning and Decision Making

Decision making has been described as a set of skills: being able to define the problem, search for alternative solutions, find the best alternative, and examine

Table 12. The Social-Competencies Assets	
Planning and decision making	Young person knows how to plan ahead and make choices.
Interpersonal competence	Young person has empathy, sensitivity, and friendship skills.
Cultural competence	Young person has knowledge of and comfort with people of different cultural/racial/ethnic backgrounds.
Resistance skills	Young person can resist negative peer pressure and dangerous situations.
Peaceful conflict resolution	Young person seeks to resolve conflict nonviolently.

the outcome of the solution (Beyth-Marom, Fischhoff, Quadrel, & Furby, 1991). Decision making is directly related to cognitive development; as such, it is constrained by the developmental immaturity of the individual. Decision making is also situation specific; adolescents may make more mature decisions within familiar rather than unfamiliar contexts (Leffert & Petersen, 1996a).

Many programs have been designed to teach decision-making skills to adolescents or to enhance the skills they already have. Some of the interest in such programs has grown out of the presupposition that adolescents are not good decision makers; if we could increase or improve young people's decision-making abilities, we might be able to offset their involvement in risky behaviors, which are thought, at least partially, to be a result of faulty decision making.

The premise of programs designed to enhance decision-making skills is that increasing adolescents' decision-making abilities would help them deal with the challenges they face (Beyth-Marom et al., 1991; Resnick, 1987). Given individual variation in cognitive development, however, and the contextual variation reflected in the content of decisions adolescents have to make, it is not surprising that global "decision-making programs" have not shown consistent positive impact. Nonetheless, planning and decision making have been shown to be directly or indirectly associated with:

- **Increased competence** in interacting with the environment (Beyth-Marom et al., 1991);
- **Increased self-esteem** (Mann, Harmoni, & Power, 1989; Mann, Harmoni, Power, Beswick, & Ormond, 1988); and
- **Decreased engagement in risky behaviors** (Moore & Gullone, 1996; Rogel, Zuehlke, Petersen, Tobin-Richards, & Shelton, 1980); **decreased marijuana use** (Bailey & Hubbard, 1990); **decreased alcohol use** (Milgram, 1996); and **delay of sexual intercourse** (Lock & Vincent, 1995).

Interpersonal Competence and Cultural Competence

Few research or evaluation reports pertain to cultural competence as a construct separate from interpersonal competence. Interpersonal competence and cultural competence are directly or indirectly associated with:

- **Protection against adversity** (Luthar, 1995; Luthar & Zigler, 1991) and **improved adjustment** (Elias et al., 1986);
- **Positive self-esteem** (Paterson, Pryor, & Field, 1995); **improved school competence, perceived self-competence** (Cauce, 1986); **improved peer competence** (Gore & Aseltine, 1995) and **peer**

acceptance (Parkhurst & Asher, 1992; Wentzel, 1994); and **improved ability to form friendships** (Vernberg, Ewell, Beery, & Abwender, 1994);

- **Increased problem-solving ability** (Mott & Krane, 1994);
- **Increased academic achievement** (Arroyo & Zigler, 1995; Chen, Rubin, & Li, 1997 [among Chinese children and adolescents]);
- **Decreased loneliness** (Inderbtizen-Pisaruk, Clark, & Solano, 1992) and **decreased depression** (Davila, Hammen, Burge, Paley, & Daley, 1995); and
- **Decreased problem behaviors such as substance use** (Barnea et al., 1992; Caplan et al., 1992) and **lower risk of negative consequences from early sexual activity** among African American youth (St. Lawrence et al., 1994).

Resistance Skills

Resistance skills relate to the ability to deal effectively with pressures to engage in a variety of risky behaviors. They are an important ingredient of many current prevention programs. A great deal of the literature pertaining to resistance skills consists of evaluations of the effectiveness of programs aimed at enhancing these skills among adolescents. Resistance skills are directly or indirectly associated with:

- **Increased self-efficacy** (Ellickson & Hays, 1990–91); **increased autonomy** (Steinberg & Silverberg, 1986); and, more generally, **improved self-competence** (Caplan et al., 1992); and
- **Decreased problem behaviors such as substance use** (Donaldson, Graham, & Hansen, 1994; Iso-Ahola & Crowley, 1991) and **alcohol use** (Donaldson, Graham, Piccinin, & Hansen, 1995; Gorman, 1995; Rohrbach, Graham, Hansen, Flay, & Johnson, 1987).

Peaceful Conflict Resolution

Popular accounts of adolescent development generally portray adolescents as moody and in conflict with their parents (Collins & Laursen, 1992; Laursen & Koplas, 1995). In reality, adolescents are not always, or even generally, in conflict with their parents or peers. They do have conflicts, particularly during early adolescence (Collins & Laursen, 1992), but conflicts with parents primarily center on rather mundane issues, such as clothing or chores.

Conflict is not aggression, nor does it necessarily result in aggression. A methodological problem in this line of research is that investigators often have confused the definition of conflict (e.g., short-lived arguing, quarreling, fighting) with that of aggression (Collins & Laursen, 1992). In contrast to occasional conflict, aggression is typically thought to be a pattern of behaviors that are quite stable over time (e.g., Olweus, 1984); aggressive children often become aggressive adolescents and adults. Aggression may be affected by various interventions. Such interventions are generally aimed at the development of more effective and acceptable methods of social interaction and conflict resolution.

Peaceful conflict resolution has been shown to be directly or indirectly associated with:

- **Increased psychosocial health and adjustment** (Hinde, 1979; Johnson, 1975); **increased self-regulation** (Johnson & Johnson, 1996); and **increased self-esteem** (Gentry & Benenson, 1993; Krappmann & Oswald, 1987; Miller, 1993);
- **Increased social support** (Johnson & Sarason, 1979; Kashani & Shepperd, 1990);
- **Increased academic achievement** (Fullan, 1991; Johnson & Johnson, 1996 [when conflict resolution occurs in academic settings that use cooperative learning]); and **improved school climate** (Sherrod, 1995);
- **Decreased problem behaviors such as antisocial behavior and early school withdrawal** (Kupersmidt & Coie, 1990); **decreased use of alcohol and other substances** (Clapper et al., 1995; Martin et al., 1994; O'Donnell, Hawkins, & Abbott, 1995); and **decreased suicidal activity** (Vannatta, 1996).

Variations in Findings

The research we reviewed confirms the positive impact of the social competencies. Few studies have addressed group differences, such as gender, in the processes related to social competence. Those that have done so have shown few group differences. For example, one study revealed no group differences in general social competencies (i.e., interpersonal effectiveness) between inner-city and suburban adolescents (Caplan et al., 1992).

Some studies suggest that social competencies may affect outcomes indirectly for youth of color. For example, in a study of almost 300 7th through 9th graders, DuBois and Hirsch (1990) found that African American young people were almost twice as likely as Caucasian youth to report having a close "other-race" school friend whom they saw frequently outside of school. They suggest that several features of neighborhoods may enable or facilitate interracial relationships among youth. The neighborhood composition may help to offset stereotypical or negative attitudes that can often develop in the school setting because of instructional practices (such as tracking). Mekos and Elder (1996) found that strong community ties are positively related to social competence among rural youth.

Studying sexual decision making among African American adolescent females, Pete and DeSantis (1990) found that they used cognitive reasoning about sexual decisions that is similar to that reported in the literature of other groups of females. In related research, Zimmerman, Sprecher, Langer, and Holloway (1995) also report no consistent ethnic group differences in the ability of young people to refuse unwanted sex. They observed, however, that females who had high self-efficacy beliefs—defined as a belief that one will be successful in life—were more likely than males to believe that they could say no to sex. These findings are consistent with Leadbeater, Hellner, Allen, and Aber (1989) and suggest few ethnic differences in decision making.

How Social Competencies Work

Social competence develops gradually over the course of childhood and adolescence, beginning in the earliest interactions of infant and parent. As mentioned earlier, much of the related research literature pertains to a more general definition of social competence. Researchers have hypothesized that social competencies provide youth with the ability to cope with a variety of stressors, such as social pressures to use alcohol or tobacco (e.g., Spivack & Shure, 1982). In general, the ability to cope with difficult situations affects aspects of interpersonal effectiveness such as being able to socialize with new people or to get to know people in new situations. Young people who have practice in applying their developing social competencies may be able to deal with interpersonal situations more effectively or with a greater measure of comfort (Hawkins & Weis, 1985). Alternatively, as Elias et al. (1986) found, social competencies may not necessarily help young people deal with stressful situations as much as they help youth reduce or avoid stress in the first place. Those researchers found that children who had been involved in a problem-solving program in 6th grade experienced fewer stressors when they made the transition to middle school than did children who were not involved in the program. They did not, however, adjust better to the stresses they did experience.

Planning and Decision Making

Social competence requires the ability to solve problems and make decisions (e.g., D'Zurilla & Goldfried, 1971). In reality, young people's ability to solve problems may be an end product of their being able to plan and make decisions as well as to use other social cognitive skills, such as being able to ask others for help (Windle, Miller-Tutzauer, Barnes, & Welte, 1991). In a small study of about 175 4th and 5th graders, Broderick (1998) suggested that females and males may have differing problem-solving styles that contribute to varying likelihoods of experiencing depression. Given a set of hypothetical academic, family, and peer problems to solve, females tended to say they would worry about the problem, feel bad about it, and think about their role in it, whereas males more often said they would try to forget about the problem or do other things to take their minds off it. The more youth used a ruminating, worrying style of problem solving, the lower their self-esteem and the greater their loneliness. If females generally use this problem-solving approach more than males, that may provide one explanation of their higher levels of depression during adolescence. Although this small study focused on younger children, other research also has shown that females may tend to ruminate or use emotionally focused methods to solve problems rather than a more active problem-solving approach (e.g., Compas, Crosan, & Grant, 1993; Nolen-Hoeksema, 1987).

As early as 1974, Spivack and Shure found that both aggressive and inhibited young people were less competent at solving problems and making decisions. For example, Spivack, Platt, and Shure (1976) examined the differences between a group of high school students with adjustment problems and a comparison group that did not have adjustment problems. The groups differed in their abilities to generate alternative solutions, to think through from the cause of a problem to its consequences (means-end thinking), and to see another person's viewpoint (role-taking skills). Both groups could recognize problem situations, and both were aware of causes and consequences. What differentiated the groups was in finding ways to solve problems.

Studies have shown that delinquent young people are particularly deficient in social problem-solving skills, such as decision making (e.g., Kennedy, 1984). Correlational studies of this kind do not, however, specify the direction of effect; it is not clear to what extent delinquency may be caused by a deficiency in decision making skills or to what extent delinquency may interfere with young people acquiring these skills (Beyth-Marom et al., 1991).

Surprisingly few studies have examined the development of decision-making skills. Moreover, few studies have examined developmental differences in adolescent and adult decision making (Furby & Beyth-Marom, 1992). Research has shown that children and youth become more capable of making decisions as they get older (e.g., Weithorn & Campbell, 1982). For example, Ebata and Moos (1994) have found that older youth generally use more coping strategies that involve logical analysis, guidance and support from others, positive rethinking of the situation, and direct action to solve problems, whereas younger adolescents tend to use more avoidance methods, such as trying not to think about the problem, distracting oneself, or expressing negative feelings. By midadolescence, decision-making abilities and reasoning are thought to be as good as those of adults (Lewis, 1981; Weithorn & Campbell, 1982). An adolescent's ability to make decisions is not always consistent, however, and may be affected by novel and stressful contexts (Hamburg, 1986).

Adolescents are more likely than older people to find themselves in situations that are new to them; they are particularly prone to considerably less sophisticated thinking than they may be capable of in situations that are more familiar or comfortable (Crockett & Petersen, 1993; Hamburg, 1986). Like adults, adolescents are susceptible to "hot cognitions" (Hamburg, 1986), thoughts that are emotionally laden and that may interfere with decision-making processes (e.g., Gilligan & Belenky, 1980). These thoughts can result in impulsive behavior that may contribute to the special risks of adolescence. In novel situations, adolescents may respond impulsively without giving consideration to either the consequences of their actions or possible alternative options (Furby & Beyth-Marom, 1992). For example, adolescents may have difficulty negotiating the complexity of social relationships as they pertain to sexuality. In a situation that is new to them, they may be overcome by their emotions, whereas an adult is better able to make decisions because of familiarity or previous exposure to similar situations (Leffert & Petersen, 1996a). Experience is key to handling some situations effectively.

Because adolescents engage in risky behaviors, many people think they make faulty decisions or that they are unaware of the risks associated with their behaviors. Research evidence does not support the contention that adolescents are prone to "irrational" risky behavior, behavior that is more likely to negatively affect their well-being or health than to positively affect it (Furby & Beyth-Marom, 1992).

Indeed, Adler (1994) has suggested that, just like adults, adolescents make rational decisions. Only when observers do not understand their intentions do their decisions "look" irrational. Adolescents' understanding of the "facts" may be different, or they may have faulty beliefs about the consequences or risks associated with a certain option. They may also reject what they believe are adult values that would lead them to make more adultlike decisions (Fischhoff & Quadrel, 1991). Part of the dilemma in thinking about adolescent decision making and risk is that "the majority of competent, healthy adolescents engage in some level of problem behavior, and most of them will grow up to be competent, healthy adults" (Maggs, Almeida, & Galambos 1995, p. 345). In a small study of about 100 Canadian 6th graders followed for four years, Maggs et al. reported that, even though adolescents rated engaging in problem behaviors as more risky than fun, it was the element of fun that explained most of the variance in whether they took that risk or not. That is, they made decisions based more on imagined positive consequences than on fear of negative consequences.

Other studies do not support these conclusions, however. For example, Small, Silverberg, and Kerns (1993) studied a large sample of about 2,400 7th through 12th graders and concluded that youth perceptions of the costs of risky behavior were more important in their decision making than their perceptions of the benefits. Perhaps significantly, Small et al. studied only alcohol use and sexual intercourse, whereas Maggs et al. studied a much larger list of problem behaviors that included missing curfews, cheating on tests, or stealing something worth less than $2. It is possible that the more adolescents view the potential costs of a behavior as serious, the more likely costs are to become the critical factor in decision making. If young people view the potential costs of a behavior as not very serious, then the "fun" factor may predominate in their decision about whether to engage in a particular behavior.

Decision making in adolescence is affected by what Elkind (1967) has termed the "personal fable." Elkind suggested that adolescents tend to harbor a belief that they are invulnerable to certain risks, such as becoming pregnant. This may lead to what appears to the observer to be rather reckless behavior (Arnett, 1995). Adolescent decision making about the use of contraception, for example, may be influenced by this sense of invulnerability. Research examining the phenomenon of invulnerability comes from studies where adolescents estimate whether the possibility of a negative outcome resulting from their behavior is lower for themselves than for other people (Arnett, 1995). "Optimistic bias" is a belief that negative events are less likely to happen to oneself than to other people. Studies demonstrate, however, that decision making naturally includes a certain degree of "optimistic bias" for all people, adults as well as adolescents. A conclusion that can be drawn from this research is that adolescents are no more likely to be optimistically biased than adults (e.g., Byrnes & McClenny, 1994; Fischhoff & Quadrel, 1991).

Interpersonal Competence and Cultural Competence

How interpersonal and cultural competence may "work" or how they may impact youth outcomes has not been frequently studied. As thinking and reasoning skills change during adolescence, one domain affected is social reasoning, which might be defined as the ability to understand social situations and complex social relationships. Elkind (1967) has suggested that social reasoning also includes the capacity to understand the perspective of others, which distinguishes the social reasoning of adolescents from that of children. In general, adolescence, particularly early adolescence, is a time of transition in social reasoning abilities. Both interpersonal and cultural competence can be considered a part of social reasoning because they involve understanding what other people are like and what their perspectives are—in other words, being able to understand the mental perspective or life experience of others.

Some research has suggested caution in assuming that social skills necessarily lead to positive outcomes. Scheier and Botvin (1998) studied more than 800 mostly White middle-school students and reported that personal competence in the form of perceived school abilities, decision-making skills, and self-control was indeed related to lower use of alcohol across the two-year study. At the same time, however, high social skills—measured as assertiveness, willingness to be confrontational in social situations, and general confidence in dealing with new social situations—were related to greater use of alcohol over the next two years. It may be that young adolescents who are especially skilled at social interaction may encounter more alcohol-using peers and opportunities to use alcohol. They particularly may benefit from efforts to enhance their academic success, decision-making skills, and resistance skills.

Researchers have suggested that all children must develop both an acceptance of themselves as well as a group identity. One aspect of group identity is to identify oneself as a member of an ethnic or cultural group. Failure to develop an ethnic identity may have a negative impact on development (Walker, Taylor, McElroy, Phillip, & Wilson, 1995). Fordham (1988) and Fordham and Ogbu (1986), for instance, provided a description of the relation between identity and academic success among African Americans. They attribute poor academic performance among African Americans to the way that African Americans have been marginalized in the dominant culture. Because of inequities in both the social and the educational systems, many African American young people have come to view academic performance as futile (Arroyo & Zigler, 1995). Fordham and Ogbu have suggested that African American young people who do succeed academically do so because of a certain "racelessness" in their behaviors and experiences. Fordham and Ogbu describe raceless behavior as young people behaving in ways that help them gain approval from their teachers, avoiding relationships with other African Americans who are not as academically motivated, modulating their voice and speech, and not participating in activities that are generally thought of as "Black" activities (Arroyo & Zigler, 1995). These young people also hide their abilities. Fordham and Ogbu suggest that these types of raceless behaviors and attitudes distance African American young people from their community and result in feelings of alienation, depression, and anxiety. In contrast, research has shown that acceptance and pride in one's own cultural heritage is an important aspect of identify development and competence.

Other researchers have similarly described the importance of developing a positive identity with one's group; without this, young people of color may reject their own ethnicity and be ostracized by the majority group (Ogbu, 1991). In contrast, Arroyo and Zigler (1995) found no differences in the achievement-related attitudes and behaviors of African American and Caucasian high-achieving students, suggesting that high achievement, in general, was associated with racelessness. They found that the racelessness construct included general achievement attitudes that were common to all high achievers, not limited to members of a specific racial group. Academically successful young people often feel they must choose between working hard at school or having peer relationships (Ford, 1992).

In a study of three groups of African American, Latina/Latino, and Asian American adolescents (8th and 11th grade), Phinney, Ferguson, and Tate (1997) found that two factors influenced attitudes toward other groups: attitudes toward one's own group and contact with other groups. They observed that favoring one's own group did not imply a less positive attitude toward another group. Indeed, students who rated members of their own group positively also tended to rate other groups positively.

Resistance Skills

In a comprehensive review of school-based prevention programs offered between 1980 and 1990, Hansen (1992) concluded that the social influence models of prevention are the most successful in the prevention of adolescent substance abuse. Ennett et al. (1994) came to the same conclusion in conducting a meta-analysis of evaluations of Project DARE, a widely used drug abuse prevention program. They reported that the didactic and exhortatory approach of DARE was not effective in preventing or reducing drug abuse, particularly when compared with other approaches that are based on social skill building and that have significant emphasis on interactive teaching strategies. Social influence models emphasize the impact of peers and other sources of social pressure. Studies of resistance skills have shown that having a greater knowledge of the social sources of pressure to use alcohol, for example, helps young people to exercise their methods of resisting those pressures. For example, Hansen et al. (1988) showed that prevention efforts that only taught adolescents ways in which they could avoid offers (of drugs, for instance) were not as effective as social influence approaches because they did not include information on how difficult turning down those offers might be. As with decision making, however, it may be that having had a number of different experiences practicing or thinking about a situation may decrease the novelty of various situations and enhance an adolescent's resistance skills.

Research on adolescents' beliefs about the normative behaviors of their peers offers an interesting slant on understanding how resistance skills may work (see Chapter 3, on boundaries and expectations, for further discussion). Donaldson et al. (1994) found that adolescents' beliefs about the prevalence and acceptability of substance use by their peers mediated resistance skills. Specifically, adolescents' resistance skills were better if they thought their peers disapproved of and did not use substances. Adolescents may have faulty or erroneous perceptions about the actual substance use of their peers. Their beliefs about what is normative or typical among their peers may influence their willingness to use the resistance skills that they know. In other words, they are less likely to use resistance skills if they believe that the behavior in question is normative among their peers.

Self-efficacy beliefs are another important aspect of resistance skills. Self-efficacy is the perception or belief that an individual holds about her or his ability to achieve a desired result. Albert Bandura (1997) has shown that self-efficacy fosters the ability to change behavior. For example, in a study of the social influence of adolescent drug use among more than 1,000 adolescents, Ellickson and Hays (1990–91) reported that both resistance self-efficacy (the belief that one can resist the pressures to use substances) and social influences affected drug use. They also found that the mechanism may operate differently depending on an adolescent's prior experience with drugs. Among young people who already are using drugs, low resistance self-efficacy and social influences that are supportive of drug use predict higher expectations by the adolescent that he or she will use drugs in the future and also influence increased drug use. Among youth who are not using drugs, low resistance self-efficacy and social influences that are supportive of drug use affect the young people's expectations of subsequent use, but these expectations do not get translated into future behavior.

Peaceful Conflict Resolution

Whereas death as a result of disease has dramatically declined over the past 40 years, accidents, homicides, and suicides among adolescents have increased as a cause of mortality during the same time period (Leffert & Petersen, 1996b; Petersen, 1991). The United States exceeds all of the developed countries in deaths among youth between 10 and 14 years of age (Hingson & Howland, 1993). Although not all of these deaths are a result of violence or conflict, adolescents in the United States are four to five times more likely to die as a result of homicide than young people in other countries, and these rates have been increasing in recent years (Center for the Study of Social Policy, 1991).

The causes of violence to and among youth are complex, involving multiple factors. Weapons are easily obtained and too often used, notwithstanding the "zero tolerance" weapons policies and increasing presence of metal detectors in schools. Access to guns has been shown to be related to suicide and violence among youth (Resnick et al., 1997). The suicide rate among adolescents has quadrupled in the past four decades and increased at a higher rate than among the general population, from 2.7 per 100,000 in 1950 to 11.3 per 100,000 in 1988 (Centers for Disease Control and Prevention, 1991; Garland & Zigler, 1993). Many factors have been shown to be risk factors for suicide, including psychiatric illness (e.g., Shaffer, Garland, Gould, Fisher, & Trautman, 1988), psychosocial factors such as poor problem-solving skills (Cole, 1989), and social factors such as an increase in the availability of firearms (e.g., Boyd, 1983; Brent et al., 1988). Adults increasingly must consider the prospect that young people will use weapons to deal with their unhappiness or their aggressive feelings and in their attempts to resolve conflicts.

Much of the literature pertaining to peaceful conflict resolution involves studies of the effects of aggression or antisocial behavior on youth outcomes such as the prediction of aggressive behavior in the future. Antisocial behavior and aggression have been found to be some of the most powerful predictors of problems in adolescence and adulthood (e.g., Parker & Asher, 1987).

Cognitive aspects are significant in how young people resolve conflicts or problems (e.g., Guerra & Slaby, 1990). Research consistently has demonstrated that aggressive children have a tendency to attribute hostile intentions to others when the social situation is ambiguous (Dodge, 1980; Dodge & Frame, 1982).

Contrary to what is often thought, most adolescents and their parents maintain warm relationships during adolescence (Hill, 1988; Rutter, Graham, Chadwick, & Yule, 1976). Despite their warmth and continued connectedness, however, interactions between youth and parents are sometimes characterized by conflict (Collins & Laursen, 1992; Montemayor, 1983), particularly during early adolescence (Steinberg, 1981). Most of these conflicts revolve around the mundane tasks of daily life (Collins & Laursen, 1992).

However, conflicts that occur frequently or that are not resolved can have negative effects. Learning to deal with conflicts in peaceful and constructive ways is central to young people's developing the skills to manage mature relationships later in life. Despite the importance of such skills, Daro and McCurdy (1994, p. 413) found that "very few" formal evaluations had been done of conflict resolution programs. When done, however, the results are generally, but not always, positive. In an extensive review of conflict resolution and peer mediation training programs in schools, Johnson and Johnson (1996) reported that in the absence of training, students generally dealt with interpersonal conflict in destructive ways; they tended not to see the others involved as people with whom they would have

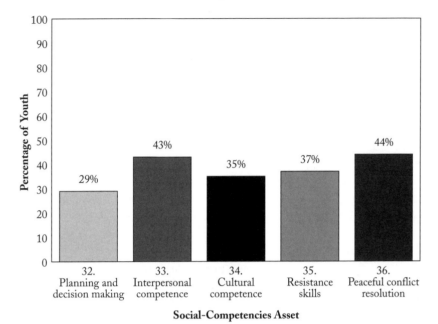

Figure 11 *Adolescents' experience of social competencies: percentage of 6th- to 12th-grade students who report experiencing each of the social-competencies assets. From unpublished Search Institute data on youth in public and/or alternative schools who completed the institute's* Profiles of Student Life: Attitudes and Behaviors *survey during the 1996–97 school year;* N = 99,462 *students in 213 U.S. communities.*

ongoing relationships, and so chose poor solutions that further damaged the possibilities of effective relationships. After training, however, students used better negotiation and conflict resolution strategies; schools reported fewer referrals and fewer suspensions based on student-student conflicts.

Adolescents' Experience of Social Competencies

It is alarming to note that so few of the youth in our sample report having the social-competencies assets. (See Figure 11.) Consistent with the trends seen in the other asset categories, we observe a decline in three of the five areas of social competence over the developmental period from 6th to 12th grades. While planning and decision-making abilities and interpersonal competence remain relatively stable, young people's reports of cultural competence, resistance skills, and conflict resolution skills drop. Unlike most of the other categories, the decline in the middle school years (grades 6 through 8) is not consistently large. The decline is steady and gradual for the assets of cultural competence and resistance skills. Peaceful conflict resolution, however, drops sharply over early adolescence and recovers only slightly in the high school grades.

As is true of the commitment-to-learning and positive-values assets, females tend to report experiencing the social-competencies assets more often than males in our sample. (With the exception of the positive-identity assets, females are more likely to report that they have most of the assets in the internal domain.) (See Chapter 8, on positive identity.) The gender differences in our aggregate sample are particularly marked in interpersonal competence and peaceful conflict resolution, with females twice as likely as males to report that they have interpersonal competence (60% versus 26%, respectively). Not surprisingly, 56% of females report the asset of peaceful conflict resolution; only 31% of males do.

What Is Missing from Our Definition of Social Competencies?

The definition of planning and decision making in the developmental asset framework includes aspects of planning ahead as well as thinking about the possible results of a decision. Based on the literature, our definition could be improved by including social problem-solving skills (e.g., analyzing problems, taking action on solving problems) that have been shown to be associated with the ability to cope with stressors (Elias et al., 1986). Our definition also would be strengthened if we included a cost-benefit analysis aspect of decision making. We do not include an assessment of whether an adolescent has weighed the relative cost of a particular decision and reflected on the benefit he or she may receive. Instead, our definition is a general self-assessment of global decision-making skills. Also, it does not reflect the context-specific nature of some decisions. Adolescents may be excellent decision makers in specific situations; for example, some may be good at making decisions about school issues and not very good at friendship-related decisions.

Interpersonal competence, as defined in our developmental asset framework, encompasses the self-perceptions of caring for others' feelings and being good at making and keeping friends. Cultural competence is defined as valuing and appreciating people of other races, ethnicities, or cultural backgrounds. It does not include skills such as the ability to handle, or be comfortable with, situations in which a young person relates with persons of other ethnicities or races. Moreover, it does not include the importance of acceptance of, and pride in, one's own ethnic or cultural heritage. In addition, race or ethnicity may be limited as a measure of cultural difference as it does not specifically address other types of cultural differences (e.g., religious differences). As Cross (1996) has pointed out, cultural diversity also is related to matters such as an individual's sexual orientation, urban or rural situation, immigrant experiences and assimilation into the majority culture, and "a group's history of oppression or economic status" (p. 3). We do not measure young people's self-reported competence with any of these other kinds of cultural differences.

Although our definition of peaceful conflict resolution includes the dimension of how a young person would respond to an unprovoked aggressive act by another adolescent, it does not include a measure of strategies used to solve interpersonal conflict or an assessment of how an adolescent would interpret an ambiguous event.

We define resistance skills to include the dimensions of knowing how to say no and being able to avoid peers who might get an adolescent "in trouble." These dimensions of resistance skills are consistent with those suggested in the literature.

Looking broadly at the research related to social competencies, some aspects of our social-competencies assets could be improved by the inclusion of some of the other skills found in some of the literature on related topics. In addition, there are conceptually meaningful areas of personal and social competence we do not measure at all, such as the ability to spend an appropriate amount of time alone. For example, while time alone is not a social competence per se, Larson (1997) has reported that youth who spend an intermediate amount of time alone are better adjusted. Specifically, in studying 5th through 9th graders, Larson concluded that 7th to 9th graders (but not 5th or 6th graders) who spent 25–45% of their nonclass time alone had better grades, were rated as better adjusted by parents and teachers, and were less depressed than peers who spent less or more time alone. Larson attributed the grade differences in the impact of solitude to a developmental role that solitude may play in early adolescence, allowing youth to make a "strategic retreat" (p. 90) from social pressures and providing them a better context for understanding themselves and for emotional coping. For those young adolescents, solitude may help enhance their overall competence and adjustment. We do not measure or consider these issues in thinking about young people's assets. This is a question of depth, not breadth: Our definitions do a good job of capturing the social competencies as they are described in the literature, but a deeper assessment (for example, more questions pertaining to a given context) could enhance our understanding of how young people develop social competence.

How Can Social Competencies Be Built?

Program evaluations and research on the prevention of adolescent problem behaviors constitute much of the available literature about how the social competencies can be built. Many of the programs cited in the literature are school based; they may include aspects of communication, decision making, negotiation, and conflict resolution. Proponents of such training programs believe that schools should teach social competence skills in the same way that they teach other skills (Hawkins & Weis, 1985).

Because the adolescent's social competence occurs within a variety of social relationships and across a number of different contexts, any attempt to build adolescents' social competence must also take into account the many relationships and contextual factors of her or his life. For example, programs targeting substance use must teach specific peer resistance skills and support what are thought to be moderating influences of substance use (such as improved parent-child communication) (Ogilvy, 1994). Moreover, studies have shown that prevention efforts (or attempts to build social competencies) must begin in late childhood, or early adolescence at the very latest, to target most health-risk behaviors (e.g., Clapper et al., 1995). For example, Elliott (1993) found that rates of alcohol use and sexual activity became normative (i.e., engaged in by 50% of adolescents) by ages 15 and 17, respectively. If the goal is to delay onset, whether through improved decision making or another strategy, the intervention must take place much earlier (Leffert & Petersen, 1996b; Petersen, 1993).

Planning and Decision Making

Efforts to build youth's planning and decision-making skills must involve a process for making rational decisions (Hansen, 1992), such as improving adolescents' knowledge, increasing their sense of options, and encouraging insight into their motivations for, and the consequences of, making decisions (Rogel et al., 1980). Teaching adolescents to be "vigilant" decision makers also is important (Mann et al., 1988). A vigilant decision maker is alert to a wide range of alternatives, carefully weighs positive and negative consequences, searches for new information, and makes plans to implement a decision. In addition, adults must help adolescents deal with potential information overload and learn how to sort through a potentially large volume of information. Gallotti and Kozberg (1996) use the process of applying to college as an example. Some young people are virtually showered with mail from prospective colleges; offering decision aids or steps to making rational decisions might be useful.

Many prevention efforts involve the adolescent in role-playing situations that she or he is likely to encounter, such as how to handle the behavior of a friend who brings alcohol to a party. Research has shown that such behavioral rehearsal is a critical element of effectiveness (e.g., Ogilvy, 1994). Also important is that prevention efforts encourage discussion among peers that allows adolescents to communicate with each other about how they feel about events, as well as how to handle them. Discussions of how to refuse a drink at a party or how not to get in a car with someone who has been drinking are the kinds of real-life discussions that could help adolescents prepare for situations that might occur (Milgram, 1996). School settings may be especially important places for young people to practice social skills because they offer many opportunities for discussion, practice, and feedback (Johnson, Jason, & Betts, 1990).

Interpersonal Competence and Cultural Competence

Interpersonal and cultural competence can be built by facilitating the creation of interracial friendship ties (DuBois & Hirsch, 1990). This might be more easily done in neighborhoods rather than schools, where grouping issues (e.g., ability tracking) sometimes make those ties difficult. Some neighborhoods may allow for access to other-race peers who go to other schools as well as a place to intensify relationships with peers from the same school. Neighborhood peer activities are also more informal and unstructured than in-school activities and are consequently more conducive to socializing. It is also likely that close friendships developed outside of the school context may carry over to school (Phinney, Ferguson, et al., 1997). In some settings, bringing adolescents into task-related contacts with adolescents from other cultural and ethnic groups will enhance cultural competence (Cotton, 1993).

One of the key dimensions of interpersonal competence is empathy, and studies suggest that parent education and support programs can play an important role in strengthening this aspect of adolescent competence. For example, in Henry, Sager, and Plunkett's (1996) study of 150 13- to 18-year-olds, adolescents who experienced encouragement, praise, and warmth from their parents had greater levels of empathy than those who did not. Parent education programs that help parents provide such encouragement, praise, and warmth lay the groundwork for children to care about others, an important part of overall interpersonal competence.

Resistance Skills

Most of the resistance skills training programs work from the premise that adolescents do not have the appropriate social skills to refuse their peers without experiencing negative consequences (e.g., Donaldson et al., 1995; Duryea & Okwumabua, 1988). Donaldson et al. suggest that social inoculation theory is often used to guide prevention program development:

> Inoculation against the inevitable social influences of early adolescence is the primary focus of resistance-skills training. Adolescents are first taught

how to recognize social pressure from peers. . . . Next they are trained to cope with high-pressure situations by developing social skills to refuse explicit alcohol and drug offers without experiencing negative social consequences (e.g., losing friends, being stereotyped by peers). (p. 292)

Equally important is providing adolescents with accurate prevalence estimates; this will assist them in building their repertoire of skills to resist the pressures that they may feel in their social world. As previously mentioned, adolescents often overestimate how many of their peers are engaging in particular behaviors, such as tobacco use. Faulty understanding of what their peers are doing may well weaken their "resolve" in exercising otherwise good resistance skills (Donaldson et al., 1994).

Attempts to build adolescent resistance skills must include periodic "booster" sessions, as the "staying power" of these efforts will be enhanced by continued support (Duryea & Okwumabua, 1988; Ellickson, Bell, & McGuigan, 1993). Ellickson and Hays (1990–91) suggest that building self-efficacy is also an important target for such efforts. Self-efficacy skills are particularly salient in the development of responsible sexual behaviors. For example, Zimmerman, Sprecher, et al. (1995) examined verbal sexual coercion (when a dating partner exerts verbal pressure to engage in sex) among a group of adolescents. They found that self-efficacy beliefs contribute to adolescents' ability to actually say no to sex. This suggests that programs that focus on teaching adolescents to "just say no" must go beyond the role playing and other techniques that give youth practice or rehearsal of these skills. They must focus on the development of generalized self-efficacy; if the adolescent believes that he or she can effect the outcome of a situation, that may make a difference.

Peaceful Conflict Resolution

Building peaceful conflict resolution skills needs to begin in childhood. Childhood aggression is a powerful predictor of later delinquent behavior. Aggressive or antisocial behaviors have been shown to be relatively stable; their presence in middle childhood is associated with higher rates and increased severity of adolescent and adult antisocial behavior (e.g., Robins, 1966). Interventions that target these behaviors must start early (O'Donnell et al., 1995).

Facilitating peaceful conflict resolution strategies among adolescents can be enhanced by increasing adolescents' social support networks. For example, in a study of approximately 150 adolescents, Kashani and Shepperd (1990) found that young people who were low in social support from family and friends were more likely to use violence to resolve their problems than those individuals who were high in social support. They suggest that attempts to build peaceful conflict resolution should include efforts to increase social support networks by helping young people gain the confidence to join social activities or clubs that may enhance their opportunities to develop friendships.

Because antisocial behavior and aggression have been shown repeatedly to be related to economic disadvantage, building skills of peaceful conflict resolution must be considered in light of contextual factors (Guerra, Huesmann, Tolan, Van Acker, & Eron, 1995). Studies have consistently shown that children and youth living in disadvantaged inner-city neighborhoods demonstrate higher levels of aggressive behaviors compared to children and youth from more advantaged circumstances (Achenbach, 1991; Eron, Walder, & Lefkowitz, 1972; Guerra et al., 1995). Stressful life events that are associated with poverty have also been found to be related to aggression (Guerra et al., 1995). Reducing these stressful events and facilitating the acquisition of adaptive coping strategies may enhance young people's ability to resolve conflicts. Children and youth who have observed aggressive parents learn that aggression, rather than other means of problem solving, is a means to resolve conflicts (Farrington, 1989). Parent education should underscore how powerful an influence parents' own behavior is on their children's behavior.

Conclusion

The social competencies are a set of skills that young people use to interact with others in a variety of different situations and contexts. They enable young people to confront new situations, face hard decisions through planning and practice, and interact with others in a manner that is skillful, socially appropriate, and appreciative of others' unique qualities. Although some of the literature pertaining to this asset category is more general rather than specific to each of the assets, social competence overall is viewed as an important part of development that can both enhance positive outcomes and provide youth with some of the things that will help them avoid risky behaviors.

Selected Readings

Arroyo, C. G., & Zigler, E. (1995). Racial identity, academic achievement, and the psychological well-being of economically disadvantaged adolescents. *Journal of Personality and Social Psychology, 69,* 903–914.

Bandura, A. (1977b). Self-efficacy: Toward a unifying theory of behavioral change. *Psychological Review, 84,* 191–215.

Collins, W. A., Laursen, B., Mortenson, N., Luebker, C., & Ferreira, M. (1997). Conflict processes and transitions in parent and peer relationships: Implications for autonomy and regulation. *Journal of Adolescent Research, 12,* 178–198.

DuBois, D. L., & Hirsch, B. J. (1990). School and neighborhood friendship patterns of Blacks and Whites in early adolescence. *Child Development, 61,* 524–536.

Elkind, D. (1984). Teenage thinking: Implications for health care. *Pediatric Nursing,* 383–385.

Furby, L., & Beyth-Marom, R. (1992). Risk-taking in adolescence: A decision-making perspective. *Developmental Review, 12,* 1–44.

Hansen, W. B. (1992). School-based substance abuse prevention: A review of the state of the art in curriculum, 1980–1990. *Health Education Research, 7,* 403–430.

Weithorn, L. A., & Campbell, S. B. (1982). The competency of children and adolescents to make informed treatment decisions. *Child Development, 53,* 1589–1598.

Shaping one's self-concept,
beliefs, capacities, roles, and
personal history is one of the
central tasks of adolescence.

8

The Positive-Identity Assets

What Is Positive Identity?

Identity development is one of the central tasks of the adolescent period (Erikson, 1968). Indeed, even in popular accounts, adolescence is often thought of as a time when substantial change in the self takes place. The idea of an "identity crisis" has commonly appeared in literary and media accounts of the adolescent passage.

Identity can be defined as an integrated view of oneself encompassing self-concept, beliefs, capacities, roles, and personal history. "[Its] formation is seen as an evolutionary process of differentiation and integration, synthesis and re-synthesis, and increasing cognitive complexity" (Adams, 1992, p. 1). Harter (1990b) has suggested that adolescents "who successfully navigate the journey of self-development should acquire a clear and consolidated sense of true self that is realistic and internalized, one that will lay the basis for future identity development" (p. 354).

The classic frameworks for conceptualizing the development of identity and changes in identity during adolescence have been provided by psychoanalysts Erik Erikson (1968) and Peter Blos (1962, 1979), who both recognized adolescence as a major time in life in which identity development takes place. Both Erikson and Blos conceptualized passive and active identity development processes. Erickson said passive identity occurs when the adolescent establishes a given identity by accepting the roles and self-images others provide (Adams,

1992), a process of "foreclosing" on a normal identity exploration process. Blos, on the other hand, described passive identity as a prolonged adolescence: The individual does not prematurely close off exploration of possible roles and self-images, but instead resists making final choices about that identity. Both Blos and Erikson suggested that adolescents with passive identity had self-doubt and uncertainty. Active identity, however, "is associated with self-assurance, self-certainty, and a sense of mastery" (Adams, 1992, p. 2). The development of active identity is based on a searching and self-selection process, in which self-chosen commitments are integrated into an organized psychic structure (Marcia, 1980).

Adolescents begin to define and integrate into their overall sense of themselves specific attributes or self-descriptions. They must also examine the roles they will play in the larger society, including occupational, religious, and political ones (Harter, 1990b). It is the positive features that result from the process of active identity seeking that we intend to describe in our conceptualization of the positive-identity assets. These assets represent how comfortable a youth is being herself or himself, whether or not the young person feels he or she has control over, and reasons for engaging in, aspects of life, and whether the youth has a degree of optimism when facing the future. (See Table 13.)

Summary of Research Findings

Personal Power

Our concepts of personal power and self-esteem overlap significantly. Personal power is defined as the adolescent feeling that he or she has some measure of control over things that happen. This sense of power is related to locus of control, a concept first introduced by Rotter (1966, 1975). Locus of control describes the causal relationships between behavior and its consequences—whether the outcome of a behavior is perceived by the individual as a result of something outside her or his control, or within it. Personal power is also associated with expectations of self-efficacy—the individual's beliefs about the likelihood that he or she will be able to effect a given outcome. Self-efficacy, in turn, is related

Table 13. The Positive-Identity Assets	
Personal power	Young person feels he or she has control over "things that happen to me."
Self-esteem	Young person reports having a high self-esteem.
Sense of purpose	Young person reports that "my life has a purpose."
Positive view of personal future	Young person is optimistic about her or his personal future.

to the concept of perceived self-competence (Harter, 1982), which generally is considered a component of self-esteem.

Personal power is directly or indirectly associated with:

- **Increased achievement** (Bouffard-Bouchard, Parent, & Larivée, 1991; Karnes & McGinnis, 1996); **increased engagement in learning** (Thomas et al., 1993); and **increased life satisfaction** (Hong & Giannakopoulos, 1994);
- **Increased problem-solving ability** (Gamble, 1994); **increased leadership** (McCullough, Ashbridge, & Pegg, 1994); and **increased coping skills** (Shulman, 1993);
- **Decreased at-risk status** (Browne & Rife, 1991; Seifer, Sameroff, Baldwin, & Baldwin, 1992); and
- **Decreased problem behaviors** (Allen, Leadbeater, & Aber, 1990); **decreased smoking** (Stacy et al., 1992); **decreased substance use** (Ellickson & Hays, 1990–91); **decreased vulnerability to life stress** (Weist et al., 1995); and **decreased depression** (McFarlane et al., 1995).

Self-Esteem

By far, the largest number of research and evaluation reports in the domain of positive identity pertain to the impact of self-esteem on youth behavior. Indeed, a tremendous amount of research has been generated about the development of self-esteem during adolescence. Some researchers have observed declines in overall self-esteem over the course of adolescence; others have noted increases during the same period (e.g., Abramowitz, Petersen, & Schulenberg, 1984). Studies of self-esteem have examined the effects of both low self-esteem and high self-esteem in youth on different types of psychosocial or behavioral outcomes (adult as well as adolescent). In general, although by no means universally, low self-esteem has been shown to be related to negative outcomes; high self-esteem, to positive outcomes.

Low self-esteem has been associated with:

- **Decreased school adjustment** (Ryan et al., 1994); and
- **Increased risk for a wide range of difficulties** (DuBois, Felner, & Brand, 1997), including **increased depression, hopelessness, and suicidal tendencies** (Overholser, Adams, Lehnert, & Brinkman, 1995); **increased loneliness,** particularly among males (Inderbitzen-Pisaruk, Clark & Solano, 1992); and **increased smoking** (Botvin et al., 1994).

In contrast, **positive or high self-esteem** has been associated with:

- **Increased positive emotional tone and relationships with peers and parents** (Deihl, Vicary, & Deike, 1997);
- **Increased positive adjustment during the junior high school transition** (Lord, Eccles, & McCarthy, 1994), as well as **increased satisfaction with life** (Neto, 1993);
- **Increased academic achievement** (Kelly & Jordan, 1990; Liu, Kaplan, & Risser, 1992; Strassburger, Rosén, Miller, & Chavez, 1990);
- **Decreased susceptibility to peer pressure** (Zimmerman, Copeland, Shope, & Dielman, 1997);
- **Increased positive attitudes about contraception as well as its increased use** (Herold, Goodwin, & Lero, 1979; Holmbeck, Crossman, Wandrei, & Gasiewski, 1994); **decreased levels of adolescent sexual activity** (Robinson & Frank, 1994); and **decreased nonmarital childbearing** (Plotnick & Butler, 1991); and
- **Improved treatment outcomes** (Richter, Brown, & Mott, 1991).

Sense of Purpose and Positive View of Personal Future

Very little in the literature directly focuses on the development of a sense of purpose per se. A sense of purpose may be thought of as finding meaning in life or as the reason(s) an individual has for doing something (Atkinson, 1987). In adolescence, the individual makes the first of many important choices to pursue a particular purpose or purposes. A sense of purpose is related to thinking about the future; they are typically studied together. A sense of purpose and a positive view of personal future are associated with:

- **Improved parent-child relationships** (Grossman & Rowat, 1995; Saucier & Ambert, 1982);
- **Increased self-esteem** (Nurmi & Pulliainen, 1991);
- **Decreased emotional or behavioral problems such as depression and sexual risk taking** (DuRant, Getts, Cadenhead, Emans, & Woods, 1995); **decreased emotional distress** (Blum & Rinehart, 1997; Resnick et al., 1997); and **reduced violence** (DuRant et al., 1994).

Variations in Findings

The research confirms the impact of positive identity but also shows variation in how identity affects different groups of youth. Most examinations of group differences in identity pertain to gender, or to the interaction of gender and race and ethnicity or other group variables.

Gender

Allen et al. (1990) examined gender differences in how expectations of self-efficacy might work when adolescents were faced with difficult situations—how their expectations were related to delinquency, substance use, and unprotected sexual intercourse. Although the gender differences were relatively small, Allen et al. found that low self-appraisal of competent behaviors (i.e., weak belief that one would be able to behave in a competent manner to achieve a particular outcome) was strongly related to delinquency and hard drug use among males and that identification with an adult's values was related to fewer problem behaviors among females.

Kelly and Jordan (1990) examined the relation of achievement and self-concept among young adolescents. They found that males reported higher levels of both scholastic and job-related self-concept than females did. The authors observed that "even though the academic accomplishments of the boys and girls in this study were equal, boys saw themselves as more capable than girls [i.e., academically superior to girls]" (p. 176). This is also true of females who are considered gifted: They appear to have lower career aspirations than males. This probably reflects their lack of confidence in their abilities.

Other researchers (Lord et al., 1994) have shown that physical appearance is a particularly important predictor of overall self-worth among young adolescent females. They tend to be more dissatisfied with their appearance than do males (Simmons & Blyth, 1987); this may take its toll on their self-esteem. In addition, "girls at this age who have a negative perception of their appearance may be at particular risk for developing symptoms, such as eating disorders, that reflect this diminished self-esteem" (Lord et al., 1994, p. 192).

The findings of high levels of self-esteem among males reported, for example, in the study by Kelly and Jordan (1990) reflect the findings observed consistently in studies of gender differences in adolescence (e.g., Simmons & Blyth, 1987). For example, Zimmerman et al. (1997) followed a group of more than 1,000 adolescents over the course of four school years to examine longitudinal trajectories of self-esteem. They assessed global self-esteem as well as self-esteem specifically related to the domains of school, peer, and family. They examined attitudinal and behavioral outcomes (i.e., peer pressure, academic achievement, alcohol use, and tolerance for deviance) among youth with different self-esteem trajectories (i.e., specific patterns of self-esteem over the course of the four years of the study). More female adolescents reported decreasing self-esteem trajectories than males did; more males reported increasing self-esteem trajectories.

Inderbitzen-Pisaruk et al. (1992) found gender differences in the factors that contributed to loneliness in a sample of almost 200 9th graders. Low self-esteem was a significant predictor of loneliness for males but not for females. The authors speculate that this may be a function of gender differences in the structure and function of adolescent friendships. They suggest that male friendships are more group oriented and centered around activities, whereas females tend to focus friendships around intimacy (Karweit & Hansell, 1983). The classic work of Douvan and Adelson (1966) suggests that males resolve identity issues in groups; if they are not group members, they may be at risk for low self-esteem and, consequently, for loneliness. Conversely, girls may do better if they form close one-on-one relationships; their self-esteem depends less on being a member of a group.

Another study (Stein, Newcomb, & Bentler, 1992) showed that late adolescent females' perceptions of themselves as having good interpersonal relationships affected their future evaluation of themselves as young adults. In contrast, males' perceptions of themselves as having opportunities for personal achievement and self-fulfillment were most important for their future self-evaluations.

Weist et al. (1995) examined the influence of life stress on psychological adjustment and school performance among a sample of urban youth. They found gender differences in some of the variables thought to mediate or moderate the adolescent's response to stress. Although family cohesion (i.e., family closeness, family support) served to protect males from the effects of stress, it did not explicitly protect females. Family cohesion, however, was related to self-concept among females. The researchers also found that external locus of control (i.e., the individual's perception of a low level of personal power) increased both males' and females' vulnerability to the effects of stress.

Race and Ethnicity

Echohawk and Parsons (1977) examined personal control among Native American youth from two Bureau of Indian Affairs boarding schools and how they perceived Caucasian youth. The Native American adolescents in this study reported high levels of external locus of control. The authors suggest that this is realistic given the real-life situations in which members of a "caste-like" minority group are indeed controlled by "powerful others" (see Ogbu, 1978). Adolescents from such groups may have fewer opportunities to explore or to "try on" different options or choices of roles or identities (Hauser & Kasendorf, 1983). For example, some youth may be unable to choose to attend institutions of higher education, where a good deal of identity exploration occurs, because of economic or other constraints. In addition, some youth face the dual challenge of needing to weigh or explore the identity possibilities that exist in two cultures, that of the majority culture as well as their own cultural group (Markstrom-Adams, 1992). It is also probable that some young people will face the compounded challenge of exploring the identity possibilities of more than two cultures.

Studies generally suggest that youth with high levels of ethnic identity also have higher levels of self-esteem. In a study of nearly 700 Hispanic, African American, and Caucasian students, Phinney, Cantu, and Kurtz (1997) reported that ethnic identity significantly contributed to self-esteem for all three ethnic groups, but that it contributed relatively small percentages to the overall variance in self-esteem. Studying more than 12,000 middle and high school students, Martinez and Dukes (1997) also concluded that ethnic identity contributed to higher self-esteem, as well as to greater self-confidence and sense of purpose in life. In their study, Caucasian youth and Native American youth had weaker ethnic identities, Asian American and multiracial youth had intermediate ethnic identities, and African American and Latina/Latino youth the strongest ethnic identities. For Caucasian youth only, their sense of being an American also was strongly associated with higher self-esteem.

Our review of the literature revealed few studies about how cultural differences may affect sense of purpose. DuRant et al. (1994, 1995) have examined how exposure to violence may affect the experience of depression, hopelessness, and purpose in life among African American adolescents living in and around public housing developments. Similar to findings from resiliency research (e.g., Werner & Smith, 1992), many adolescents in these studies were resilient in the face of multiple and serious environmental stressors such as living in poor communities with high unemployment and being exposed to, or being victims of, violence. DuRant et al. (1994) found that adolescents who reported lower levels of hopelessness and a higher sense of purpose in life who also believed they would be alive at age 25 (i.e., that they had a future) were less likely to engage in violent behavior. The researchers also found that adolescents who attended religious services more often, whose household was headed by an employed adult, and whose family had a higher socioeconomic status were more likely to have a higher sense of purpose in life, fewer feelings of hopelessness, and a greater belief that they would be alive at age 25.

How Positive Identity Works

Positive identity develops gradually over the course of childhood and adolescence. It is, however, a central task of adolescence.

Personal Power

As described earlier, personal power is related to locus of control and self-efficacy beliefs. Over the past three decades, many studies have been conducted on locus of control; a good deal of research evidence suggests that the individual who has an internal locus of control (i.e., who believes that consequences are a result that he or she can effect) are quite different from the individual who has an external locus of control (i.e., who believes that consequences are a result of something the individual can effect only inadequately or not at all). For example, if an adolescent attributes her or his achievement at school to hard work or ability, he or she maintains an internal locus of control. If achievement is attributed instead to luck or chance, the adolescent maintains an external locus of control. Studies (e.g., Douglas & Powers, 1982; Karnes & D'Ilio, 1991) consistently have shown that higher achievement is related to internal locus of control (see also Chapter 5, on commitment to learning).

Studies (e.g., Seifer et al., 1992) have also shown that having an internal locus of control protects youth from social and emotional risk. Personal characteristics such as locus of control and self-efficacy can protect against problem behaviors (Garmezy, 1985). For example, Luthar and Zigler (1992) studied the relation between intelligence and psychosocial factors such as locus of control among a sample of 144 adolescents in an inner-city school. They found that psychosocial assets may protect intelligent inner-city adolescents from a pattern of rejecting academic efforts in favor of other activities. Instead, youth will maximize effort at school if they "believe that events in their lives are determined largely by their own efforts (internal locus of control)" (p. 296).

Personal power and locus of control are also linked to self-efficacy; an adolescent's belief that consequences are a result of something internal suggests that he or she can exercise some influence or at the very least, that he or she has the ability to effect an outcome. Bandura (1977a, 1986, 1997) has long suggested that self-efficacy affects what individuals will try to do, how much effort they may be willing to expend to achieve a particular outcome, and their persistence in the face of things that may get in the way of a desired outcome. For example, Stacy et al. (1992) found that self-efficacy was the only factor that moderated the effect of peers' social influence on smoking. They concluded that the greater the belief in one's ability to resist social influences, the less strength that friends' social influence actually may have. For some youth, culturally valued expressions of personal power can have negative effects in mainstream settings such as school. For example, Stevens (1997) concluded from a study of African American middle school females that loudness and arguing, with each other and with authority figures, are a means by which these females assert their cultural value in a society that devalues African American women: "The behavior may well indicate resiliency and serve as a protective element in negotiating hostile racist environments" (p. 165). Nevertheless, loud, defiant behavior in school usually leads to negative consequences. Thus, how and in what circumstances youth display their personal power may be influenced by cultural as well as developmental issues.

Self-Esteem

Self-esteem pertains to the way in which the individual evaluates her or his self-concept(s); it is thought to be an important aspect of an individual's overall well-being. Self-esteem has been associated with a variety of psychosocial outcomes as well as many developmental tasks. Because of the important developmental challenges facing young people during adolescence, changes in self-esteem during this period have been of particular interest to researchers. As mentioned earlier, positive or high self-esteem has been shown to be associated with positive developmental outcomes (e.g., Hirsch and DuBois, 1991). Conversely, low self-esteem has repeatedly been shown to be related to various problem behaviors (e.g., DuBois et al., 1997; Ryan et al., 1994).

The adolescent's self-concept or self-image typically is composed of a global sense of herself or himself as a person as well as self-perceptions in different domains (Harter, 1986, 1990a). Researchers have assessed self-esteem in specific domains such as physical attractiveness, peer relationships or acceptance, academic competence, athletic competence, and behavior (e.g., Harter, 1982, 1990a). Although global assessments of self-esteem are typically highly correlated with self-esteem in specific domains, developmental trends may vary for an individual across domains (e.g., Fend & Schrörer, 1985). For example, a young person could see herself or himself as athletically competent but as lacking competence in academics. Self-esteem is the evaluative aspect of self-concept; it cuts across all of the domains that make up a young person's life.

Researchers have demonstrated that self-esteem may decline when the adolescent is faced with simultaneous changes, including school transitions that occur concurrently with pubertal change (e.g., Blyth, Simmons, & Carlton-Ford, 1983; Petersen, Kennedy, & Sullivan, 1991). In general, although there may be a good deal of individual variation in how adolescents handle or cope with stressful events or developmental transitions, adolescents do better if they can face challenges sequentially rather than simultaneously (Coleman, 1974). Resiliency or protective factors such as social support may, however, weaken the impact that multiple challenges have on adolescent self-esteem (e.g., Wigfield, Eccles, Mac Iver, Reuman, & Midgley, 1991).

Researchers continue to study the general stability of a youth's self-esteem during adolescence. Some researchers have found that on the whole, self-esteem either slightly increases or is relatively stable over the course of adolescence (McCarthy & Hoge, 1982; Nottelmann, 1987). Alsaker and Olweus (1992) found that self-esteem was relatively stable for short periods of time (e.g., a year), but changed over longer periods, particularly among young adolescents.

Other researchers have reported somewhat different findings. For example, in a longitudinal study of more than 1,000 adolescents (beginning when the subjects were in 6th grade and continuing through 10th grade), Zimmerman et al. (1997) reported that self-esteem declined slightly over the course of grades 6 through 10. They were specifically interested, however, in patterns of self-esteem: What happens over time to young people who have consistently high self-esteem, moderately high and rising self-esteem, steadily decreasing self-esteem, or consistently low self-esteem? The study, which replicates the earlier work of Hirsch and DuBois (1991), provides an interesting glimpse at how individual differences in patterns of self-esteem may influence, or be influenced by, other developmental factors (e.g., susceptibility to peer pressure, school grades, alcohol use, and tolerance for deviance).

Data from their findings are presented in Figure 12, which shows how young people's self-esteem trajectories affect their susceptibility to peer pressure. The young people with consistently high self-esteem are less susceptible to peer pressure than other youth; this holds true as the youth moves from the 6th to the 10th grade (the study used the 6th, 7th, 8th, and 10th grades as time points). The figure graphically portrays the impact that different pathways of development may have on psychosocial outcomes. Zimmerman et al. (1997) suggest that young people with consistently high or rising self-esteem have the skills and resources to cope with stressors. Consistently high or rising self-esteem may actually enhance other factors (such as having supportive and caring parents and teachers) as well as moderate the negative effects of risk factors such as the susceptibility to peer pressure.

All groups of youth in the study by Zimmerman et al. (1997) experienced increasing susceptibility to peer pressure over the course of adolescence, but the slope of the decreasing self-esteem group is steeper. Susceptibility to peer pressure rose the least over time among the group with moderate and rising self-esteem and the group with consistently high self-esteem. The researchers concluded that high or increasing self-esteem can serve a protective role.

In another study of the individual variation of self-esteem over the course of adolescence, Deihl et al. (1997) followed 142 adolescents from rural Appalachia over a four-year period, from immediately following the transition to junior high school through the transition to high school. Similar to the previously described study, they identified three distinct groups of adolescents: those with consistently high self-esteem over the course of the study, those with a small increase in self-esteem over the four-year period, and those with consistently low self-esteem. Overall, and consistent with the research of others (e.g., O'Malley

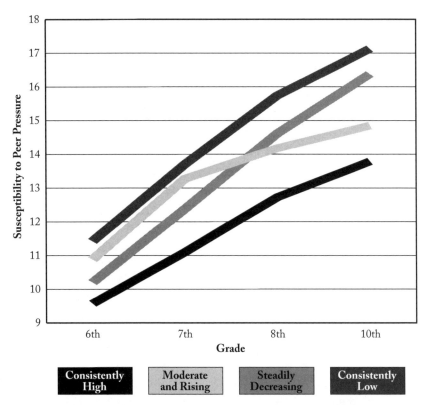

Figure 12 *Susceptibility to peer pressure by self-esteem trajectory. From "A Longitudinal Study of Self-Esteem: Implications for Adolescent Development," by M. A. Zimmerman, L. A. Copeland, J. T. Shope, and T. E. Dielman, 1997,* Journal of Youth and Adolescence, 26, *p. 129. Copyright 1997 by Plenum Publishing Corporation. Reprinted with permission.*

& Bachman, 1983), the authors found that self-esteem generally increased from 7th through 10th grades. They characterized the group with consistently high self-esteem as resilient adolescents who were able to cope with the changes and challenges of adolescence without suffering declining self-esteem. They also reported more positive peer and family relationships along with a more positive emotional status compared with the other two groups. Their resiliency may have served to protect them from most threats to their self-esteem.

Lord et al. (1994) also observed that protective aspects of both academic and nonacademic self-perceptions "facilitate positive gains in self-esteem across the transition to junior high school" (p. 189). Specifically, they found that 6th graders with confidence in academic, social, and athletic abilities showed gains in global self-esteem following the school transition. In contrast, worrying and self-consciousness were more likely to be associated with declines in self-esteem.

The work that Eccles and colleagues have done on stage-environment "fit" (Eccles et al., 1993) has demonstrated the importance of the fit between an adolescent's environment and her or his developmental needs. In this context, this means that when children enter adolescence, the family, schools, and other settings in which they interact must renegotiate the power balance between adult and adolescent to reflect the latter's growing needs for autonomy and self-control. When parents and other adults are able to adjust to children's changing developmental needs, there will be a better match or fit between the adolescent and the environment (see also Chapter 5, on commitment to learning).

Lord et al. (1994) also demonstrated that the fit between the adolescent and the environment affects self-esteem. A responsive and sensitive family environment may serve to protect adolescents when they make the transition to junior high school; adolescents who reported "less opportunity to express their own desires and opinions and who perceived a lack of attunement between themselves and their parents" (p. 191) did not do as well during the transition to junior high school compared with adolescents whose family environment was a better match with their developmental needs.

Another type of developmental fit may involve the racial composition of schools. Gray-Little and Carels (1997), for example, studied more than 100,000 5th-, 8th-, and 11th-grade students and reported that for 5th and 8th graders, African American and Caucasian students with the highest achievement were in schools that were largely Caucasian. For 11th graders, African American and Caucasian students with the highest achievement and self-esteem attended schools with more balanced racial compositions. Self-esteem also was highest for African American 5th graders in largely White schools, and for Caucasian 8th graders in either balanced or mostly White schools. School racial composition made no difference for African American 8th graders, however. Overall, the results suggest that for the majority of Caucasian and African American students, the environment most conducive to their self-esteem and achievement is either racially balanced or predominantly Caucasian. These research findings suggest that to the extent that Caucasian students go to schools made up mostly of African American students (less common) or to the extent that African American students attend such schools (much more common), their self-esteem and achievement may suffer.

Sense of Purpose and Positive View of Personal Future

A sense of purpose and a positive view of the future are related to an overall feeling of support and the presence of a secure environment (see Chapter 1, on support, and Chapter 2, on empowerment). They are also associated with psychological well-being. For example, in a study of adolescents with separated or divorced parents, Grossman and Rowat (1995) found that the quality of the parental relationships, not the parents' marital status (i.e., married, separated, or divorced), mattered most in predicting the adolescents' sense of a personal future. Specifically, they found that poor parental relationships were related to a low sense of future for the adolescent. The authors suggest that "this lack of parental support may impede the family's capacity to serve as a secure environment in which learning and growth may take place" (p. 257).

A sense of purpose and a positive view of the future also have implications for stressful life experiences. Young people who feel that they do not have a future may be at risk for a number of different emotional and behavioral problems. As DuRant et al. (1995) found, hopelessness is related to family conflict, corporal punishment, and exposure to violence.

In their analysis of the National Longitudinal Study on Adolescent Health, Resnick et al. (1997) found that emotional distress and suicide were associated with adolescents' perceived risk of an untimely death (i.e., lack of a positive view of personal future), regardless of the age of the adolescent. In addition, among young adolescents (7th and 8th graders), interpersonal violence was also associated with a higher perceived risk of an untimely death. In contrast, adolescents who report a higher sense of purpose in life and who believed that they would be alive at 25 were less likely to be involved in violent activities, even if they lived in an environment that might be likely to produce a sense of not being able to change one's life (DuRant et al., 1994).

Adolescents' Experience of Positive Identity

Although it is heartening to see that 70% of the young people in Search Institute's large sample report a positive view of their personal future and somewhat more than half of youth feel that they have a sense of purpose, it is alarming that fewer than half of adolescents in our sample report positive self-esteem or a sense of personal power. (See Figure 13.) Although reports of the other assets in the positive-identity domain remain relatively stable over the developmental period (personal power increases substantially over the high school years), self-esteem levels show a net overall decline from 6th to 12th grade. Reports of this asset dip beginning in 7th grade, remain low through 10th grade, and then recover almost to 6th-grade levels for the 11th and 12th grade.

Although more consistent with the findings of Alsaker and Olweus (1992), these findings differ from those of most other researchers (e.g., McCarthy & Hoge, 1982; O'Malley & Bachman, 1983). For example, most research findings, contrary to popular beliefs, show steadily increasing trends in self-esteem over adolescence. This positive trend is seen in all self-esteem data on U.S. youth.

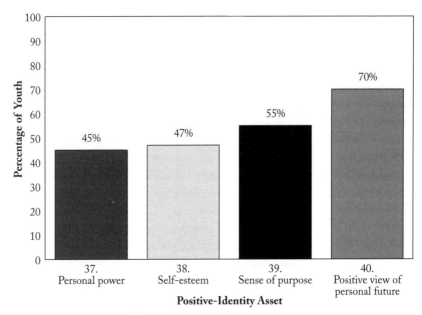

Figure 13 *Adolescents' experience of positive identity: percentage of 6th- to 12th-grade students who report experiencing each of the positive-identity assets. From unpublished Search Institute data on youth in public and/or alternative schools who completed the institute's* Profiles of Student Life: Attitudes and Behaviors *survey during the 1996–97 school year; N = 99,462 in 213 U.S. communities.*

However, many of these studies did not examine gender differences. Consistently in adolescent research (e.g., Simmons & Blyth, 1987), females report lower self-esteem than males. Although we note an overall decline in self-esteem from 6th to 12th grade, longitudinal research is needed to fully understand this pattern.

Adolescents show some increase in sense of purpose from 6th to 12th grade, after a decline in early to midadolescence. The "recovery," observed beginning in the 11th grade, may reflect growing clarity about plans for the future, as has been reported in the literature (e.g., Abramowitz, Petersen, and Schulenberg, 1984). "Positive view of the future" is the positive-identity asset reported by the greatest number of youth in our sample; almost three quarters of youth report having this asset. Our sample shows clear gender differences in self-esteem and sense of purpose, both of which are reported more frequently by males.

What Is Missing from Our Definition of Positive Identity?

Our definitions of the positive-identity assets appear to reflect the construct of identity as it is described in the literature. Personal power reflects both an assessment of internal locus of control and the ability to cope with or change things in the environment (i.e., self-efficacy). Although they constitute a global assessment of self-esteem, the individual items that we use to tap this construct are considered well established and reliable (Rosenberg, 1965; Rosenberg & Simmons, 1972).

Our measure of a sense of purpose and positive view of the future does not include any specific assessment of planning for the future, such as exploring or taking steps toward setting and achieving career, job, educational, or other life goals. Our measure could be improved by understanding how adolescents' abilities or desires to plan for the future may reflect how they actually view their futures.

How Can Positive Identity Be Built?

Most of the program evaluations and research literature reviewed here pertain to building positive identity in youth specifically by building their self-esteem. Many programs, even those that are not focused on self-esteem or other aspects of identity development, include some aspect of self-esteem enhancement as a program component (Leffert et al., 1996).

Studies have shown that school-based efforts may nurture feelings of self-worth in both children and adolescents. They have also shown the importance of parent, teacher, and community involvement in fostering self-esteem among adolescents, regardless of racial or gender differences (Robinson & Frank, 1994). Page (1992) noted that it is easy for schools and other social institutions to focus on "externals" such as appearance and achievement and that our society often rewards external attributes such as beauty or athletic ability. Indeed, Page challenges educators to emphasize the "inherent value of young people as unique human beings. Feelings of unconditional self-worth are achieved when individuals come to realize that they are important and worthwhile regardless of performance or appearance" (p. 154).

Parent-child relationships are particularly important in building self-esteem as well as the other positive-identity assets. For instance, research has shown that self-esteem is positively related to intimate and nurturing relationships with parents (e.g., Buri, Kirchner, & Walsh, 1987; Coopersmith, 1967; Lackovic-Grgin et al., 1994) and negatively related to parental overcontrol and punitiveness (e.g., Hill, Holmbeck, Marlow, Green, & Lynch, 1985; Papini & Sebby, 1987). (See Chapter 1, on support.)

DuBois and colleagues (e.g., DuBois et al., 1997) have suggested that programs designed to promote or enhance self-esteem must be domain specific, targeting particular areas of self-esteem such as schoolwork and family relationships. For example, McCarthy and Hoge (1982) suggest that feedback from teachers may have particular influence on academic self-esteem; this underscores the important distinction between a global sense of oneself compared with a domain-specific self-image (e.g., Harter, 1990b).

Zimmerman et al. (1997) suggest that "efforts either to prevent and stabilize decreasing self-esteem or to build self-esteem may have vital effects on other outcomes for youth" (p. 137). They also suggest that the notion of "one size fits all" may not be helpful in designing prevention or promotion programs. Different strategies for building self-esteem among youth with different profiles (e.g., youth with consistently low self-esteem, youth with decreasing self-esteem) may be more effective and a better way of allocating limited resources.

In a study of more than 400 6th graders, half of whom were defined as "at risk," Browne and Rife (1991) examined the psychosocial domains of self-concept and locus of control. Consistent with other research (e.g., Nystrom, 1989), they found that empowerment strategies can enhance the development of an internal locus of control. These can occur in community mentorship programs, partnership programs with colleges and universities, parents' awareness about educational and career opportunities, and parent-school partnerships that work toward addressing the particular needs of youth in high-risk situations.

DuRant et al. (1994) suggest that the most effective means of building the identity assets such as a sense of purpose is to use a social cognitive approach based on social learning theory (Bandura, 1997). Such approaches assume that adolescents become involved in risky behaviors through socially learned experiences. Thus, adolescents "need to be provided not only with the reasons to alter high-risk behavior but with the means, resources, and social supports to do so" (DuRant et al., 1994, p. 616). Institutional and community change is particularly important in such efforts.

Social learning theory also emphasizes that low levels of self-efficacy are a result of past failures with competent behaviors, which reduces the individual's persistence in attempting to continue competent behaviors in the future. Allen et al. (1990) found that adolescents with high rates of problem behaviors were less positive about how competent behaviors would work for them; they suggest that adolescents may turn to problem behaviors as a result of their negative self-appraisals of competence. Interventions, then, must be designed to promote competent behavior, but must also consider the influence of adolescents' expectations about how likely it is that competent behaviors will benefit them.

Conclusion

The process of defining oneself on a number of different fronts and consolidating those definitions into an integrated whole is one of the essential tasks of adolescence. The positive-identity assets cut across many of the issues found in the research and speak to the importance of active and realistic exploration of role opportunities. Implicit in the realization of a positive outcome is the availability, in the adolescent's environment, of such opportunities. Therefore, the process of identity development will best occur if young people feel they have the ability to effect its outcome, feel good about themselves, have developing clarity about roles and purpose(s), and possess the expectation of a positive future.

Selected Readings

Bandura, A. (1997). *Self-efficacy: The exercise of control.* New York: W. H. Freeman.

Blum, R. W., & Rinehart, P. M. (1997). *Reducing the risk: Connections that make a difference in the lives of youth.* Minneapolis: University of Minnesota, Division of General Pediatrics and Adolescent Health.

Deihl, L. M., Vicary, J. R., & Deike, R. C. (1997). Longitudinal trajectories of self-esteem from early to middle adolescence and related psychosocial variables among rural adolescents. *Journal of Research on Adolescence, 7,* 393–411.

DuRant, R. H., Getts, A., Cadenhead, C., Emans, S. J., & Woods, E. (1995). Exposure to violence and victimization and depression, hopelessness, and purpose in life among adolescents living in and around public housing. *Journal of Developmental and Behavioral Pediatrics, 16,* 233–237.

Eccles, J. S., Midgley, C., Wigfield, A., Miller Buchanan, C., Reuman, D., Flanagan, C., & Mac Iver, D. (1993). Development during adolescence: The impact of stage/environment fit on young adolescents' experiences in schools and in families. *American Psychologist, 48,* 90–101.

Harter, S. (1990b). Self and identity development. In S. S. Feldman & G. R. Elliott (Eds.), *At the threshold: The developing adolescent* (pp. 352–387). Cambridge, MA: Harvard University Press.

Lord, S. E., Eccles, J. S., & McCarthy, K. A. (1994). Surviving the junior high school transition: Family processes and self-perceptions as protective and risk factors. *Journal of Early Adolescence, 14,* 162–199.

Marcia, J. E. (1980). Identity in adolescence. In J. Adelson (Ed.), *Handbook of adolescent psychology* (pp. 149–173). New York: John Wiley.

Zimmerman, M. A., Copeland, L. A., Shope, J. T., & Dielman, T. E. (1997). A longitudinal study of self-esteem: Implications for adolescent development. *Journal of Youth and Adolescence, 26,* 117–141.

Postscript: Lessons from the Research

We have reviewed and synthesized the results of more than 1,200 scientific studies and other sources pertaining to the positive development of adolescents. In doing so, we have thought deeply for two years about what the research says about the framework of developmental assets for youth, the ways in which the framework is strong, and in what respects it may be weak. We have tried through these labors to come to a better understanding of adolescent development and what adults must do to promote positive youth development.

Overarching Themes and Conclusions

A number of conclusions stand out among our overall impressions from the scientific literature, each of which is explored in more depth below:

1. The asset framework is a solidly supported way of communicating essential features of healthy development during adolescence.
2. Some categories of assets, as well as individual assets, have a stronger research base than others.
3. Although it is quite comprehensive, the framework of 40 assets does not capture everything young people need.
4. The assets are interdependent.
5. The asset framework raises numerous critical questions about adolescent development that remain to be addressed by researchers.

6. The assets are important for all youth, but the levels and patterns of assets that work for individual youth in different contexts seem to vary.

7. Building developmental assets is only part of what communities need to do to ensure healthy development for all adolescents.

8. Supportive and caring relationships are more fundamental than programs to the process of enhancing or building assets.

1. The asset framework is a solidly supported way of communicating essential features of healthy development during adolescence.
We began this synthesis of the research with some skepticism. We were not purposefully looking for studies to "back up" Search Institute's framework of developmental assets, but wanted instead to comprehensively scan the literature to see whether this conceptualization of adolescent development made sense, and how and for whom it did not. We have tried to be critical with regard to what seems to be missing from developmental assets as Search Institute defines them, or where our measurement seems especially limited.

This review of a large body of research has convinced us that, despite the inadequacies present in any framework, the developmental asset approach and the framework of 40 assets seem to rest on a broad and deep foundation of scientific support. The effects of these positive developmental experiences and qualities have generally been well established, in terms of both preventing risky behavior among youth and promoting positive behavior. Individuals, organizations, and communities that base their programs and policies about youth on those assets generally are on firm scientific ground in doing so.

2. Some categories of assets, as well as individual assets, have a stronger research base than others.
The research is particularly large and confirming of the power of support, boundaries and expectations, constructive use of time, and commitment to learning, and to a somewhat lesser extent, of positive identity. In contrast, there is limited research on the effects of the experiences highlighted in the empowerment assets.

Our conceptualizations of the asset categories generally are well grounded in the research, but the conceptualizations of empowerment, positive values, and social competencies may be less represented in the literature than the others. Although these asset categories are supported by the research, they simply seem incomplete as a group. We have suggested other kinds of values and social competencies, and additional or alternative ways of assessing empowerment than those we currently measure. Thus, there is ample room for both conceptual and empirical work that might lead us to describe those constructs more comprehensively, yet with the same economy as the other categories seem to have been described.

3. Although it is quite comprehensive, the framework of 40 assets does not capture everything young people need.

As suggested above and in various places throughout this book, our review of this large body of empirical literature and our continued reflection on these constructs suggest that there are a number of positive developmental features that we do not measure or include as part of the developmental asset framework. In addition, we have noted assets that might be better understood or more "complete" through the addition of new questions or items on the survey used to measure developmental assets.

We have never intended to suggest that these 40 assets were everything that children and adolescents need to grow up healthy. For example, the developmental assets do not reflect that children and adolescents need food, shelter, and basic medical care, or that far too many children and adolescents in the United States are living in poverty. Instead, we think of the developmental assets as a set of positive developmental features that get people thinking and talking about the importance of raising healthy children and adolescents, and how important healthy development is for the promotion of both near-term and long-term outcomes. As such, many other things (including many that were mentioned in this book) might be compiled into a list of positive features for adolescents.

Thus, the greatest contribution of Search Institute's framework of developmental assets is not in precisely identifying and measuring an indisputable, authoritative list of everything young people need. Rather, the greatest contribution may be in offering a solidly supported framework that provokes reflection and dialogue—followed by action—in families, neighborhoods, schools, organizations, and communities about how we in our society can better care for our youngest generations.

4. The assets are interdependent.

The developmental assets and their overarching categories do not operate as separate, isolated influences in young people's lives. We have tried to capture some of the complex interactions that occur among the assets, showing how—among many other interactions—support, expectations, social competencies, and commitment to learning all seem to work to influence each other in essentially a circular fashion. Youth who have support, for example, tend to have the other assets, which in turn tend to reinforce and promote each other.

One of the challenging issues is how to create this same circular pattern for all youth, not just a select few. Asset building is not a zero-sum game: There is nothing wrong with young people with many developmental assets having their asset base strengthened even more. At the same time, it is critically important to build strengths for those young people who currently experience few of these assets. For example, regardless of the number of deficits youth have (e.g., being home alone too much, being physically abused), adolescents with 31 to 40 of the developmental assets are more likely to engage in thriving behavior than youth with average levels of assets (11–20 assets) (Benson, Scales, and Roehlkepartain, 1999). Our goal must be to ensure that all youth have high levels of the assets.

5. The asset framework raises numerous critical questions about adolescent development that remain to be addressed by researchers.

For example, the review of the support assets (Chapter 1) confirms that adults other than parents play important roles in promoting adolescent well-being. At the very least, youth need an adult, whether parent or not, to care deeply about them. What happens if youth have multiple caring adults in their lives? What is the differential impact on youth of having three, four, or five caring adults versus having only one?

Our review of the literature also reinforces the importance of neighborhood support. What is the best way to conceptualize and define this idea? Is the number of adults in the neighborhood who care about youth really the best way to understand the impact of neighborhood-level variables? What about the degree to which neighbors, parents, teachers, and other adults in young people's lives talk to each other and are themselves connected, not just that they are connected to a young person? What difference does it make in the lives of youth who perceive their neighbors to have that connection compared with youth who do not see such relationships among their neighbors and the other adults in their lives?

Similarly, there is scant research that directly answers the most basic of questions: What is the impact of youth feeling valued by adults? Questions such as these abound in regard to all the categories of assets. The asset framework offers a fertile source of research energy that can greatly enhance our collective understanding of how adolescents develop and what communities must do to ensure their healthy development.

6. The assets are important for all youth, but the levels and patterns of assets that work for individual youth in different contexts seem to vary.

All young people need support and boundaries, for example, but the effective levels and kinds of support and boundaries depend on the youth to whom we refer. The following examples represent a few of the many individual differences that appear in the literature:

- Many African American adolescents perceive teacher support to be high when teachers give them a great deal of homework, but that connection does not seem nearly as strong for White youth.
- Parents raising adolescents in an urban context may provide greater safety for their children by being stricter than parents raising their children in other settings.
- The middle school transition can be particularly difficult for females, especially those who mature biologically ahead of their peers.

There are many other examples of how context and individual differences interact to affect young people's experience of the assets. This review underscores the importance of asking not only *if* a particular process or program is effective, but also *for whom* and under what circumstances?

7. Building developmental assets is only part of what communities need to do to ensure healthy development for all adolescents.
Search Institute has highlighted the difference between an asset-building approach and more traditional problem-prevention efforts. Focusing on building strengths, on the role everyone plays in building assets, and on viewing youth themselves as resources and not just as sources of problems to be prevented often produces a greater sense of hope in communities than do more common approaches that focus on naming and reducing or preventing problems such as substance abuse or adolescent pregnancy. This review of the literature indicates that building developmental assets can have pervasive positive effects on youth outcomes.

However, just as the assets may work somewhat differently for different youth, it is also true that asset building alone does not make a healthy community or one that equitably ensures healthy development for *all* youth. Our own analyses of aggregate data from nearly 100,000 6th to 12th graders shows that various assets working together can enable us to predict roughly 20–50% of the variation in youth experiencing patterns of risky behavior and somewhat less in thriving outcomes (Leffert et al., in press; Scales, Benson, et al., 1998).

Some youth, by virtue of individual or environmental factors in their lives (e.g., various learning or developmental disabilities, drug-abusing parents, poverty) are at great risk of experiencing negative outcomes. Other youth are already abusing alcohol and other drugs; perpetrating or being victims of violence; failing in school; or stealing, cheating, and lying on a regular basis. Without targeted prevention and treatment efforts, asset-building relationships and opportunities alone will not be sufficient to enable most youth to overcome such problems.

Asset building alone obviously will not create jobs, make racism, sexism, and other forms of discrimination disappear, or radically raise the quality of the most resource-poor schools in America's inner cities. Asset building is an essential aspect of communities responding to the developmental needs of adolescents, but, if done in isolation, it leaves a complete community response to what youth collectively need as unfinished as a house with a foundation but no walls or roof.

8. Supportive and caring relationships are more fundamental than programs to the process of enhancing or building assets.

There is no question that youth programs that are guided in their design around positive developmental features, such as those captured in the asset framework, have demonstrated success in reducing risks and promoting positive youth outcomes. But regardless of the asset category, this review underscores that the success of programs lies largely in supportive and caring relationships among young people and their peers, and among youth and caring adults.

Some of the asset categories are more obviously about relationships, such as support or social competencies. But the research evidence shows repeatedly that the positive effects of other asset categories (such as commitment to learning and constructive use of time) occur in large part because of the social interactions they foster. Adults expressing care, setting standards, modeling behavior, peers communicating effectively with each other, reinforcing norms, cooperating and resolving problems peacefully—all contribute to young people's sense of rootedness and competence.

This research confirmation of the fundamental importance of relationships also reinforces the corollary notion that asset building is for everyone, not only professionals or volunteers specially trained to work in youth programs and formal activities. The informal acts of relationship that youth experience every day, cumulatively, likely are more important than the programs in which they participate. Thus, this review offers support for the value of mobilizing community residents to make asset building for youth a more intentional part of their lives.

Implications

This review and synthesis of the scientific literature points to several implications for various readers.

For Researchers

We have tried to raise questions about what is missing from our conceptualization of the assets and to suggest what needs to be additionally measured. For example, the limited quantitative research on the constructs related to the empowerment assets suggests the need for further research on what young people need to feel safe, valued, and useful. Additional research also would help us understand what the most important social competencies and positive values might be.

Moreover, this review has illuminated the need for more research on how the assets interact with each other and may operate for different youth and in different contexts. For example, how critical are boundaries and expectations in young people's development of a solid commitment to learning, especially among youth who might experience obstacles to, or prejudice against, their achievement because of their ethnic or cultural background, gender, or socioeconomic status? We have raised numerous such issues and questions throughout this book that may be fruitfully pursued by researchers.

For Policy Makers and Funders

Several conclusions are important for policy makers and funders. Programs and policies based on the developmental asset framework clearly are sound. The research evidence is large for the effects of those assets on the positive outcomes policy makers—and all of us—desire. The assets contribute to the reduction of risky behaviors, increases in positive behaviors, and overall resilience.

However, we caution policy makers and funders, as well as practitioners, not to misinterpret the evidence. The research we have reviewed here consistently suggests that the developmental assets work more often indirectly and in interaction with other assets, with many assets each contributing small amounts to the achievement of particular positive outcomes such as school success or doing community service. Many assets seem to be important in ways we only partially understand. The power lies not in any isolated asset, but in the accumulation and interaction of many assets.

Community Leaders and People Who Work with Youth and Families

We hope that this review provides assurance to community leaders and people who work with youth and families that the scientific underpinnings of the developmental asset framework are sound. The evidence shows that assets make a positive difference in young people's lives and that community residents, programs, and institutions have critical roles to play in building every asset category, especially the external assets, which are more directly under their control.

The opportunities communities offer for youth to use their time constructively, to serve and contribute to community betterment, to hear consistent messages about expected behaviors, and to feel cared about and supported by all adults, clearly matter.

The research suggests that the more intentional communities and those who work with youth and families become in building assets, the more they will reduce or prevent negative outcomes among adolescents and the more they will stimulate the positive skills, values, commitments, and self-perceptions that enable youth to be healthy, productive, principled, and caring.

Moreover, it should be clear from this review how many of the assets are built by family life, both directly and indirectly, and how important family support and expectations are. The studies we have reviewed consistently suggest that family support and expectations are even more important than a youth's socioeconomic background in affecting various outcomes. Indeed, family support can often moderate the negative effects of socioeconomic constraints. When we help families build their children's developmental infrastructure, we can help our most vulnerable young people rise above what may be a crumbling economic and physical infrastructure around them.

Individuals Matter

Finally, the scientific literature does not help us come to a valid conclusion about which of the assets or categories is "most important." In contrast, as we reviewed study after study, we were struck both by the predictable power of the assets for adolescents in general and by the idiosyncratic ways in which particular combinations of assets, working within varying contexts for specific adolescents, may have their most profound effects. In the end, how the assets "work" is a function of the characteristics of the individual adolescent and how he or she is embedded in multiple nested and interacting worlds of family, school, friends, and community.

In analyses of the Search Institute data we have cited elsewhere in this book (Leffert et al., in press; Scales, Benson, et al., 1998), we found much the same trend: Some assets (such as time in youth programs and achievement motivation) contribute more to predicting positive outcomes and reduced risk. But numerous assets also contribute just a little, suggesting that they play indirect and sometimes almost undetectable supporting roles in an adolescent's life; without them, the power of the apparent "most important" assets is likely to diminish.

In the final analysis, we can say with a great deal of confidence that the assets work to reduce young people's risks and promote their well-being, but a vast uncharted territory remains to be explored to learn precisely how the assets help youth achieve those developmental goals. Focusing on developmental assets clearly puts all of us on the right path—as researchers, policy makers, funders, community leaders, and those who work with youth and their families—but our journey has just begun.

References

Abbott, R., Sutton, B., Jackson, M. C., Jr., & Logan, B. W. (1976). *Process and impact evaluation: The Detroit 4-H program* (final report). East Lansing: Michigan State University.

Abramowitz, R. H., Petersen, A. C., & Schulenberg, J. E. (1984). Changes in self-image during early adolescence. In D. Offer, E. Ostrov, & K. Howard (Eds.), *Patterns of adolescent self-image* (pp. 19–28). San Francisco: Jossey-Bass.

Achenbach, T. M. (1991). *Integrative guide for the 1991 CBCL/4-18 YSR, and TRF profiles.* Burlington: University of Vermont, Department of Psychiatry.

Achor, S., & Morales, A. (1990). Chicanas holding doctoral degrees: Social reproduction and cultural ecological approaches. *Anthropology and Education Quarterly, 21,* 269–287.

Adams, G. R. (1992). Introduction and overview. In G. R. Adams, T. P. Gullotta, & R. Montemayor (Eds.), *Advances in adolescent development: Vol. 4. Adolescent identity formation* (pp. 1–8). Newbury Park, CA: Sage.

Adlaf, E. M., & Smart, R. G. (1985). Drug use and religious affiliation, feelings and behaviour. *British Journal of Addiction, 80,* 163–171.

Adler, N. (1994). *Adolescent sexual behavior looks irrational—but looks are deceiving.* Washington, DC: Federation of Behavioral, Psychological, and Cognitive Sciences.

Ainley, M. D. (1993). Styles of engagement with learning: Multidimensional assessment of their relationship with strategy use and school achievement. *Journal of Educational Psychology, 85,* 395–405.

Alan Guttmacher Institute (1994). *Sex and America's teenagers.* New York: Author.

Alban Institute. (1997). Trend scan: The view from here. *Congregations, 23,* 5–11.

Allen, J. P., Leadbeater, B. J., & Aber, J. L. (1990). The relationship of adolescents' expectations and values to delinquency, hard drug use, and unprotected sexual intercourse. *Development and Psychopathology, 2,* 85–98.

Allen, J. P., Philliber, S., Herrling, S., & Kuperminc, G. P. (1997). Preventing teen pregnancy and academic failure: Experimental evaluation of a developmentally based approach. *Child Development, 68,* 729–742.

Aloise-Young, P. A., Graham, J. W., & Hansen, W. B. (1994). Peer influence on smoking initiation during early adolescence: A comparison of group members and group outsiders. *Journal of Applied Psychology, 79,* 281–287.

Alsaker, F. D., & Olweus, D. (1992). Stability and global self-evaluations in early adolescence: A cohort longitudinal study. *Journal of Research on Adolescence, 47,* 123–145.

American Psychological Association (1997). What makes kids care? Teaching gentleness in a violent world. In *ParenthoodWeb.* Available World Wide Web: http://www.parenthoodweb. com/.

Anderman, E. M., & Kimweli, D. M. S. (1997). Victimization and safety in schools serving early adolescents. *Journal of Early Adolescence, 17,* 408–438.

Anderson, A. R., & Henry, C. S. (1994). Family system characteristics and parental behaviors as predictors of adolescent substance use. *Adolescence, 29,* 405–420.

Arhar, J. M., & Kromrey, J. D. (1993, April). *Interdisciplinary teaming in the middle level school: Creating a sense of belonging for at-risk middle level students.* Paper presented at the annual meeting of the American Educational Research Association, Atlanta, GA.

Arnett, J. (1995). The young and the reckless: Adolescent reckless behavior. *Current Directions in Psychological Science, 4,* 67–71.

Arroyo, C. G., & Zigler, E. (1995). Racial identity, academic achievement, and the psychological well-being of economically disadvantaged adolescents. *Journal of Personality and Social Psychology, 69,* 903–914.

Astone, N. M., & McLanahan, S. S. (1991). Family structure, parental practices and high school completion. *American Sociological Review, 56,* 309–320.

Atkinson, R. (1987). The development of purpose in adolescence: Insights from the narrative approach. *Adolescent Psychiatry, 14,* 149–161.

Bailey, S. L., & Hubbard, R. L. (1990). Developmental variation in the context of marijuana initiation among adolescents. *Journal of Health and Social Behavior, 31,* 58–70.

Bandura, A. (1977a). *Social learning theory.* Englewood Cliffs, NJ: Prentice-Hall.

Bandura, A. (1977b). Self-efficacy: Toward a unifying theory of behavioral change. *Psychological Review, 84,* 191–215.

Bandura, A. (1986). *Social foundations of thought and action.* Englewood Cliffs, NJ: Prentice-Hall.

Bandura, A. (1997). *Self-efficacy: The exercise of control.* New York: W. H. Freeman.

Bandura, A., Ross, D., & Ross, S. A. (1963). Imitation of film-mediated aggressive models. *Journal of Abnormal and Social Psychology, 66,* 3–11.

Bankston, C. L., & Zhou, M. (1995). Religious participation, ethnic identification, and adaptation of Vietnamese adolescents in an immigrant community. *Sociological Quarterly, 36,* 523–534.

Barber, B., & Eccles, J. S. (1997, April). *Student council, volunteering, basketball, or marching band: What kind of extracurricular involvement matters?* Symposium paper presented at the biennial meeting of the Society for Research on Child Development, Washington, DC.

Barber, B. K. (1996). Parental psychological control: Revisiting a neglected construct. *Child Development, 67,* 3296–3319.

Barber, B. K., & Olsen, J. A. (1997). Socialization in context: Connection, regulation, and autonomy in the family, school, and neighborhood, and with peers. *Journal of Adolescent Research, 12,* 287–315.

Barnea, Z., Teichman, M., & Rahav, G. (1992). Personality, cognitive, and interpersonal factors in adolescent substance use: A longitudinal test of an integrative model. *Journal of Youth and Adolescence, 21*, 187–201.

Barnes, G. M. (1984). Adolescent alcohol abuse and other problem behaviors: Their relationships and common parental influences. *Journal of Youth and Adolescence, 13*, 329–348.

Barnes, G. M., & Farrell, M. P. (1992). Parental support and control as predictors of adolescent drinking, delinquency, and related problem behaviors. *Journal of Marriage and the Family, 54*, 763–776.

Barringer, F. (1993, June 2). School hallways as gauntlets of sexual taunts. *New York Times*, p. A12.

Batchelder, T. H., & Root, S. (1994). Effects of an undergraduate program to integrate academic learning and service: Cognitive, prosocial cognitive, and identity outcomes. *Journal of Adolescence, 17*, 341–355.

Battistich, V., Solomon, D., Watson, M., Solomon, J., & Schaps, E. (1989). Effects of an elementary school program to enhance prosocial behavior on children's cognitive-social problem-solving skills and strategies. *Journal of Applied Developmental Psychology, 10*, 147–169.

Baum, C. G., & Forehand, R. (1981). Long term follow-up assessment of parent training by use of multiple outcome measures. *Behavior Therapy, 12*, 643–652.

Baum, S. M., Renzulli, J. S., & Hébert, T. P. (1995). Reversing underachievement: Creative productivity as a systematic intervention. *Gifted Child Quarterly, 39*, 224–235.

Bauman, K. E., Botvin, G. J., Botvin, E. M., & Baker, E. (1992). Normative expectations and the behavior of significant others: An integration of traditions in research on adolescents' cigarette smoking. *Psychological Reports, 71*, 568–570.

Baumrind, D. (1971). Current patterns of parental authority. *Developmental Psychology Monographs, 4* (1, Pt. 2).

Baumrind, D. (1978). Parental disciplinary patterns and social competence in children. *Youth and Society, 9*, 239–276.

Beane, J., Turner, J., Jones, D., & Lipka, R. (1981). Long term effects of community service programs. *Curriculum Inquiry, 11*, 143–155.

Bear, G. G. (1989). Social cognitive influences on early adolescents' decisions to copy software in hypothetical situations. *Journal of Early Adolescence, 9*, 499–515.

Benard, B. (1990). *Turning the corner: From risk to resiliency.* Portland, OR: Northwest Regional Educational Laboratory, Western Regional Center Drug-Free Schools and Communities.

Benard, B. L. (1991). *Fostering resiliency in kids: Protective factors in the family, school, and community.* San Francisco: Far West Laboratory for Educational Research and Development. (ERIC Document Reproduction Service No. ED 335 781)

Benson, P. L. (1997). *All kids are our kids: What communities must do to raise caring and responsible children and adolescents.* San Francisco: Jossey-Bass.

Benson, P. L., & Donahue, M. J. (1989). Ten-year trends in at-risk behaviors: A national study of Black adolescents. *Journal of Adolescent Research, 4*, 125–139.

Benson, P. L., Donahue, M. J., & Erickson, J. A. (1989). Adolescence and religion: A review of the literature from 1970 to 1986. In M. L. Lynn and D. O. Mobery (Eds.), *Research in the Social Scientific Study of Religion, 1* (pp. 153–181). Greenwich, CT: JAI Press.

Benson, P. L., Leffert, N., Scales, P. C., & Blyth, D. A. (1998). Beyond the "village" rhetoric: Creating healthy communities for children and adolescents. *Applied Developmental Science, 2*, 138–159.

Benson, P. L., Masters, K. S., & Larson, D. B. (1997). Religious influences on child and adolescent development. In J. D. Noshpitz & N. E. Alessi (Eds.), *Handbook of child and adolescent psychiatry: Vol. 4. Varieties of Development* (pp. 206–219). New York: John Wiley & Sons.

Benson, P. L., Scales, P. C., and Roehlkepartain, E. C. (1999). *A fragile foundation: The state of developmental assets among American youth.* Minneapolis, MN: Search Institute.

Berends, M. (1995). Educational stratification and students' social bonding to school. *British Journal of Sociology of Education, 16,* 327–352.

Bergin, D. A. (1992). Leisure activity, motivation, and academic achievement in high school students. *Journal of Leisure Research, 24,* 225–239.

Berndt, T. J., & Miller, K. E. (1990). Expectancies, values, and achievement in junior high school. *Journal of Educational Psychology, 82,* 319–326.

Best, K. M., Hauser, S. T., & Allen, J. P. (1997). Predicting young adult competencies: Adolescent era parent and individual differences. *Journal of Adolescent Research, 12,* 90–112.

Beutel, A., & Marini, M. M. (1995). Gender and values. *American Sociological Review, 60,* 436–448.

Beyth-Marom, R., Fischhoff, B., Quadrel, M. J., & Furby, L. (1991). Teaching decision-making to adolescents: A critical review. In J. Baron & R. V. Brown (Eds.), *Teaching decision making to adolescents* (pp. 19–59). Hillsdale, NJ: Lawrence Erlbaum.

Bilchik, S. (1995). *Delinquency prevention works.* Washington, DC: Department of Justice, Office of Juvenile Justice and Delinquent Prevention.

Bisnaire, L. M., Firestone, P., & Rynard, D. (1990). Factors associated with academic achievement in children following parental separation. *American Journal of Orthopsychiatry, 60,* 67–76.

Block, J., Block, J. H., & Keyes, S. (1988). Longitudinally foretelling drug usage in adolescence: Early childhood personality and environmental precursors. *Child Development, 59,* 336–355.

Blos, P. (1962). *On adolescence: A psychoanalytic interpretation.* New York: Free Press.

Blos, P. (1979). *The adolescent passage: Developmental issues.* New York: International Universities Press.

Blum, R. W., & Rinehart, P. M. (1997). *Reducing the risk: Connections that make a difference in the lives of youth.* Minneapolis: University of Minnesota, Division of General Pediatrics and Adolescent Health.

Blyth, D., Simmons, R. G., & Carlton-Ford, S. (1983). The adjustment of early adolescents to school transitions. *Journal of Early Adolescence, 3,* 105–120.

Blyth, D. A., & Leffert, N. (1995). Communities as contexts for adolescent development: An empirical analysis. *Journal of Adolescent Research, 10,* 64–87.

Blyth, D. A., Saito, R., & Berkas, T. (1997). A quantitative study of the impact of service-learning programs. In A. S. Waterman (Ed.), *Service-learning: Applications from the research* (pp. 39–56). Mahwah, NJ: Lawrence Erlbaum.

Blyth, D. A., & Traeger, C. (1988). Adolescent self-esteem and perceived relationships with parents and peers. In S. Salzinger, J. S. Antrobus, & M. Hammer (Eds.), *Social networks of children, adolescents, and college students* (pp. 171–194). Hillsdale, NJ: Lawrence Erlbaum.

Bø, I. (1995). The sociocultural environment as a source for growth among 15–16-year-old boys. *Children's Environments, 12,* 469–478.

Bogenschneider, K., Small, S. A., & Tsay, J. L. (1997). Child, parent, and contextual influences on perceived parenting competence among parents of adolescents. *Journal of Marriage and the Family, 59,* 345–362.

Botvin, G. J., Botvin, E. M., Baker, E., Dusenbury, L., & Goldberg, C. (1992). The false consensus effect: Predicting adolescents' tobacco use from normative expectations. *Psychological Reports, 70,* 171–178.

Botvin, G. J., Epstein, J. A., Schinke, S. P., & Diaz, T. (1994). Predictors of cigarette smoking among inner-city minority youth. *Journal of Developmental and Behavioral Pediatrics, 15,* 67–73.

Bouffard-Bouchard, T., Parent, S., & Larivée, S. (1991). Influence of self-efficacy on self-regulation and performance among junior and senior high-school age students. *International Journal of Behavioral Development, 14,* 153–164.

Boyd, J.H. (1983). The increasing rate of suicide by firearms. *New England Journal of Medicine, 308,* 872–874.

Braddock, J. H., II, Royster, D. A., Winfield, L. F., & Hawkins, R. (1991). Bouncing back: Sports and academic resilience among African-American males. *Education and Urban Society, 24,* 113–131.

Brent, D. A., Perper, J. A., Goldstein, C. E., Kolko, D. J., Allan, M. J., Allman, C. J., & Zelenak, J. P. (1988). Risk factors for adolescent suicide: A comparison of adolescent suicide victims with suicidal inpatients. *Archives of General Psychiatry, 45,* 581–588.

Brewster, K. L. (1994). Race differences in sexual activity among adolescent women: The role of neighborhood characteristics. *American Sociological Review, 59,* 408–424.

Brewster, K. L., Billy, J. O., & Grady, W. R. (1993). Social context and adolescent behavior: The impact of community on the transition to sexual activity. *Social Forces, 71,* 713–740.

Broderick, P. C. (1998). Early adolescent gender differences in the use of ruminative and distracting coping strategies. *Journal of Early Adolescence, 18,* 173–191.

Brody, G. H., Stoneman, Z., & Flor, D. (1996). Parental religiosity, family processes, and youth competence in rural, two-parent African American families. *Developmental Psychology, 32,* 696–706.

Bronfenbrenner, U. (1979). *The ecology of human development: Experiments by nature and design.* Cambridge, MA: Harvard University Press.

Bronfenbrenner, U. (1991). What do families do? *Family Affairs, 4* (1–2), 1–6.

Bronner, E. (1998, January 12). College freshmen aiming for high marks in income. *New York Times,* p. A10.

Brook, J. S., Whiteman, M., & Finch, S. (1993). Role of mutual attachment in drug use: A longitudinal study. *Journal of the American Academy of Child and Adolescent Psychiatry, 32,* 982–989.

Brooks-Gunn, J., & Duncan, G. J. (1997). The effects of poverty on children. *The Future of Children, 7,* 55–71.

Brooks-Gunn, J., Duncan, G. J., Klebanov, P. K. & Sealand, N. (1993). Do neighborhoods influence child and adolescent development? *American Journal of Sociology, 99,* 353–395.

Brooks-Gunn, J., Guo, G., & Furstenberg, F. F., Jr. (1993). Who drops out of and who continues beyond high school? A 20-year follow-up of Black urban youth. *Journal of Research on Adolescence, 3,* 271–294.

Brown, B. A., Frankel, B. G., & Fennell, M. P. (1989). Hugs or shrugs: Parental and peer influence on continuity of involvement in sport by female adolescents. *Sex Roles, 20,* 397–412.

Brown, B. B. (1990). Peer groups and peer cultures. In S. S. Feldman & G. R. Elliott (Eds.), *At the threshold: The developing adolescent* (pp. 171–196). Cambridge, MA: Harvard University Press.

Brown, L. A. (1982). *A national assessment of the career and occupational development needs of 4-H youth.* Unpublished doctoral dissertation, University of Maryland, College Park.

Browne, C. S., & Rife, J. C. (1991). Social, personality, and gender differences in at-risk and not-at-risk sixth-grade students. *Journal of Early Adolescence, 11,* 482–495.

Büchel, F., & Duncan, G. J. (1998). Do parents' social activities promote children's school attainments? Evidence from the German Socioeconomic Panel. *Journal of Marriage and the Family, 60,* 95–108.

Bulcroft, R. A., Carmody, D. C., & Bulcroft, K. A. (1996). Patterns of parental independence giving to adolescents: Variations by race, age, and gender of child. *Journal of Marriage and the Family, 58,* 866–883.

Buri, J. R., Kirchner, P. A., & Walsh, J. M. (1987). Familial correlates of self-esteem in young American adults. *Journal of Social Psychology, 127,* 583–588.

Burkett, S. R. (1977). Religion, parental influence, and adolescent alcohol and marijuana use. *Journal of Drug Issues, 7,* 263–273.

Byrnes, J. P., & McClenny, B. (1994). Decision-making in young adolescents and adults. *Journal of Experimental Child Psychology, 58,* 359–388.

Cairns, R. B., & Cairns, B. D. (1994). *Lifelines and risks: Pathways of youth in our time.* Cambridge: Cambridge University Press.

Calabrese, R. L., & Schumer, H. (1986). The effects of service activities on adolescent alienation. *Adolescence, 21,* 675–687.

Call, K. T., Mortimer, J. T., & Shanahan, M. J. (1995). Helpfulness and the development of competence in adolescence. *Child Development, 66,* 129–138.

Caplan, M., Weissberg, R. P., Grober, J. S., Sivo, P. J., Grady, K., & Jacoby, C. (1992). Social competence promotion with inner-city and suburban young adolescents: Effects on social adjustment and alcohol use. *Journal of Consulting and Clinical Psychology, 60,* 56–63.

Cardenas Ramirez, B. (1992). The implications of an asset orientation for urban change strategies. In *Building strong communities: Strategies for urban change* (pp. 49–55). Baltimore: Annie E. Casey Foundation and New York: Ford Foundation and Rockefeller Foundation.

Carnegie Council on Adolescent Development (1989). *Turning points: Preparing American youth for the 21st century.* Washington, DC: Author.

Carnegie Council on Adolescent Development (1992a). *A matter of time: Risk and opportunity in the nonschool hours. Recommendations for strengthening community programs for youth.* Washington, DC: Author.

Carnegie Council on Adolescent Development (1992b). *What young adolescents want and need from out-of-school programs: A focus group report.* Washington, DC: Author. (ERIC Document Reproduction Service No. ED 358 180)

Cauce, A. M. (1986). Social networks and social competence: Exploring the effects of early adolescent friendships. *American Journal of Community Psychology, 14,* 607–628.

Cauce, A. M., Felner, R. D., & Primavera, J. (1982). Social support in high-risk adolescents: Structural components and adaptive impact. *American Journal of Community Psychology, 10,* 417–428.

Cawelti, G. (Ed.). (1995). *Handbook of research on improving student achievement.* Arlington, VA: Educational Research Service.

Centers for Disease Control and Prevention (1991, September 20). *Morbidity and Mortality Weekly Report* (Vol. 40, No. 37, pp. 633–635). Atlanta, GA: U.S. Department of Health and Human Services, Public Health Service, Centers for Disease Control and Prevention.

Center for the Study of Social Policy (1991). *Kids count data book: State profiles of child well-being.* Greenwich, CT: Annie E. Casey Foundation.

Center for Youth Development and Policy Research (1994). *Definitions of youth development, youth participation and community development.* Notes from the Wingspread Conference on Youth Participation and Neighborhood Development. Washington, DC: Author.

Chandler, K., Nolin, M. J., & Davies, E. (1995). *Student strategies to avoid harm at school: Statistics in brief.* Rockville, MD: Westat.

Chase-Lansdale, P. L., Wakschlag, L. S., & Brooks-Gunn, J. (1995). A psychological perspective on the development of caring in children and youth: The role of the family. *Journal of Adolescence, 18,* 515–556.

Chaskin, R. J., & Hawley, T. (1994). *Youth and caring: Developing a field of inquiry and practice.* Chicago: University of Chicago, Chapin Hall Center for Children.

Chaskin, R. J., & Rauner, D. M. (1995). Youth and caring: An introduction. *Phi Delta Kappan, 76,* 667–674.

Chassin, L., & Barrera, M. (1993). Substance use escalation and substance use restraint among adolescent children of alcoholics. *Psychology of Addictive Behaviors, 7,* 3–20.

Chassin, L., Pillow, D., Curran, P., Molina, B., & Barrera, M. (1993). Relation of parental alcoholism to early adolescent substance use: A test of three mediating mechanisms. *Journal of Abnormal Psychology, 102,* 3–19.

Chassin, L. A., Presson, C. C., Sherman, S. J., Montello, D., & McGrew, J. (1986). Changes in peer and parent influence during adolescence: Longitudinal versus cross-sectional perspectives on smoking initiation. *Developmental Psychology, 22,* 327–334.

Chavkin, N. F., & Gonzalez, D. L. (1995). *Forging partnerships between Mexican American parents and the schools.* Charleston, WV: ERIC Clearinghouse on Rural Education and Small Schools. (ERIC Document Reproduction Service No. ED 388 489)

Checkoway, B. (1996). *Young people creating community change.* Battle Creek, MI: W. K. Kellogg Foundation.

Chen, C., & Stevenson, H. W. (1989). Homework: A cross-cultural examination. *Child Development, 60,* 551–561.

Chen, C., & Stevenson, H. W. (1995). Motivation and mathematics achievement: A comparative study of Asian-American, Caucasian-American, and East Asian high school students. *Child Development, 66,* 1215–1234.

Chen, X., Rubin, K. H., & Li, D. (1997). Relation between academic achievement and social adjustment: Evidence from Chinese children. *Developmental Psychology, 33,* 518–525.

Child abuse and neglect national incidence study. (1996, September 23). *Washington Social Legislation Bulletin, 34,* 165–168.

Children want the good news about being a kid to make headlines. (1994, March 2). *Raleigh News and Observer,* p. 7A.

Christenson, S. L., Rounds, T., & Gorney, D. (1992). Family factors and student achievement: An avenue to increase students' success. *School Psychology Quarterly, 7,* 178–206.

Clapper, R. L., Buka, S. L., Goldfield, E. C., Lipsitt, L. P., & Tsuang, M. T. (1995). Adolescent problem behaviors as predictors of adult alcohol diagnoses. *International Journal of the Addictions, 30,* 507–523.

Clark, Reginald (1988). *Critical factors in why disadvantaged students succeed or fail in school.* Washington, DC: Academy for Educational Development.

Clark-Lempers, D. S., Lempers, J. D., & Ho, C. (1991). Early, middle, and late adolescents' perceptions of their relationships with significant others. *Journal of Adolescent Research, 6,* 296–315.

Coates, D. L. (1985). Relationships between self-concept measures and social network characteristics for Black adolescents. *Journal of Early Adolescence, 5,* 319–338.

Coates, D. L. (1987). Gender differences in the structure and support characteristics of Black adolescents' social networks. *Sex Roles, 17,* 667–687.

Cochran, J. K., Wood, P. B., & Arneklev, B. J. (1994). Is the religiosity-delinquency relationship spurious? Social control theories. *Journal of Research in Crime and Delinquency, 31,* 92–123.

Cochran, M., & Bø, I. (1989). The social networks, family involvement, and pro- and antisocial behavior of adolescent males in Norway. *Journal of Youth and Adolescence, 18,* 377–398.

Cohen, P. A., Kulik, J. A., & Kulik, C. C. (1982). Educational outcomes of tutoring: A meta-analysis of findings. *American Educational Research Journal, 19,* 237–248.

Cole, D. A. (1989). Psychopathology of adolescent suicide: Hopelessness, coping beliefs, and depression. *Journal of Abnormal Psychology, 98,* 248–255.

Coleman, J. S. (1974). *Youth: Transition to adulthood* (Report of the Panel on Youth of the President's Science Advisory Committee). Chicago: University of Chicago Press.

Coley, R. L., & Hoffman, L. W. (1996). Relations of parental supervision and monitoring to children's functioning in various contexts: Moderating effects of families and neighborhoods. *Journal of Applied Developmental Psychology, 17,* 51–68.

Collingwood, T. R., Reynolds, R., Kohl, H., Smith, W., & Sloan, S. (1991). Physical fitness effects of substance abuse risk factors and use patterns. *Journal of Drug Education, 21,* 73–84.

Collingwood, T. R., Sunderlin, J., & Kohl, H. W. (1994). The use of a staff training model for implementing fitness programming to prevent substance abuse with at-risk youth. *American Journal of Health Promotion, 9,* 20–23, 33.

Collins, W. A., & Laursen, B. (1992). Conflict and relationships in the transition to adolescence: Continuity and change in interaction, affect and cognition. In C. U. Shantz & W. W. Hartup (Eds.), *Conflict in child and adolescent development* (pp. 216–241). Cambridge: Cambridge University Press.

Collins, W. A., Laursen, B., Mortensen, N., Luebker, C., & Ferreira, M. (1997). Conflict processes and transitions in parent and peer relationships: Implications for autonomy and regulation. *Journal of Adolescent Research, 12,* 178–198.

Compas, B. E., Crosan, P. G., & Grant, K. E. (1993). Promoting positive mental health during adolescence. In S. G. Millstein, A. C. Petersen, & E. O. Nightingale (Eds.), *Promoting the health of adolescents: New directions for the twenty-first century* (pp. 159–179). New York: Oxford University Press.

Conger, K. J., Conger, R. D., & Scaramella, L. V. (1997). Parents, siblings, psychological control, and adolescent adjustment. *Journal of Adolescent Research, 12,* 113–138.

Connell, J. P., Aber, J. L., & Walker, G. (1995). How do urban communities affect youth? Using social science research to inform the design and evaluation of comprehensive community initiatives. In J. P. Connell, A. C. Kubish, L. Schorr, & C. H. Weiss (Eds.), *New approaches to evaluating community initiatives: Concepts, methods, and contexts* (pp. 93–125). Washington, DC: Aspen Institute.

Connell, J. P., Halpern Felsher, B. L., Clifford, E., Crichlow, W., & Usinger, P. (1995). Hanging in there: Behavioral, psychological, and contextual factors affecting whether African-American adolescents stay in high school. Special issue: Creating supportive communities for adolescent development: Challenges to scholars. *Journal of Adolescent Research, 10,* 41–63.

Connell, J. P., Spencer, M. B., & Aber, J. L. (1994). Educational risk and resilience in African-American youth: Context, self, action, and outcomes in school. *Child Development, 65,* 493–506.

Conrad, D. E. (1980). The differential impact of experiential learning programs on secondary school students. (Doctoral dissertation, University of Minnesota, 1980). *Dissertation Abstracts International, 41,* 919.

Conrad, D. E., & Hedin, D. (1981). National assessment of experiential education: Summary and implications. *Journal of Experiential Education, 4,* 6–20.

Conti, R., Amabile, T. M., & Pollak, S. (1995). The positive impact of creative activity: Effects of creative task engagement and motivational focus on college students' learning. *Personality and Social Psychology Bulletin, 21,* 1107–1116.

Cook, T. D., Church, M. B., Ajanaku, S., Shadish, W. R., Kim, J., & Cohen, R. (1996). The development of occupational aspirations and expectations among inner-city boys. *Child Development, 67,* 3368–3385.

Coombs, R. H., Paulson, M. J., & Richardson, M. A. (1991). Peer vs. parental influence in substance use among Hispanic and Anglo children and adolescents. *Journal of Youth and Adolescence, 20,* 73–88.

Coon, H., Carey, G., & Fulker, D. W. (1992). Community influences on cognitive ability. *Intelligence, 16,* 169–188.

Cooper, C. R., Grotevant, H. D., & Condon, S. M. (1983). Individuality and connectedness in the family as a context for adolescent identity formation and role-taking skill. *New Directions for Child Development, 22,* 43–60.

Coopersmith, S. (1967). *The antecedents of self-esteem.* San Francisco: Freeman.

Coordinating Council on Juvenile Justice and Delinquency Prevention (1996). *Combating violence and delinquency: The national juvenile justice action plan.* Washington, DC: Author.

Corno, L. (1996). Homework is a complicated thing. *Educational Researcher, 25,* 27–30.

Cotterell, J. L. (1992). The relation of attachments and support to adolescent well-being and school adjustment. *Journal of Adolescent Research, 7,* 28–42.

Cotton, K. (1993). Fostering intercultural harmony in schools: Research finding. In *School Improvement Research Series.* Available World Wide Web: http://www.nwrel.org/scpd/sirs/8/topsyn7.html.

Cotton, K., & Savard, W. G. (1982). *Parent involvement in instruction, K-12: Research synthesis.* St. Ann, MO, and Portland, OR: CEMREL, Inc., and Northwest Regional Educational Lab.

Crockett, L. J., & Petersen, A. C. (1993). Adolescent development: Health risks and opportunities for health promotion. In S. G. Millstein, A. C. Petersen, & E. O. Nightingale (Eds.), *Promoting the health of adolescents: New directions for the twenty-first century* (pp. 13–37). New York: Oxford University Press.

Cross, C. T. (1990). *Who is the American eighth grader?* Washington, DC: Department of Education, Office of Educational Research and Improvement.

Cross, C. T. (1991). NELS 88: A look at the American 8th grade student. *Middle Ground, Winter, 6–7.*

Cross, T. (1996). Developing a knowledge base to support cultural competence. *Family Resource Coalition Report, 14,* 2–7.

Crosman, M. D. (1989). *The effects of required community service on the development of self-esteem, personal and social responsibility of high school students in a Friends' school.* Unpublished doctoral dissertation, Lancaster Theological Seminary, Lancaster, PA.

Csikszentmihalyi, M., & Henshaw, D. (1997, April). Community involvement in school and quality of experience. In B. I. Bertenthal & N. S. Newcombe (Co-Chairs), *Adolescent involvement in community activities: Antecedents, correlates, and outcomes.* Symposium conducted at the biennial meeting of the Society for Research in Child Development, Washington, DC.

Csikszentmihalyi, M., & Larson, R. (1984). *Being adolescent: Conflict and growth in the teenage years.* New York: Basic Books.

Damon, W., & Colby, A. (1996). Education and moral commitment. *Journal of Moral Education, 25,* 31–37.

Damon, W., & Gregory, A. (1997). The youth charter: Towards the formation of adolescent moral identity. *Journal of Moral Education, 26,* 117–130.

D'Angelo, L. L., Weinberger, D. A., & Feldman, S. S. (1995). Like father, like son? Predicting male adolescents' adjustment from parents' distress and self-restraint. *Developmental Psychology, 31,* 883–896.

Daniels, J., D'Andrea, M., & Heck, R. (1995). Moral development and Hawaiian youths: Does gender make a difference? *Journal of Counseling and Development, 74,* 90–93.

Danish, S. J., Petitpas, A. J., & Hale, B. D. (1990). Sport as a context for developing competence. In T. P. Gullotta, G. R. Adams, & R. Montemayor (Eds.), *Advances in adolescent development: Vol. 3. Developing social competency in adolescence* (pp. 169–194). Newbury Park, CA: Sage.

Danziger, S. K., & Farber, N. B. (1990). Keeping inner-city youths in school: Critical experiences of young Black women. Special issue: Persistent poverty. *Social Work Research and Abstracts, 26,* 32–39.

Darmody, J. P. (1991). The adolescent personality, formal reasoning, and values. *Adolescence, 26,* 731–742.

Daro, D., & McCurdy, K. (1994). Preventing child abuse and neglect: Programmatic interventions. *Child Welfare, 73,* 405–430.

Dassance, J. (1998). Assets and faith: A Black church perspective [interview]. In E. C. Roehlkepartain, *Building assets in congregations: A practical guide for helping youth grow up healthy* (p. 15). Minneapolis, MN: Search Institute.

Davey, L. F. (1993). *Developmental implications of shared and divergent perceptions in the parent-adolescence relationship.* Paper presented at the biennial meeting of the Society for Research in Child Development, New Orleans, LA.

Davila, J., Hammen, C., Burge, D., Paley, B., & Daley, S. E. (1995). Poor interpersonal problem solving as a mechanism of stress generation in depression among adolescent women. *Journal of Abnormal Psychology, 104,* 592–600.

Davis, J. E., & Jordan, W. J. (1994). The effects of school context, structure, and experiences on African American males in middle and high school. Special issue: Pedagogical and contextual issues affecting African American males in school and society. *Journal of Negro Education, 63,* 570–587.

Dawson, D. A. (1991). Family structure and children's health and well-being: Data from the 1988 National Health Interview Survey on Child Health. *Journal of Marriage and the Family, 53,* 573–584.

Dean, K. C., & Yost, P. R. (1991). *A synthesis of the research on, and a descriptive overview of Protestant, Catholic, and Jewish religious youth programs in the United States.* Washington, DC: Carnegie Council on Adolescent Development.

Deihl, L. M., Vicary, J. R., & Deike, R. C. (1997). Longitudinal trajectories of self-esteem from early to middle adolescence and related psychosocial variables among rural adolescents. *Journal of Research on Adolescence, 7,* 393–411.

DeJong, W. (1987). A short-term evaluation of project DARE (Drug Abuse Resistance Education): Preliminary indications of effectiveness. *Journal of Drug Education, 17,* 279–294.

Delamater, J., & MacCorquodale, P. (1978). Premarital contraceptive usage: A test of two models. *Journal of Marriage and the Family, 40,* 235–247.

Delaney, M. E. (1996). Across the transition to adolescence: Qualities of parent/adolescent relationships and adjustment. *Journal of Early Adolescence, 16,* 274–300.

Demo, D. H. (1985). The measurement of self-esteem: Refining our methods. *Journal of Personality and Social Psychology, 48,* 1490–1502.

Dewsbury-White, K. E. (1993). *The relationship of service-learning project models to subject-matter achievement of middle school students.* Unpublished doctoral dissertation, Michigan State University, East Lansing.

Dickens, M. N., & Cornell, D. G. (1993). Parent influences on the mathematics self-concept of high ability adolescent girls. Special issue: Mathematics. *Journal for the Education of the Gifted, 17,* 53–73.

Dishion, T. J., Andrews, D. W., & Crosby, L. (1995). Antisocial boys and their friends in early adolescence: Relationship characteristics, quality, and interactional process. *Child Development, 66,* 139–151.

Dodge, K. A. (1980). Social cognition and children's aggressive behavior. *Child Development, 51,* 162–170.

Dodge, K. A., & Frame, C. L. (1982). Social cognitive biases and deficits in aggressive boys. *Child Development, 53,* 629–635.

Donahue, M. J. (1987). *Technical report of the national demonstration project field test of "Human sexuality: Values and choices."* Minneapolis, MN: Search Institute.

Donahue, M. J., & Benson, P. L. (1995). Religion and the well-being of adolescents. *Journal of Social Issues, 51,* 145–160.

Donaldson, S. I., Graham, J. W., & Hansen, W. B. (1994). Testing the generalizability of intervening mechanism theories: Understanding the effects of adolescent drug use prevention interventions. *Journal of Behavioral Medicine, 17,* 195–216.

Donaldson, S. I., Graham, J. W., Piccinin, A. M., & Hansen, W. B. (1995). Resistance-skills training and onset of alcohol use: Evidence for beneficial and potentially harmful effects in public schools and in private Catholic schools. *Health Psychology, 14,* 291–300.

Donnermeyer, J. F., & Park, D. S. (1995). Alcohol use among rural adolescents: Predictive and situational factors. *International Journal of the Addictions, 30,* 459–479.

Dornbusch, S. M., Ritter, P. L., Leiderman, P. H., Roberts, D. F., & Fraleigh, M. J. (1987). The relation of parenting style to adolescent school performance. *Child Development, 58,* 1244–1257.

Douglas, P., & Powers, S. (1982). Relationship between achievement locus of control and expectancy of success of academically talented high school students. *Psychological Reports, 51* (part 2), 1259–1262.

Douvan, E., & Adelson, J. (1966). *The adolescent experience.* New York: John Wiley and Sons.

Dryfoos, J. G. (1990). *Adolescents at risk—Prevalence and prevention.* New York: Oxford University Press.

Dubas, J. S., Graber, J. A., & Petersen, A. C. (1991). The effects of pubertal development on achievement during adolescence. Special issue: Development and education across adolescence. *American Journal of Education, 99,* 444–460.

Dubas, J. S., & Snider, B. A. (1993). The role of community-based youth groups in enhancing learning and achievement through nonformal education. In R. M. Lerner (Ed.), *Early adolescence: Perspectives on research, policy, and intervention* (pp. 159–174). Hillsdale, NJ: Lawrence Erlbaum.

DuBois, D. L., Felner, R. D., & Brand, S. (1997). Self-esteem profiles and adjustment in early adolescence: A two-year longitudinal investigation. In D. L. DuBois (Chair), *Trajectories and profiles of self-esteem in adolescence: Identification and implications for adjustment*. Symposium conducted at the biennial meeting of the Society for Research on Child Development, Washington, DC.

DuBois, D. L., Felner, R. D., Brand, S., Adan, A. M., & Evans, E. G. (1992). A prospective study of life stress, social support, and adaptation in early adolescence. *Child Development, 63,* 542–557.

DuBois, D. L., Felner, R. D., Meares, H., & Krier, M. (1994). Prospective investigation of the effects of socioeconomic disadvantage, life stress, and social support on early adolescent adjustment. *Journal of Abnormal Psychology, 103,* 511–522.

DuBois, D. L., & Hirsch, B. J. (1990). School and neighborhood friendship patterns of Blacks and Whites in early adolescence. *Child Development, 61,* 524–536.

Duke, M., Johnson, T. C., & Nowicki, S. J., Jr. (1977). Effects of sports fitness camp experience on locus of control orientation in children, ages 6 to 14. *Research Quarterly, 48,* 280–283.

Duncan, G. J. (1994). Families and neighbors as sources of disadvantage in schooling decisions of White and Black adolescents. *American Journal of Education, 103,* 20–53.

DuRant, R. H., Cadenhead, C., Pendergrast, R. A., Slavens, G., & Linder, C. W. (1994). Factors associated with the use of violence among urban Black adolescents. *American Journal of Public Health, 84,* 612–617.

DuRant, R. H., Getts, A., Cadenhead, C., Emans, S. J., & Woods, E. (1995). Exposure to violence and victimization and depression, hopelessness, and purpose in life among adolescents living in and around public housing. *Journal of Developmental and Behavioral Pediatrics, 16,* 233–237.

Duryea, E. J., & Okwumabua, J. (1988). Effects of a preventive alcohol education program after three years. *Journal of Drug Education, 18,* 23–31.

D'Zurilla, T. J., & Goldfried, M. R. (1971). Problem solving and behavior modification. *Journal of Abnormal Psychology, 78,* 17–126.

Earls, F., McGuire, J., & Shay, S. (1994). Evaluating a community intervention to reduce the risk of child abuse: Methodological strategies in conducting neighborhood surveys. *Child Abuse and Neglect, 18,* 473–485.

East, P. L. (1996). The younger sisters of childbearing adolescents: Their attitudes, expectations, and behaviors. *Child Development, 67,* 267–282.

East, P. L., Felice, M. E., & Morgan, M. C. (1993). Sisters' and girlfriends' sexual and childbearing behavior: Effects on early adolescent girls' sexual outcomes. *Journal of Marriage and the Family, 55,* 953–963.

Ebata, A. T., & Moos, R. H. (1994). Personal, situational, and contextual correlates of coping in adolescence. *Journal of Research on Adolescence, 4,* 99–125.

Eccles, J. (1997). User-friendly science and mathematics: Can it interest girls and minorities in breaking through the middle school wall? In David Johnson (Ed.), *Minorities and girls in school: Effects on achievement and performance* (pp. 65–104). Thousand Oaks, CA: Sage.

Eccles, J. S., Buchanan, C. M., Flanagan, C., Fuligni, A., Midgley, C., & Yee, D. (1991). Control versus autonomy during early adolescence. *Journal of Social Issues, 47,* 53–68.

Eccles, J. S., Early, D., Fraser, K., Belansky, E., & McCarthy, K. (1997). The relation of connection, regulation, and support for autonomy to adolescents' functioning. *Journal of Adolescent Research, 12,* 263–286.

Eccles, J. S., & Harold, R. D. (1993). Parent-school involvement during the early adolescent years. *Teachers College Record, 94,* 568–587.

Eccles, J. S., Lord, S. E., Roeser, R. W., Barber, B. L., & Jozefowicz, D. M. H. (1997). The association of school transitions in early adolescence with developmental trajectories through high school. In J. Schulenberg, J. L. Maggs, & K. Hurrelmann (Eds.), *Health risks and developmental transitions during adolescence* (pp. 283–320). Cambridge: Cambridge University Press.

Eccles, J. S., & Midgley, C. (1990). Changes in academic motivation and self-perception during early adolescence. In R. Montemayor, G. R. Adams, & T. P. Gullotta (Eds.), *Advances in adolescent development: Vol. 2. From childhood to adolescence: A transitional period* (pp. 134–155). Newbury Park, CA: Sage.

Eccles, J. S., Midgley, C., Wigfield, A., Miller Buchanan, C., Reuman, D., Flanagan, C., & Mac Iver, D. (1993). Development during adolescence: The impact of stage-environment fit on young adolescents' experiences in schools and in families. *American Psychologist, 48,* 90–101.

Echohawk, M., & Parsons, O. A. (1977). Leadership vs. behavioral problems and belief in personal control among American Indian youth. *Journal of Social Psychology, 102,* 47–54.

Egeland, B., Jacobvitz, D., & Sroufe, L. A. (1988). Breaking the cycle of abuse. *Child Development, 59,* 1080–1088.

Eggert, L. L., & Herting, J. R. (1991). Preventing teenage drug abuse: Exploratory effects of network social support. *Youth and Society, 22,* 482–524.

Eisenberg, N., Carlo, G., Murphy, B., & Van Court, P. (1995). Prosocial development in late adolescence: A longitudinal study. *Child Development, 66,* 1179–1197.

Eisenberg, N., & McNally, S. (1993). Socialization and mothers' and adolescents' empathy-related characteristics. *Journal of Research on Adolescence, 3,* 171–191.

Eisenberg, N., Miller, P. A., Shell, R., McNally, S., & Shea, C. (1991). Prosocial development in adolescence: A longitudinal study. *Developmental Psychology, 27,* 849–857.

Elias, M., Gara, M., Ubriaco, M., Rothbaum, P. A., Clabby, J. F., & Schuyler, T. (1986). Impact of a preventive social problem solving intervention on children's coping with middle-school stressors. *American Journal of Community Psychology, 14,* 259–275.

Elkind, D. (1967). Egocentrism in adolescence. *Child Development, 38,* 1025–1034.

Ellickson, P. L., Bell, R. M., & McGuigan, K. (1993). Preventing adolescent drug use: Long-term results of a junior high program. *American Journal of Public Health, 83,* 856–861.

Ellickson, P. L., & Hays, R. D. (1990–91). Beliefs about resistance self-efficacy and drug prevalence: Do they really affect drug use? Special issue: Nonexperimental methods for studying addictions. *International Journal of the Addictions, 25,* 1353–1378.

Elliott, D. S. (1993). Health enhancing and health compromising lifestyles. In S. G. Millstein, A. C. Petersen, & E. O. Nightingale (Eds.), *Promoting the health of adolescents: New directions for the twenty-first century* (pp. 119–145). New York: Oxford University Press.

Elliott, D. S., Wilson, W. J., Huizinga, D., Sampson, R. J., Elliott, A., & Rankin, B. (1996). The effects of neighborhood disadvantage on adolescent development. *Journal of Research in Crime and Delinquency, 33,* 389–426.

Elmen, J. (1991). Achievement orientation in early adolescence: Developmental patterns and social correlates. *Journal of Early Adolescence, 10,* 125–151.

Ennett, S. T., Tobler, N. S., Ringwalt, C. L., & Flewelling, R. L. (1994). How effective is Drug Abuse Resistance Education? A meta-analysis of Project DARE outcome evaluations. *American Journal of Public Health, 84,* 1394–1401.

Ensminger, M. E. (1990). Sexual activity and problem behaviors among Black, urban adolescents. *Child Development, 61,* 2032–2046.

Ensminger, M. E., Lamkin, R. P., & Jacobson, N. (1996). School leaving: A longitudinal perspective including neighborhood effects. *Child Development, 67,* 2400–2416.

Ensminger, M. E., & Slusarcick, A. L. (1992). Paths to high school graduation or dropout: A longitudinal study of a first-grade cohort. *Sociology of Education, 65,* 95–113.

Entwisle, D. R., Alexander, K. L., & Olson, L. S. (1994). The gender gap in math: Its possible origins in neighborhood effects. *American Sociological Review, 59,* 822–838.

Entwistle, N. J., Kozeki, B., & Tait, H. (1989). Pupils' perceptions of school and teachers: II. Relationships with motivation and approaches to learning. *British Journal of Educational Psychology, 59,* 340–350.

Epstein, J. L. (1987). Parent involvement: What research says to administrators. *Education and Urban Society, 19,* 119–136.

Erikson, E. H. (1968). *Identity: Youth and crisis.* New York: Norton.

Eron, L. D., Walder, L. O., & Lefkowtiz, M. M. (1972). *The learning of aggression in children.* Boston: Little, Brown.

Estrada, P. (1995). Adolescents' self-reports of prosocial responses to friends and acquaintances: The role of sympathy-related cognitive, affective, and motivational processes. *Journal of Research on Adolescence, 5,* 173–200.

Fallon, B. J., & Bowles, T. V. (1997). The effect of family structure and family functioning on adolescents' perceptions of intimate time spent with parents, siblings, and peers. *Journal of Youth and Adolescence, 26,* 25–43.

Farkas, S., Johnson, J., Duffett, A., & Bers, A. (1997). *Kids these days: What Americans really think about the next generation.* New York: Public Agenda.

Farrell, A. D., & Danish, S. J. (1993). Peer drug associations and emotional restraint: Causes or consequences of adolescents' drug use? *Journal of Consulting and Clinical Psychology, 61,* 327–334.

Farrington, D. P. (1989). Early predictors of adolescent aggression and adult violence. *Violence and Victims, 4,* 79–100.

Feiring, C., & Lewis, M. (1991). The transition from middle childhood to early adolescence: Sex differences in the social network and perceived self-competence. *Sex Roles, 24,* 489–509.

Feiring, C., & Lewis, M. (1993). Do mothers know their teenagers' friends? Implications for individuation in early adolescence. *Journal of Youth and Adolescence, 22,* 337–354.

Feldman, S. S., & Elliott, G. R. (Eds.), (1990). *At the threshold: The developing adolescent.* Cambridge, MA: Harvard University Press.

Feldman, S. S., & Weinberger, D. A. (1994). Self-restraint as a mediator of family influences on boys' delinquent behavior: A longitudinal study. *Child Development, 65,* 195–211.

Feldman, S. S., & Wentzel, K. R. (1990). Relations among family interaction patterns, classroom self-restraint, and academic achievement in preadolescent boys. *Journal of Educational Psychology, 82,* 813–819.

Felner, R. D., Ginter, M., & Primavera, J. (1982). Primary prevention during school transitions: Social support and environmental structure. *American Journal of Community Psychology, 10,* 277–290.

Felner, R., Jackson, A., Kasak, D., Mulhall, P., Brand, S., & Flowers, N. (1997). The impact of school reform for the middle grades: A longitudinal study of a network engaged in Turning Points-based comprehensive school transformation. In R. Takanishi & D. Hamburg (Eds.), *Preparing adolescents for the twenty-first century: Challenges facing Europe and the United States* (pp. 38–69). Cambridge: Cambridge University Press.

Fend, H., & Schrörer, S. (1985). The formation of self-concepts in the context of educational systems. *International Journal of Behavioral Development, 8,* 423–444.

Fine, M., Weis, L., & Powell, L. C. (1997). Communities of difference: A critical look at de-segregated spaces created for and by youth. *Harvard Educational Review, 67,* 247–284.

Finn, J. D. (1993). *School engagement & students at risk.* Washington, DC: National Center for Education Statistics. (ERIC Document Reproduction Service No. ED 363 322)

Fischhoff, B., & Quadrel, M. J. (1991). Adolescent alcohol decisions. *Alcohol, Health, and Research World, 15,* 43–51.

Flannery, D. J., Vazsonyi, A. T., Torquati, J., & Fridrich, A. (1994). Ethnic and gender differences in risk for early adolescent substance use. *Journal of Youth and Adolescence, 23,* 195–213.

Fletcher, A. (1997, April). *Parental influences on adolescent involvement in community activities.* Symposium at the biennial meetings of the Society for Research in Child Development, Washington, DC.

Ford, D. Y. (1992). Self-perceptions of underachievement and support for the achievement ideology among early adolescent African-Americans. *Journal of Early Adolescence, 12,* 228–252.

Ford, K., & Norris, A. E. (1993). Urban Hispanic adolescents and young adults: Relationship of acculturation to sexual behavior. *Journal of Sex Research, 30,* 316–323.

Ford, M. E., Wentzel, K. R., Wood, D., Stevens, E., & Siesfeld, G. A. (1989). Processes associated with integrative social competence: Emotional and contextual influences on adolescent social responsibility. *Journal of Adolescent Research, 4,* 405–425.

Fordham, S. (1988). Racelessness as a factor in Black students' school success: Pragmatic strategy or pyrrhic victory? *Harvard Educational Review, 58,* 54–84.

Fordham, S., & Ogbu, J. U. (1986). Black students' school success: "Coping with the burden of 'acting white.'" *Urban Review, 18,* 176–206.

Frey, C. U., & Röthlisberger, C. (1996). Social support in healthy adolescents. *Journal of Youth and Adolescence, 25,* 17–31.

Fry, D. P. (1988). Intercommunity differences in aggression among Zapotec children. *Child Development, 59,* 1008–1019.

Fuchs, V. R., & Reklis, D. M. (1992). America's children: Economic perspectives and policy options. *Science, 255,* 41–46.

Fuligni, A. J. (1997). The academic achievement of adolescents from immigrant families: The roles of family background, attitudes, and behavior. *Child Development, 68,* 351–363.

Fuligni, A. J., & Stevenson, H. W. (1995). Time use and mathematics achievement among American, Chinese, and Japanese high school students. *Child Development, 66,* 830–842.

Fullan, M. (with S. Stiegelbauer). (1991). *The new meaning of educational change.* New York: Teachers College Press.

Furby, L., & Beyth-Marom, R. (1992). Risk-taking in adolescence: A decision-making perspective. *Developmental Review, 12,* 1–44.

Furstenberg, F. (1993). How families manage risk and opportunity in dangerous neighborhoods. In W. J. Wilson (Ed.), *Sociology and the public agenda* (pp. 231–258). Newbury Park, CA: Sage.

Galambos, N. L., & Maggs, J. L. (1991). Out-of-school care of young adolescents and self-reported behavior. *Developmental Psychology, 27,* 644–655.

Galan, F. J. (1988). Alcoholism prevention and Hispanic youth. *Journal of Drug Issues, 18,* 49–58.

Galotti, K. M., & Kozberg, S. F. (1996). Adolescents' experience of a life-framing decision. *Journal of Youth and Adolescence, 25,* 3–16.

Gamble, W. C. (1994). Perceptions of controllability and other stressor event characteristics as determinants of coping among young adolescents and young adults. *Journal of Youth and Adolescence, 23,* 65–84.

Gambone, M. A., & Arbreton, A. J. A. (1997). *Safe havens: The contributions of youth organizations to healthy adolescent development.* Philadelphia: Public/Private Ventures.

Garbarino, J. (1995). *Raising children in a socially toxic environment.* San Francisco: Jossey-Bass.

Garbarino, J., & Kostelny, K. (1994). Family support and community development. In S. L. Kagan & B. Weissbourd (Eds.), *Putting families first: America's family support movement and the challenge of change* (pp. 297–320). San Francisco: Jossey-Bass.

Gardner, D. (1995). *Improving our schools 1995: The first annual report of student and parent perspectives on Broward's public schools.* Fort Lauderdale, FL: Broward County School Board.

Garland, A. F., & Zigler, E. (1993). Adolescent suicide prevention: Current research and social policy implications. *American Psychologist, 48,* 169–182.

Garmezy, N. (1985). Stress-resistant children: The search for protective factors. In J. E. Stevenson (Ed.), *Recent research in developmental psychopathology. Journal of Child Psychology and Psychiatry Book Supplement, No. 4* (pp. 213–233). Oxford: Pergamon Press.

Garmezy, N. (1991). Resiliency and vulnerability to adverse developmental outcomes associated with poverty. *American Behavioral Scientist, 34,* 416–430.

Garmezy, N. (1993). Children in poverty: Resilience despite risk. *Psychiatry, 56,* 127–136.

Garton, A. F., & Pratt, C. (1991). Leisure activities of adolescent school students: Predictors of participation and interest. *Journal of Adolescence, 114,* 305–321.

Gauze, C., Bukowski, W. M., Aquan-Assee, J., & Sippola, L. K. (1996). Interactions between family environment and friendship and associations with self-perceived well-being during early adolescence. *Child Development, 67,* 2201–2216.

Gentry, B., & Benenson, W. (1993). School-to-home transfer of conflict management skills among school-age children. *Families in Society, 74,* 67–73.

Gibson, J. W., & Kempf, J. (1990). Attitudinal predictors of sexual activity in Hispanic adolescent females. *Journal of Adolescent Research, 5,* 414–430.

Giles, D. E., Jr., & Eyler, J. (1994). The impact of a college community service laboratory on students' personal, social, and cognitive outcomes. *Journal of Adolescence, 17,* 327–339.

Gilligan, G., & Belenky, M. F. (1980). A naturalistic study of abortion decisions. In R. Selman & R. Yando (Eds.), *Clinical-developmental psychology* (Vol. 7, pp. 69–90). San Francisco: Jossey-Bass.

Ginsburg, K. R., Slap, G. B., Cnaan, A., Forke, C. M., Balsley, C. M., & Rouselle, D. M. (1995). Adolescents' perceptions of factors affecting their decisions to seek health care. *Journal of the American Medical Association, 273,* 1913–1918.

Glaser, M. A., Larsen, W. C., & Salem Nichols, R. (1992). After the alternative elementary program: A promise of continued student success? *Urban Review, 24,* 55–71.

Glasgow, K. L., Dornbusch, S. M., Troyer, L., Steinberg, L., & Ritter, P. L. (1997). Parenting styles, adolescents' attributions, and educational outcomes in nine heterogeneous high schools. *Child Development, 68,* 507–529.

Goodenow, C. (1992, April). *School motivation, engagement, and sense of belonging among urban adolescent students.* Paper presented at the annual meeting of the American Educational Research Association, San Francisco, CA. Ann Arbor, MI: Society for the Psychological Study of Social Issues.

Goodenow, C. (1993a). Classroom belonging among early adolescent students: Relationships to motivation and achievement. *Journal of Early Adolescence, 13,* 21–43.

Goodenow, C. (1993b). The psychological sense of school membership among adolescents: Scale development and educational correlates. *Psychology in the Schools, 30,* 79–90.

Gore, S., & Aseltine, R. H., Jr. (1995). Protective processes in adolescence: Matching stressors with social resources. *American Journal of Community Psychology, 23,* 301–327.

Gorman, D. M. (1995). Are school-based resistance skills training programs effective in preventing alcohol misuse? *Journal of Alcohol and Drug Education, 41,* 74–98.

Gottfredson, G. D., & Gottfredson, D. C. (1989). *School climate, academic performance, attendance, and dropout.* Washington, DC: Department of Education, Office of Educational Research and Improvement.

Graham, J. E., Updegraff, K. A., Tomascik, C. A., & McHale, S. M. (1997). Someone who cares: Evaluation of school advisor programs in two community settings. *Applied Developmental Science, 1,* 28–42.

Graham, J. W., Marks, G., & Hansen, W. B. (1991). Social influence processes affecting adolescent substance use. *Journal of Applied Psychology, 76,* 291–298.

Graham, S., Weiner, B., & Benesh-Weiner, M. (1995). An attributional analysis of the development of excuse giving in aggressive and nonaggressive African American boys. *Developmental Psychology, 31,* 274–284.

Gray-Little, B., & Carels, R. A. (1997). The effects of racial dissonance on academic self-esteem and achievement in elementary, junior high, and high school students. *Journal of Research on Adolescence, 7,* 109–131.

Gregory, L. W. (1995). The "turnaround" process: Factors influencing the school success of urban youth. Special issue: Creating supportive communities for adolescent development: Challenges to scholars. *Journal of Adolescent Research, 10,* 136–154.

Grolnick, W. S., & Slowiaczek, M. L. (1994). Parents' involvement in children's schooling: A multidimensional conceptualization and motivational model. *Child Development, 65,* 237–252.

Grossman, J. B., & Garry, E. M. (1997, April). Mentoring—A proven delinquency prevention strategy. *Juvenile Justice Bulletin,* 1–7.

Grossman, M., & Rowat, K. M. (1995). Parental relationships, coping strategies, received support, and well-being in adolescents of separated or divorced and married parents. *Research in Nursing and Health, 18,* 249–261.

Grotevant, H. D., & Cooper, C. R. (1985). Patterns of interaction in family relationships and the development of identity exploration in adolescence. *Child Development, 56,* 415–428.

Grotevant, H. D., & Cooper, C. R. (1986). Individuation in family relationships: A perspective on individual differences in the development of identity and role-taking skill in adolescence. *Human Development, 29,* 82–100.

Guerra, N. G., Huesmann, L. R., Tolan, P. H., Van Acker, R., & Eron, L. D. (1995). Stressful events and individual beliefs as correlates of economic disadvantage and aggression among urban children. *Journal of Consulting and Clinical Psychology, 63,* 518–528.

Guerra, N. G., & Slaby, R. G. (1990). Cognitive mediators of aggression in adolescent offenders: II. Intervention. *Developmental Psychology, 26,* 269–277.

Gutierres, S. E., Molof, M., & Ungerleider, S. (1994). Relationship of "risk" factors to teen substance use: A comparison of abstainers, infrequent users, and frequent users. *International Journal of the Addictions, 29,* 1559–1579.

Haffner, D. W. (Ed.) (1995) *Facing facts: Sexual health for America's adolescents.* New York: Sexuality Information and Education Council of the United States and National Commission on Adolescent Sexual Health.

Hagborg, W. J. (1991). A study of homework time of a high school sample. *Perceptual and Motor Skills, 73,* 103–106.

Hahn, A., Leavitt, T., & Aaron, P. (1994). *Evaluation of the Quantum Opportunities Program (QOP). Did the program work? A report on the post secondary outcomes and cost-effectiveness of the QOP Program (1989–1993).* Waltham, MA: Brandeis University, Center for Human Resources. (ERIC Document Reproduction Service No. ED 385 621)

Hallinan, M. T., & Williams, R. A. (1990). Students' characteristics and the peer-influence process. *Sociology of Education, 63,* 122–132.

Halpern, R. (1992). The role of after-school programs in the lives of inner-city children: A study of the Urban Youth Network. *Child Welfare, 71,* 215–230.

Hamburg, B. (1986). Subsets of adolescent mothers: Developmental, biomedical, and psychosocial issues. In B. Lancaster & B. A. Hamburg (Eds.), *School-age pregnancy and parenthood: Biosocial dimensions* (pp. 115–145). New York: Aldine de Gruyter.

Hamburg, B. A. (1990). *Life skills training: Preventive interventions for young adolescents* (Carnegie Council on Adolescent Development, Working Papers). Washington, DC: Carnegie Council on Adolescent Development.

Hamilton, S. F., & Fenzel, L. M. (1988). The impact of volunteer experience on adolescent social development: Evidence of program effects. *Journal of Adolescent Research, 3,* 65–80.

Hamilton, S. F., & Zeldin, R. S. (1987). Learning civics in the community. *Curriculum Inquiry, 17,* 407–420.

Hanks, M. P., & Eckland, B. K. (1976). Athletics and social participation in the educational attainment process. *Sociology of Education, 49,* 271–294.

Hansen, W. B. (1992). School-based substance abuse prevention: A review of the state of the art in curriculum, 1980–1990. *Health Education Research, 7,* 403–430.

Hansen, W. B., Graham, J. W., Wolkenstein, B. H., Lundy, B. Z., Pearson, J., Flay, B. R., & Anderson Johnson, C. (1988). Differential impact of three alcohol prevention curricula on hypothesized mediating variables. *Journal of Drug Education, 18,* 143–153.

Hanson, S. L., & Ginsburg, A. L. (1988). Gaining ground: Values and high school success. *American Educational Research Journal, 25,* 334–365.

Harnisch, D. L. (1985, October). *An investigation of the factors associated with effective public high schools.* Paper presented at the annual meeting of the Mid-Western Educational Research Association, Chicago, IL.

Harold, G. T., & Conger, R. D. (1997). Marital conflict and adolescent distress: The role of adolescent awareness. *Child Development, 68,* 333–350.

Harter, S. (1982). The perceived competence scale for children. *Child Development, 53,* 87–97.

Harter, S. (1986). Cognitive-developmental processes in the integration of concepts about emotion and the self. *Social Cognition, 4,* 119–151.

Harter, S. (1990a). Processes underlying adolescent self-concept formation. In R. Montemayor, G. R. Adams, & T. P. Gullotta (Eds.), *Advances in adolescent development: Vol. 2. From childhood to adolescent: A transitional period?* (pp. 205–239). Newbury Park, CA: Sage.

Harter, S. (1990b). Self and identity development. In S. S. Feldman & G. R. Elliott (Eds.), *At the threshold: The developing adolescent* (pp. 352–387). Cambridge, MA: Harvard University Press.

Harter, S., Marold, D. B., & Whitesell, N. R. (1992). Model of psychosocial risk factors leading to suicidal ideation in young adolescents. *Development and Psychopathology, 4,* 167–188.

Harter, S., Marold, D. B., Whitesell, N. R., & Cobbs, G. (1996). A model of the effects of perceived parent and peer support on adolescent false self behavior. *Child Development, 67,* 360–374.

Hartos, J. L., & Power, T. G. (1997). Mothers' awareness of their early adolescents' stressors: Relation between awareness and adolescent adjustment. *Journal of Early Adolescence, 17,* 371–389.

Hauser, S. T., & Kasendorf, E. (1983). *Black and White identity formation.* Malabar, FL: Robert E. Krieger.

Hauser, S. T., Powers, S. I., Noam, G. G., Jacobson, A. M., Weiss, B., & Follansbee, D. J. (1984). Familial contexts of adolescent ego development. *Child Development, 55,* 195–213.

Hawkins, J. D., Catalano, R. F., & Miller, J. Y. (1992). Risk and protective factors for alcohol and other drug problems in adolescence and early adulthood: Implications for substance abuse prevention. *Psychological Bulletin, 112,* 64–105.

Hawkins, J. D., & Lam, T. (1987). Teacher practices, social development, and delinquency. In J. D. Burchard & S. N. Burchard (Eds.), *Prevention of delinquent behavior* (pp. 241–274). Newbury Park, CA: Sage.

Hawkins, J. D., & Weis, J. G. (1985). The social development model: An integrated approach to delinquency prevention. *Journal of Primary Prevention, 6,* 73–97.

Hawkins, R., Royster, D. A., & Braddock, J. H. (1992). *Athletic investment and academic resilience among African-American females and males in the middle grades. Research report No. 3.* Cleveland, OH: Cleveland State University, Urban Child Research Center. (ERIC Document Reproduction Service No. 361 450)

Hay, I. (1993). Motivation, self-perception and gifted students. *Gifted Education International, 9,* 16–21.

Hayward, B. J., & Tallmadge, G. K. (1995). *Strategies for keeping kids in school: Evaluation of dropout prevention and reentry projects in vocational education. Final report.* Washington, DC: Department of Education, Office of the Under Secretary. (ERIC Document Reproduction Service No. ED 385 767)

Hechinger, F. M. (1992). Programs for young people: The youth organization as family supplement. *Fateful choices: Healthy youth for the 21st century.* New York: Carnegie Corporation of New York.

Hecht, D., & Fusco, D. (1995). *The effects of participation in the Helper Model of service learning in early adolescence* (Final report to DeWitt Wallace-Reader's Digest Fund). New York: City University of New York, Center for Advanced Study in Education.

Hedin, D., Hannes, K., & Saito, R. (1985). *Minnesota youth poll: Youth look at themselves and the world.* St. Paul: University of Minnesota, Minnesota Report AD-MR-2666.

Heinsohn, A. L., & Cantrell, M. J. (1986). *Pennsylvania 4-H impact study: An evaluation of teens' life skills development* (final report). University Park: Pennsylvania State University.

Henderson, A. T., & Berla, N. (Eds.). (1994). *A new generation of evidence: The family is critical to student achievement.* St. Louis, MO, and Flint, MI: Danforth Foundation and Mott (C. S.) Foundation. (ERIC Document Reproduction Service No. ED 375 968)

Henry, C. S., Sager, D. W., & Plunkett, S. W. (1996). Adolescents' perceptions of family system characteristics, parent-adolescent dyadic behaviors, adolescent qualities, and adolescent empathy. *Family Relations, 45,* 283–292.

Herman, M. R., Dornbusch, S. M., Herron, M. C., & Herting, J. R. (1997). The influence of family regulation, connection, and psychological autonomy on six measures of adolescent functioning. *Journal of Adolescent Research, 12,* 34–67.

Herman-Stahl, M., & Petersen, A. C. (1996). The protective role of coping and social resources for depressive symptoms among young adolescents. *Journal of Youth and Adolescence, 25,* 733–753.

Herold, E. S., Goodwin, M. S., & Lero, D. S. (1979). Self-esteem, locus of control, and adolescent contraception. *Journal of Psychology, 101,* 83–88.

Hershberger, S. L., & D'Augelli, A. R. (1995). The impact of victimization on the mental health and suicidality of lesbian, gay, and bisexual youths. *Developmental Psychology, 31,* 65–74.

Hill, J. P. (1983). *Participatory education and youth development in secondary schools.* Philadelphia: Research for Better Schools. (ERIC Document Reproduction Service No. ED 242 701)

Hill, J. P. (1988). Adapting to menarche: Familial control and conflict. In M. R. Gunnar & W. A. Collins (Eds.), *Minnesota symposium on child psychology* (Vol. 21, pp. 43–77). Hillsdale, NJ: Lawrence Erlbaum.

Hill, J. P., Holmbeck, G. N., Marlow, L., Green, T. M., & Lynch, M. E. (1985). Menarcheal status and parent-child relations in families of seventh-grade girls. *Journal of Youth and Adolescence, 14,* 301–316.

Hinde, R. (1979). *Towards understanding relationships.* London: Academic Press.

Hingson, R., & Howland, J. (1993). Promoting safety in adolescents. In S. G. Millstein, A. C. Petersen, & E. O. Nightingale (Eds.), *Promoting the health of adolescents: New directions for the twenty-first century* (pp. 305–327). New York: Oxford University Press.

Hirsch, J. H., & DuBois, D. L. (1991). Self-esteem in early adolescence: The identification and prediction of contrasting longitudinal trajectories. *Journal of Youth and Adolescence, 20,* 53–72.

Hodgkinson, V. A., & Weitzman M. S. (with Crutchfield, E. A., & Heffron, A. J.). (1996). *Volunteering and giving among teenagers 12 to 17 years of age.* Washington, DC: Independent Sector.

Hoge, D. R., Smit, E. K., & Hanson, S. L. (1990). School experiences predicting changes in self-esteem of sixth- and seventh-grade students. *Journal of Educational Psychology, 82,* 117–127.

Holmbeck, G. N., Crossman, R. E., Wandrei, M. L., & Gasiewski, E. (1994). Cognitive development, egocentrism, self-esteem, and adolescent contraceptive knowledge, attitudes, and behavior. *Journal of Youth and Adolescence, 23,* 169–193.

Hong, S. M., & Giannakopoulos, E. (1994). The relationship of satisfaction with life to personality characteristics. *Journal of Psychology, 128,* 547–558.

Hops, H., Tildesley, E., Lichtenstein, E., Ary, D., & Sherman, L. (1990). Parent-adolescent problem-solving interactions and drug use. *American Journal of Drug and Alcohol Abuse, 16,* 239–258.

Hot issues in education. (1997, October 15). *Education Week, 17,* 4.

Huang, S. L., & Waxman, H. C. (1995). Motivation and learning-environment differences between Asian-American and White middle school students in mathematics. *Journal of Research and Development in Education, 28,* 208–219.

Hudkins, S. J. (1995). Parvis e glandibus quercus: "Great oaks from little acorns grow." *Journal of Extension* [On-line], *33.* Available World Wide Web: almanac@joe.org.

Hunter, A. G. (1997). Counting on grandmothers: Black mothers' and fathers' reliance on grandmothers for parenting support. *Journal of Family Issues, 18,* 251–269.

Hutchinson, M. K., & Cooney, T. M. (1998). Patterns of parent-teen sexual risk communication: Implications for intervention. *Family Relations, 47,* 185–194.

Inderbitzen-Pisaruk, H., Clark, M. L., & Solano, C. H. (1992). Correlates of loneliness in midadolescence. *Journal of Youth and Adolescence, 21,* 151–167.

Irby, M. A., & McLaughlin, M. W. (1990). When is a gang not a gang? When it's a tumbling team. *Future Choices, 2,* 31–39.

Iso-Ahola, S., & Hatfield, B. (1986). *Psychology of sports: A social psychological approach.* Dubuque, IA: William C. Brown.

Iso-Ahola, S. E., & Crowley, E. D. (1991). Adolescent substance abuse and leisure boredom. *Journal of Leisure Research, 23,* 260–271.

Jackson, R. M., & Meara, N. M. (1981). Father identification, achievement, and occupational behavior of rural youth: 10-year follow-up. *Journal of Vocational Behavior, 19,* 212–226.

Jacobson, S. W. (1979). Matching behavior in the young infant. *Child Development, 50,* 425–430.

Jarrett, R. L. (1995). Growing up poor: The family experiences of socially mobile youth in low-income African American neighborhoods. *Journal of Adolescent Research, 10,* 111–135.

Jenkins, J. E. (1996). The influence of peer affiliation and student activities on adolescent drug involvement. *Adolescence, 31,* 297–306.

Jensen, L., Newell, R. J., & Holman, T. (1990). Sexual behavior, church attendance, and permissive beliefs among unmarried young men and women. *Journal for the Scientific Study of Religion, 29,* 113–117.

Jerry-Szpak, J., & Brown, H. P. (1994). Alcohol use and misuse: The hidden curriculum of the adolescent athlete. *Journal of Child and Adolescent Substance Abuse, 3,* 57–67.

Jessor, R. (1993). Successful adolescent development among youth in high-risk settings. *American Psychologist, 48,* 117–126.

Jessor, R., Van Den Bos, J., Vanderryn, J., Costa, F. M., & Turbin, M. S. (1995). Protective factors in adolescent problem behavior: Moderator effects and developmental change. *Developmental Psychology, 31,* 923–933.

Jessor, R. R., & Jessor, S. L. (1975). Adolescent development and the onset of drinking: A longitudinal study. *Journal of Studies on Alcohol, 36,* 27–51.

Jessor, R. R., & Jessor, S. L. (1977). *Problem behavior and psychological development: A longitudinal study of youth.* New York: Academic Press.

Johnson, B. M., Shulman, S., & Collins, W. A. (1991). Systemic patterns of parenting as reported by adolescents: Developmental differences and implications for psychosocial outcomes. *Journal of Adolescent Research, 6,* 235–252.

Johnson, D. W. (1975). *Cooperative competencies and the prevention and treatment of drug abuse.* (ERIC Document Reproduction Service No. ED 108 066)

Johnson, D. W., & Johnson, R. T. (1996). Conflict resolution and peer mediation programs in elementary and secondary schools: A review of the research. *Review of Educational Research, 66,* 459–506.

Johnson, E. A. (1993). *The relationship of self-blame and responsibility attributions and motivations, for schoolwork and conduct, to self-worth and self-perceptions.* Paper presented at the biennial meeting of the Society for Research in Child Development, New Orleans, LA.

Johnson, J. H., Jason, L. A., & Betts, D. M. (1990). Promoting social competencies through educational efforts. In T. P. Gullotta, G. R. Adams, & R. Montemayor (Eds.), *Advances in adolescent development: Vol. 3. Developing social competency in adolescence* (pp. 139–168). Newbury Park, CA: Sage.

Johnson, J. H., & Sarason, I. G. (1979). Moderator variables in stress research. In I. G. Sarason & C. D. Spielberger (Eds.), *Stress and anxiety* (Vol. 6, pp. 151–167). Washington, DC: Hemisphere.

Johnston, L. D., Bachman, J. G., & O'Malley, P. M. (1980). *Highlights from student drug use in America 1975–1980.* Rockville, MD: National Institute on Drug Abuse.

Jones, C. H., Slate, J. R., Blake, P. C., & Holifield, S. D. (1992). Two investigations of the academic skills of junior and senior high school students. *High School Journal, 76,* 24–29.

Jones, S. E. (1990). *Long-term investments in youth: The need for comprehensive programs for disadvantaged young men in urban areas.* Washington, DC: Union Institute, Center for Public Policy. (ERIC Document Reproduction Service No. ED 328 657)

Juhasz, A. M., & Sonnenshein-Schneider, M. (1987). Adolescent sexuality: Values, morality and decision-making. *Adolescence, 22,* 579–590.

Juvonen, J., & Murdock, T. B. (1995). Grade-level differences in the social value of effort: Implications for self-preservation tactics of early adolescents. *Child Development, 66,* 1694–1705.

Kablaoui, B. N., & Pautler, A. J. (1991). The effects of part-time work experience on high school students. *Journal of Career Development, 17,* 195–211.

Kandel, D. (1980). Drug and drinking behavior among youth. *Annual Review of Sociology, 6,* 235–285.

Kann, L., Kinchen, S. A., Williams, B. I., Ross, J. G., Lowry, R., Hill, C. V., Grunbaum, J. A., Blumson, P. S., Collins, J. L., & Kolbe, L. J. (1998, August 14). Youth risk behavior surveillance—United States, 1997. *Morbidity and Mortality Weekly Report, 47* (SS-3), 1–89.

Karnes, F. A., Deason, D. M., & D'Ilio, V. (1993). Leadership skills and self-actualization of school-age children. *Psychological Reports, 73* (part 1), 861–862.

Karnes, F. A., & D'Ilio, V. R. (1991). Locus of control in rural southern elementary gifted students. *Psychological Reports, 69,* 927–928.

Karnes, F. A., & McGinnis, J. C. (1996). Scores on indicators of leadership skills, locus of control, and self-actualization for student leaders in grades 6 to 10. *Psychological Reports, 78,* 1235–1240.

Karweit, N., & Hansell, S. (1983). Sex differences in adolescent relationships: Friendship and status. In J. Epstein & N. Karweit (Eds.), *Friends in school: Patterns of selection and influence in secondary schools* (pp. 115–130). New York: Academic Press.

Kasen, S., Cohen, P., & Brook, J. S. (1998). Adolescent school experiences and dropout, adolescent pregnancy, and young adult deviant behavior. *Journal of Adolescent Research, 13,* 49–72.

Kashani, J. H., & Shepperd, J. A. (1990). Aggression in adolescents: The role of social support and personality. *Canadian Journal of Psychiatry, 35,* 311–315.

Kasser, T., Ryan, R. M., Zax, M., & Sameroff, A. J. (1995). The relations of maternal and social environments to late adolescents' materialistic and prosocial values. *Developmental Psychology, 31,* 907–914.

Keith, T. Z., Reimers, T. M., Fehrmann, P. G., Pottebaum, S. M., & Aubey, L. W. (1986). Parental involvement, homework, and TV time: Direct and indirect effects on high school achievement. *Journal of Educational Psychology, 78*, 373–380.

Kelly, J. A., & Worell, L. (1978). Personality characteristics, parent behaviors, and sex of subject in relation to cheating. *Journal of Research in Personality, 12*, 179–188.

Kelly, K. R., & Jordan, L. K. (1990). Effects of academic achievement and gender on academic and social self-concept: A replication study. *Journal of Counseling and Development, 69*, 173–177.

Keltikangas-Järvinen, L., & Lindeman, M. (1997). Evaluation of theft, lying, and fighting in adolescence. *Journal of Youth and Adolescence, 26*, 467–483.

Kennedy, R. E. (1984). Cognitive behavioral interventions with delinquents. In A. W. Meyers & W. E. Craighead (Eds.), *Cognitive behavior therapy with children* (pp. 351–376). New York: Plenum Press.

Kidder, R. M., & Loges, W. E. (1997). *Global values, moral boundaries: A pilot survey.*

King, V., Elder, G. H., Jr., & Whitbeck, L. B. (1997). Religious involvement among rural youth: An ecological and life-course perspective. *Journal of Research on Adolescence, 7*, 431–456.

Kirby, D., Short, L., Collins, J., Rugg, D., Kolbe, L., Howard, M., Miller, B., Sonenstein, F., & Zabin, L. S. (1994). School-based programs to reduce sexual risk behavior: A review of effectiveness. *Public Health Reports, 109*, 339–360.

Kleiber, D., Larson, R., & Csikszentmihalyi, M. (1986). The experience of leisure in adolescence. *Journal of Leisure Research, 18*, 169–176.

Knight, S. L. (1991). The effects of students' perceptions of the learning environment on their motivation in language arts. *Journal of Classroom Interaction, 26*, 19–23.

Kohn, A. (1997). How not to teach values: A critical look at character education. *Phi Delta Kappan, 78*, 428–439.

Komro, K. A., Perry, C. L., Murray, D. M., Veblen-Mortensen, S., Williams, C. L., & Anstine, P. S. (1996). Peer-planned social activities for preventing alcohol use among young adolescents. *Journal of School Health, 66*, 328–334.

Kramer, L. R. (1992). Young adolescents' perceptions of school. In J. L. Irvin (Ed.), *Transforming middle level education: Perspectives and possibilities* (pp. 28–45). Boston: Allyn & Bacon.

Krappmann, L., & Oswald, H. (1987, April). *Negotiation strategies in peer conflicts: A follow-up study in natural settings.* Paper presented at the biannual meeting of the Society for Research in Child Development, Baltimore, MD. (ERIC Document Reproduction Service No. ED 282 641)

Krevans, J., & Gibbs, J. C. (1996). Parents' use of inductive discipline: Relations to children's empathy and prosocial behavior. *Child Development, 67*, 3263–3277.

Kubis, M. E. (1994). *The relationship between home literary environments and attitudes toward reading in ninth-grade students.* Unpublished doctoral dissertation, Georgia State University, Atlanta. (ERIC Document Reproduction Service No. ED 385 822)

Kumpfer, K. L., & Turner, C. W. (1990/1991). The social ecology model of adolescent substance abuse: Implications for prevention. Special issue: Preventive interventions for children at risk. *International Journal of the Addictions, 25*, 435–463.

Kunjufu, J. (1988). *To be popular or smart? The Black peer group.* Chicago: African American Images.

Kupersmidt, J. B., & Coie, J. D. (1990). Preadolescent peer status, aggression, and school adjustment as predictors of externalizing problems in adolescence. *Child Development, 61,* 1350–1362.

Kurdek, L. A., & Fine, M. A. (1994). Family acceptance and family control as predictors of adjustment in young adolescents: Linear, curvilinear, or interactive effects? *Child Development, 65,* 1137–1146.

Kurdek, L. A., Fine, M. A., & Sinclair, R. J. (1995). School adjustment in sixth graders: Parenting transitions, family climate, and peer norm effects. *Child Development, 66,* 430–445.

Kurth-Schai, R. (1988). Collecting the thoughts of children: A delphic approach. *Journal of Research and Development in Education, 21,* 53–59.

Kuther, T. L., & Fisher, C. B. (1998). Victimization by community violence in young adolescents from a suburban city. *Journal of Early Adolescence, 18,* 53–76.

Lackovic-Grgin, K., Dekovic, M., & Opacic, G. (1994). Pubertal status, interaction with significant others, and self-esteem of adolescent girls. *Adolescence, 29,* 691–700.

Ladd, G. W., Kochenderfer, B. J., & Coleman, C. C. (1997). Classroom peer acceptance, friendship, and victimization: Distinct relational systems that contribute uniquely to children's school adjustment? *Child Development, 68,* 1181–1197.

Ladewig, H., & Thomas, J. K. (1987). *Does 4-H make a difference?* Unpublished manuscript, Texas A & M University, College Station, TX.

Lamborn, S. D., Fischer, K. W., & Pipp, S. (1994). Constructive criticism and social lies: A developmental sequence for understanding honesty and kindness in social interactions. *Developmental Psychology, 30,* 495–508.

Lamborn, S. D., Mounts, N. S., Steinberg, L., & Dornbusch, S. M. (1991). Patterns of competence and adjustment among adolescents from authoritative, authoritarian, indulgent and neglectful families. *Child Development, 62,* 1049–1065.

Landrine, H., Richardson, J. L., Klonoff, E. A., & Flay, B. (1994). Cultural diversity in the predictors of adolescent cigarette smoking: The relative influence of peers. *Journal of Behavioral Medicine, 17,* 331–346.

Larson, R. (1994). Youth organizations, hobbies, and sports as developmental contexts. In R. K. Lilbereisen & E. Todt (Eds.), *Adolescence in context: The interplay of family, school, peers, and work in adjustment.* New York: Springer-Verlag.

Larson, R. W. (1997). The emergence of solitude as a constructive domain of experience in early adolescence. *Child Development, 68,* 80–93.

Larson, R. W., & Csikszentmihalyi, M. (1980). The significance of time alone in adolescent development. *Journal of Current Adolescent Medicine, 2,* 33–40.

Larson, R. W., & Richards, M. H. (1989). Introduction: The changing life space of early adolescence. *Journal of Youth and Adolescence, 18,* 501–509.

Laursen, B., & Koplas, A. L. (1995). What's important about important conflicts? Adolescents' perceptions of daily disagreements. *Merrill Palmer Quarterly, 41,* 536–553.

Lawson, H. A, & Briar-Lawson, K. (1997). *Connecting the dots: Progress toward the integration of school reform, school-linked services, parent involvement and community schools.* Oxford, OH: The Danforth Foundation and the Institute for Educational Renewal at Miami University.

Lawton, M. (1998, April 15). Latino students' math scores climb while family income drops. *Education Week, 7,* 14.

Leadbeater, B. J., Hellner, I., Allen, J. P., & Aber, J. L. (1989). Assessment of interpersonal negotiation strategies in youth engaged in problem behaviors. *Developmental Psychology, 25,* 465–472.

Lee, C. C. (1984). An investigation of psychosocial variables related to academic success for rural Black adolescents. *Journal of Negro Education, 53,* 424–434.

Lee, V. E., & Bryk, A. S. (1989). A multilevel model of the social distribution of high school achievement. *Sociology of Education, 62,* 172–192.

Lee, V. E., & Smith, J. R. (1993). Effects of school restructuring on the achievement and engagement of middle-grade students. *Sociology of Education, 66,* 164–187.

Lee, V. E., Winfield, L. F., & Wilson, T. C. (1991). Academic behaviors among high-achieving African-American students. *Education and Urban Society, 24,* 65–86.

Leffert, N., Benson, P. L., & Roehlkepartain, J. L. (1997). *Starting out right: Developmental assets for children.* Minneapolis, MN: Search Institute.

Leffert, N., Benson, P. L., Scales, P. C., Sharma, A. R., Drake, D. R., Blyth, D. A. (in press). Developmental assets: Measurement and prediction of risk behaviors among adolescents. *Applied Developmental Science.*

Leffert, N., & Herring, H. (1998). *Shema: Listening to Jewish youth.* Minneapolis, MN: Search Institute.

Leffert, N., & Petersen, A. C. (1996a). Biology, challenge, and adaptation: Effects on physical and mental health. In M. Bornstein & J. Genevro (Eds.), *Child development and behavioral pediatrics* (pp. 129–154). Hillsdale, NJ: Lawrence Erlbaum.

Leffert, N., & Petersen, A. C. (1996b). Healthy adolescent development: Risks and opportunities. In P. Kato & T. Mann (Eds.), *Handbook of diversity issues in health psychology* (pp. 117–140). New York: Plenum Press.

Leffert, N., Saito, R. N., Blyth, D. A., & Kroenke, C. H. (1996). *Making the case: Measuring the impact of youth development programs.* Minneapolis, MN: Search Institute.

Leifman, H., Kühlhorn, E., Allebeck, P., Andréasson, S., & Romelsjö, A. (1995). Abstinence in late adolescence: Antecedents to and covariates of a sober lifestyle and its consequences. *Social Science and Medicine, 41,* 113–121.

Lempers, J. D., Clark-Lempers, D., & Simons, R. L. (1989). Economic hardship, parenting, and distress in adolescence. *Child Development, 60,* 25–39.

Lennings, C. J. (1993). The role of activity in adolescent development: A study of employment. *Adolescence, 28,* 701–710.

Leon, G. R., Fulkerson, J. A., Perry, C. L., & Dube, A. (1994). Family influences, school behaviors, and risk for the later development of an eating disorder. *Journal of Youth and Adolescence, 23,* 499–515.

Leone, C. M., & Richards, M. H. (1989). Classwork and homework in early adolescence: The ecology of achievement. Special issue: The changing life space of early adolescence. *Journal of Youth and Adolescence, 18,* 531–548.

Lerner, R. M. (1987). A life-span perspective for early adolescence. In R. M. Lerner & T. T. Foch (Eds.), *Biological-psychosocial interactions in early adolescence.* Hillsdale, NJ: Lawrence Erlbaum.

Leung, J., & Leung, K. (1992). Life satisfaction, self-concept, and relationship with parents in adolescence. *Journal of Youth and Adolescence, 21,* 653–665.

Levental, H., & Keeshan, P. (1993). Promoting healthy alternatives to substance abuse. In S. G. Millstein, A. C. Petersen, & E. O. Nightingale (Eds.), *Promoting the health of adolescents: New directions for the twenty-first century* (pp. 260–284). New York: Oxford University Press.

Levine, F. J., & Rosich, K. J. (1996). The community as a social context. *Social causes of violence: Crafting a science agenda.* Washington, DC: American Sociological Association.

Lewis, C. (1981). How adolescents approach decisions: Changes over grades seven to twelve and policy implications. *Child Development, 52,* 538–544.

Ley, T. C., Schaer, B. B., & Dismukes, B. W. (1994). Longitudinal study of the reading attitudes and behaviors of middle school students. *Reading Psychology, 15,* 11–38.

Lindsay, P. (1984). High school size, participation in activities, and young adult social participation: Some enduring effects of schooling. *Educational Evaluation and Policy Analysis, 6,* 73–83.

Linquanti, R. (1992). Using community-wide collaboration to foster resiliency in kids: A conceptual framework. Portland, OR: Western Regional Center for Drug-Free Schools and Communities.

Litchfield, A. W., Thomas, D. L., & Li, B. D. (1997). Dimensions of religiosity as mediators of the relations between parenting and adolescent deviant behavior. *Journal of Adolescent Research, 12,* 199–226.

Liu, X., Kaplan, H. B., & Risser, W. (1992). Decomposing the reciprocal relationships between academic achievement and general self-esteem. *Youth and Society, 24,* 123–148.

Lock, S. E., & Vincent, M. L. (1995). Sexual decision-making among rural adolescent females. *Health Values: The Journal of Health Behavior, Education and Promotion, 19,* 47–58.

Lorch, B. R., & Hughes, R. H. (1985). Religion and youth substance use. *Journal of Religion and Health, 24,* 197–208.

Lord, S. E., Eccles, J. S., & McCarthy, K. A. (1994). Surviving the junior high school transition: Family processes and self-perceptions as protective and risk factors. *Journal of Early Adolescence, 14,* 162–199.

Luchs, K. P. (1980). Selected changes in urban high school students after participation in community based learning and service activities. (Doctoral dissertation, University of Maryland, 1980). *Dissertation Abstracts International, 42,* 3371.

Lunenburg, F. C., & Schmidt, L. J. (1989). Pupil control ideology, pupil control behavior and the quality of school life. *Journal of Research and Development in Education, 22,* 36–44.

Luthar, S. S. (1995). Social competence in the school setting: Prospective cross-domain associations among inner-city teens. *Child Development, 66,* 416–429.

Luthar, S. S., & Zigler, E. (1991). Vulnerability and competence: A review of research on resilience in childhood. *American Journal of Orthopsychiatry, 61,* 6–22.

Luthar, S. S., & Zigler, E. (1992). Intelligence and social competence among high-risk adolescents. *Development and Psychopathology, 4,* 287–299.

Maccoby, E., & Martin, J. (1983). Socialization in the context of the family: Parent-child interaction. In E. M. Hetherington (Ed.), *Handbook of child psychology: Vol. IV. Socialization, personality, and social development* (4th ed., pp. 1–101). New York: Wiley.

Maccoby, E. E. (1984). Middle childhood in the context of the family. In W. A. Collins (Ed.), *Development during middle childhood: The years from six to twelve* (pp. 184–239). Washington, DC: National Academy Press.

Maggs, J. L., Almeida, D. M., & Galambos, N. L. (1995). Risky business: The paradoxical meaning of problem behavior for young adolescents. *Journal of Early Adolescence, 15,* 344–362.

Mahoney, J. L., & Cairns, R. B. (1997). Do extracurricluar activities protect against early school dropout? *Developmental Psychology, 33,* 241–253.

Mallinckrodt, B. (1992). Childhood emotional bonds with parents, development of adult social competencies, and availability of social support. *Journal of Counseling Psychology, 39,* 453–461.

Mann, L., Harmoni, R., & Power, C. (1989). Adolescent decision-making: The development of competence. *Journal of Adolescence, 12,* 265–278.

Mann, L., Harmoni, R., Power, C., Beswick, G., & Ormond, C. (1988). Effectiveness of the GOFER course in decision making for high school students. *Journal of Behavioral Decision Making, 1,* 159–168.

Marcia, J. E. (1980). Identity in adolescence. In J. Adelson (Ed.), *Handbook of adolescent psychology* (pp. 149–173). New York: Wiley.

Margalit, M., & Eysenck, S. (1990). Prediction of coherence in adolescence: Gender differences in social skills, personality, and family climate. *Journal of Research in Personality, 24,* 510–521.

Marjoribanks, K. (1990). The predictive validity of a teachers' support scale in relation to adolescents' aspirations. *Educational and Psychological Measurement, 50,* 647–651.

Marjoribanks, K. (1996). Ethnicity, family achievement syndrome, and adolescents' aspirations: Rosen's framework revisited. *Journal of Genetic Psychology, 157,* 349–359.

Markstrom-Adams, C. (1992). A consideration of factors in identity formation. In G. R. Adams, T. P. Gullotta, & R. Montemayor (Eds.), *Advances in adolescent development: Vol. 4. Adolescent identity formation* (pp. 173–192). Newbury Park, CA: Sage.

Markus, G. B., Howard, J. P. F., & King, D. C. (1993). Integrating community service and classroom instruction enhances learning: Results from an experiment. *Educational Evaluation and Policy Analysis, 15,* 410–419.

Marsh, D. D. (1973). Education for political involvement: A pilot study of twelfth graders. (Doctoral dissertation, University of Wisconsin, 1973). *Dissertation Abstracts International, 35,* 172.

Marsh, H. W. (1991). Employment during high school: Character building or a subversion of academic goals? *Sociology of Education, 64,* 172–189.

Martin, C. S., Earleywine, M., Blackson, T. C., Vanyukov, M. M., Moss, H. B., & Tarter, R. E. (1994). Aggressivity, inattention, hyperactivity, and impulsivity in boys at high and low risk for substance abuse. *Journal of Abnormal Child Psychology, 22,* 177–203.

Martinez, R. O., & Dukes, R. L. (1997). The effects of ethnic identity, ethnicity, and gender on adolescent well-being. *Journal of Youth and Adolescence, 26,* 503–516.

Maryland State Department of Education (1990). *In the middle: Addressing the needs of at risk students during the middle learning years. Technical team report. Submitted to the Commission for Students At Risk of School Failure.* Baltimore: Author. (ERIC Document Reproduction Service No. ED 326 333)

Maslow, A. (1962). *Toward a psychology of being.* Princeton, NJ: Van Nostrand.

Mason, C. A., Cauce, A. M., Gonzales, N., & Hiraga, Y. (1996). Neither too sweet nor too sour: Problem peers, maternal control, and problem behavior in African American adolescents. *Child Development, 67,* 2115–2130.

Massad, C. M. (1981). Sex role identity and adjustment during adolescence. *Child Development, 52,* 1290–1298.

Masselam, V. S., Marcus, R. F., & Stunkard, C. L. (1990). Parent-adolescent communication, family functioning, and school performance. *Adolescence, 25,* 725–737.

Masten, A. S., Coatsworth, J. D., Neemann, J., Gest, S. D., Tellegen, A., & Garmezy, N. (1995). The structure and coherence of competence from childhood through adolescence. *Child Development, 66,* 1635–1659.

Maton, K. I. (1990). Meaningful involvement in instrumental activity and well-being: Studies of older adolescents and at risk urban teen-agers. *American Journal of Community Psychology, 18,* 297–320.

Mauldin, T., & Meeks, C. B. (1990). Sex differences in children's time use. *Sex Roles, 22,* 537–554.

McCarthy, J. D., & Hoge, D. R. (1982). Analysis of age effects in longitudinal studies of adolescent self-esteem. *Developmental Psychology, 18,* 372–379.

McCullough, P. M., Ashbridge, D., & Pegg, R. (1994). The effect of self-esteem, family structure, locus of control, and career goals on adolescent leadership behavior. *Adolescence, 29,* 605–611.

McDevitt, T. M., Lennon, R., & Kopriva, R. J. (1991). Adolescents' perceptions of mothers' and fathers' prosocial actions and empathic responses. *Youth and Society, 22,* 387–409.

McDonald, L., & Sayger, T. V. (1996). *Impact of a family and school based prevention program on protective factors for high risk youth: Issues in evaluation.* Madison: Wisconsin Center for Education Research.

McFarlane, A. H., Bellissimo, A., & Norman, G. R. (1995). The role of family and peers in social self-efficacy: Links to depression in adolescence. *American Journal of Orthopsychiatry, 65,* 402–410.

McGee, Z. T. (1992). Social class differences in parental and peer influence on adolescent drug use. *Deviant Behavior, 13,* 349–372.

McGill, J. C. (1992). *The relationship of community service learning to developing mature interpersonal relationships in a sample of university students.* Unpublished doctoral dissertation, American University, Washington, DC.

McGuire, K. D., & Weisz, J. R. (1982). Social cognition and behavior correlates of preadolescent chumship. *Child Development, 53,* 1478–1484.

McKeowan, R. E., Garrison, C. Z., Jackson, K. L., Cuffe, S. P., Addy, C. L., & Waller, J. L. (1997). Family structure and cohesion, and depressive symptoms in adolescents. *Journal of Research on Adolescence, 7,* 267–281.

McKnight, J. L., & Kretzmann, J. (1990). *Mapping community capacity.* Evanston, IL: Northwestern University, Institute for Policy Research, Neighborhood Innovations Network.

McLaughlin, M. W., & Irby, M. A. (1994). Urban sanctuaries: Neighborhood organizations that keep hope alive. *Phi Delta Kappan, 76,* 300–306.

McLaughlin, M. W., Irby, M. A., & Langman, J. (1994). *Urban sanctuaries: Neighborhood organizations in the lives and futures of inner-city youth.* San Francisco: Jossey-Bass.

McLeod, J. D., & Edwards, K. (1995). Contextual determinants of children's responses to poverty. *Social Forces, 73,* 1487–1516.

McNeill, S., & Petersen, A. C. (1985). Gender role and identity in early adolescence: Reconsideration of theory. *Academic Psychology Bulletin, 7,* 299–315.

McStudy program aids working teens. (1997). *Assets: The Magazine of Ideas for Healthy Communities & Healthy Youth, 2,* 6.

Meeks, C. B., & Mauldin, T. (1990). Children's time in structured and unstructured leisure activities. *Lifestyles, 11,* 257–281.

Mekos, D., & Elder, G. H., Jr. (1996, March). Community ties and the development of competence in rural youth. In M. Shanahan & L. Crockett (Co-chairs), *Growing up in rural families: Community, psychological well-being, and the life course.* Symposium conducted at the biennial meeting of the Society for Research on Adolescence, Boston, MA.

Melchior, A. (1997). *Interim report: National evaluation of Learn and Serve America school and community-based programs.* Washington, DC: Corporation for National Service.

Melton, G. B. (1992). It's time for neighborhood research and action. *Child Abuse and Neglect, 16,* 909–913.

Merrick, W. A. (1992). Dysphoric moods in depressed and non-depressed adolescents. In M. DeVries (Ed.), *The experience of psychopathology: Investigating mental disorders in their natural settings* (pp. 148–156). Cambridge: Cambridge University Press.

Middleton, E. B. (1993). *The psychological and social effects of community service tasks on adolescents.* Unpublished doctoral dissertation, Purdue University, West Lafayette, IN.

Midgley, C., Feldlaufer, H., & Eccles, J. (1989). Change in teacher efficacy and student self- and task-related beliefs in mathematics during the transition to junior high school. *Journal of Educational Philosophy, 81,* 247–258.

Milgram, G. G. (1996). Responsible decision making regarding alcohol: A re-emerging prevention/education strategy for the 1990's. *Journal of Drug Education, 26,* 357–365.

Miller, B. C., McCoy, J. K., Olson, T. D., & Wallace, C. M. (1986). Parental discipline and control attempts in relation to adolescent sexual attitudes and behavior. *Journal of Marriage and the Family, 48,* 503–512.

Miller, B. C., Norton, M. C., Fan, X., & Christopherson, C. R. (1998). Pubertal development, parental communication, and sexual values in relation to adolescent sexual behaviors. *Journal of Early Adolescence, 18,* 27–52.

Miller, D. (1991). Do adolescents help and share? *Adolescence, 26,* 449–456.

Miller, D. L., & Kelley, M. L. (1991). Interventions for improving homework performance: A critical review. *School Psychology Quarterly, 6,* 174–185.

Miller, K. (1993, March). *Same sex and opposite sex friendship quality and perceived social competence: Developmental overlap.* Paper presented at the meeting of the Society for Research in Child Development, New Orleans, LA.

Millstein, S. G., Petersen, A. C., & Nightingale, E. O. (Eds.). (1993). *Promoting the health of adolescents: New directions for the twenty-first century.* New York: Oxford University Press.

Moffitt, M. A., & Wartella, E. (1992). Youth and reading: A survey of leisure reading pursuits of female and male adolescents. *Reading Research and Instruction, 31,* 1–17.

Montemayor, R. (1983). Parents and adolescents in conflict: All families some of the time and some families most of the time. *Journal of Early Adolescence, 3,* 83–104.

Moore, C. W., & Allen, J. P. (1996). The effects of volunteering on the young volunteer. *Journal of Primary Prevention, 17,* 231–258.

Moore, K. A., & Glei, D. (1995). Taking the plunge: An examination of positive youth development. *Journal of Adolescent Research, 10,* 15–40.

Moore, S., & Gullone, E. (1996). Predicting adolescent risk behavior using a personalized cost-benefit analysis. *Journal of Youth and Adolescence, 25,* 343–359.

Morrison, T. G., McLeod, L. D., Morrison, M. A., Anderson, D., & O'Connor, W. E. (1997). Gender stereotyping, homonegativity, and misconceptions about sexually coercive behavior among adolescents. *Youth and Society, 28,* 351–382.

Morrow, K. V., & Styles, M. B. (1995). *Building relationships with youth in program settings: A study of Big Brothers/Big Sisters.* Philadelphia: Public/Private Ventures.

Mortimer, J. T., Finch, M., Shanahan, M., & Ryu, S. (1992). Work experience, mental health, and behavioral adjustment in adolescence. *Journal of Research on Adolescence, 2,* 25–57.

Mortimer, J. T., Finch, M. D., Ryu, S., Shanahan, M. J., & Call, K. T. (1993). *The effects of work intensity on adolescent mental health, achievement and behavioral adjustment: New evidence from a prospective study.* Paper presented at the biennial meeting of the Society for Research in Child Development, New Orleans, LA. Bethesda, MD: National Institute of Mental Health, DHHS.

Mott, P., & Krane, A. (1994). Interpersonal cognitive problem-solving and childhood social competence. *Cognitive Therapy and Research, 18,* 127–141.

Mounts, N. S., & Steinberg, L. (1995). An ecological analysis of peer influence on adolescent grade point average and drug use. *Developmental Psychology, 31,* 915–922.

Mulvey, E. P., Arthur, M. W., & Reppucci, N. D. (1997). The prevention of juvenile delinquency: A review of the research. *Prevention Researcher, 4,* 1–7.

Muskal, F., & Chairez, M. (1990). *Mobility strategies of successful Hispanic high school students.* Stockton, CA: University of the Pacific. (ERIC Document Reproduction Service No. ED 369 862)

National Center for Education Statistics (1990). *National education longitudinal study of 1988.* Washington, DC: Author.

National Center for Education Statistics (1995). Extracurricular participation and student engagement. In *Educational policy issues: Statistical perspectives* [On-line]. Available World Wide Web: http://www.ed.gov/NCES/pubs/95741.html.

National Clearinghouse on Families and Youth. (1996). *Reconnecting youth and community: A youth development approach.* Washington, DC: U.S. Department of Health and Human Services, Administration for Children, Youth, and Families, Family and Youth Services Bureau.

National Clearinghouse on Families and Youth. (1997). *Understanding youth development: Promoting positive pathways of growth.* Washington, DC: U.S. Department of Health and Human Services, Administration for Children, Youth, and Families, Family and Youth Services Bureau.

National Commission on Children (1991). *Speaking of kids: A national survey of children and parents.* Washington, DC: Author.

National Commission on Civic Renewal (1988). *A nation of spectators: How civic disengagement weakens America and what we can do about it.* Washington, DC: Author.

National Crime Prevention Council (1995). *How communities can bring up youth free from fear and violence.* Washington, DC: Author.

National Research Council, Board on Children, Youth, and Families (1996). *Youth development and neighborhood influences: Challenges and opportunities.* Washington, DC: Author.

National School Safety Center (1989). *Role models, sports, and youth* (NSSC resource paper). Malibu, CA: Author.

NCPCA reports 1996 child abuse survey results. (1997, April 28). *Washington Social Legislation Bulletin, 35,* 29–31.

Nelson, C., & Keith, J. (1990). Comparisons of female and male early adolescent sex role attitude and behavior development. *Adolescence, 25,* 183–204.

Neto, F. (1993). The satisfaction with life scale: Psychometrics properties in an adolescent sample. *Journal of Youth and Adolescence, 22,* 125–134.

Nettles, S. M. (1991). Community contributions to school outcomes of African-American students. *Education and Urban Society, 24,* 132–147.

Neufeldt, V. (Ed.). (1988). *Webster's new world college dictionary.* (3rd ed.). New York: Simon & Schuster.

Newmann, F. M., & Rutter, R. A. (1983). *The effects of high school community service programs on students' social development* (Final report to the National Institute of Education, Washington, DC). Madison: Wisconsin Center for Education Research.

Newmann, F. M., & Wehlage, G. G. (1995). *Successful school restructuring: A report to the public and educators.* Madison: University of Wisconsin, Center on Organization and Restructuring of Schools.

Nielsen, D. M., & Metha, A. (1994). Parental behavior and adolescent self-esteem in clinical and nonclinical samples. *Adolescence, 29,* 525–542.

Noguera, P. A. (1995). Preventing and producing violence: A critical analysis of responses to school violence. Special issue: Violence and youth. *Harvard Educational Review, 65,* 189–212.

Nolen, S. B., & Haladyna, T. M. (1990). Motivation and studying in high school science. *Journal of Research in Science Teaching, 27,* 115–126.

Nolen-Hoeksema, S. (1987). Sex differences in unipolar depression: Evidence and theory. *Psychological Bulletin, 101,* 259–282.

Nolen-Hoeksema, S., Morrow, J., & Fredrickson, B. (1993). Response styles and the duration of episodes of depressed mood. *Journal of Abnormal Psychology, 102,* 20–28.

Nolin, M. J., Davies, E., & Chandler, K. (1995). *Student victimization at school: Statistics in brief.* Rockville, MD: Westat.

Nottelmann, E. D. (1987). Competence and self-esteem during transition from childhood to adolescence. *Developmental Psychology, 23,* 441–450.

Nucci, L., & Turiel, E. (1993). God's word, religious rules, and their relation to Christian and Jewish children's concepts of morality. *Child Development, 64,* 1475–1491.

Nurmi, J., & Pulliainen, H. (1991). The changing parent-child relationship, self-esteem, and intelligence as determinants of orientation to the future during early adolescence. *Journal of Adolescence, 14,* 35–51.

Nystrom, J. (1989). Empowerment models for delivery of social work services in public schools. *Social Work in Education, 11,* 160–170.

O'Connell, B. E. (1983). *Long term effects of school-community service projects.* Unpublished doctoral dissertation, State University of New York, Buffalo, NY.

Oden, S. (1995). Studying youth programs to assess influences on youth development: New roles for researchers. *Journal of Adolescent Research, 10,* 173–186.

O'Donnell, J., Hawkins, J. D., & Abbott, R. D. (1995). Predicting serious delinquency and substance use among aggressive boys. Special section: Prediction and prevention of child and adolescent antisocial behavior. *Journal of Consulting and Clinical Psychology, 63,* 529–537.

Ogbu, J. (1991). Immigrant and involuntary minorities in comparative perspective. In M. G. Gibson & J. U. Ogbu (Eds.), *Minority status and schooling* (pp. 3–33). New York: Garland.

Ogbu, J. U. (1978). *Minority education and caste: The American system in cross-cultural perspective.* New York: Academic Press.

Ogbu, J. U., & Simons, H. D. (1994). *Cultural models of school achievement: A quantitative test of Ogbu's theory. Cultural models of literacy: A comparative study. Project 12.* Washington, DC: Department of Education, Office of Educational Research and Improvement. (ERIC Document Reproduction Service No. ED 376 515)

Ogilvy, C. M. (1994). Social skills training with children and adolescents: A review of the evidence on effectiveness. *Educational Psychology: An International Journal of Experimental Educational Psychology, 14,* 73–83.

Olweus, D. (1984). Development of stable aggressive reaction patterns in males. In R. Blanchard & C. Blanchard (Eds.), *Advances in the study of aggression* (Vol. 2, pp. 103–137). New York: Academic Press.

O'Malley, P. M., & Bachman, J. G. (1983). Self-esteem: Change and stability between ages 13 and 23. *Developmental Psychology, 19*, 257–268.

O'Neil, J. (1990). *Changing perspectives: Youth as resources.* Washington, DC: National Crime Prevention Council.

Orr, J. D., & Gobeli, V. C. (1986). *4-H teen leadership development in Nebraska.* Lincoln: University of Nebraska, Nebraska Cooperative Extension Service, Institute of Agriculture and Natural Resources.

Otto, L. B., & Atkinson, M. P. (1997). Parental involvement and adolescent development. *Journal of Adolescent Research, 12*, 68–89.

Overholser, J. C., Adams, D. M., Lehnert, K. L., & Brinkman, D. C. (1995). Self-esteem deficits and suicidal tendencies among adolescents. *Journal of the American Academy of Child and Adolescent Psychiatry, 34*, 919–928.

Page, R. M. (1992). Feelings of physical unattractiveness and hopelessness among high school students. *High School Journal, 75*, 150–155.

Page, R. M., & Tucker, L. A. (1994). Psychosocial discomfort and exercise frequency: An epidemiological study of adolescents. *Adolescence, 29*, 183–191.

Palmer, R. B., Dakof, G. A., & Liddle, H. A. (1993). Family processes, family interventions, and adolescent school problems: A critical review and analysis. In K. L. Alves-Zervos & J. R. Shafer (Eds.), *Synthesis of research and practice: Implications for achieving schooling success for children at risk* (pp. 101–136). Philadelphia: Temple University, National Center on Education in the Inner Cities.

Papini, D. R., & Sebby, R. A. (1987). Adolescent pubertal status and affective family relationships: A multivariate assessment. *Journal of Youth and Adolescence, 16*, 1–15.

Parker, J. G., & Asher, S. R. (1987). Peer relations and later personal adjustment: Are low accepted children "at risk?" *Psychological Bulletin, 102*, 357–389.

Parkhurst, J. T., & Asher, S. R. (1992). Peer rejection in middle school: Subgroup differences in behavior, loneliness, and interpersonal concerns. *Developmental Psychology, 28*, 231–241.

Paterson, J., Pryor, J., & Field, J. (1995). Adolescent attachment to parents and friends in relation to aspects of self-esteem. *Journal of Youth and Adolescence, 24*, 365–376.

Patrick, H., Hicks, L., & Ryan, A. M. (1997). Relations of perceived social efficacy and social goal pursuit to self-efficacy for academic work. *Journal of Early Adolescence, 17*, 109–128.

Patterson, G. R., Chamberlain, P., & Reid, J. B. (1982). A comparative evaluation of a parent-training program. *Behavior Therapy, 13*, 638–650.

Patterson, G. R., & Fleischman, M. J. (1979). Maintenance of treatment effects: Some considerations concerning family systems and follow-up data. *Behavior Therapy, 10* (2), 168–185.

Patterson, G. R., & Stouthamer-Loeber, M. (1984). The correlation of family management practices and delinquency. *Child Development, 55*, 1299–1307.

Paulson, M. J., Coombs, R. H., & Richardson, M. A. (1990). School performance, academic aspirations, and drug use among children and adolescents. *Journal of Drug Education, 20*, 289–303.

Paulson, S. E. (1994). Relations of parenting style and parental involvement with ninth-grade students' achievement. *Journal of Early Adolescence, 14*, 250–267.

Peer groups–positive or negative influence on adolescents? (1996, October). *High Strides, 15*.

Pentz, M. A., Dwyer, J. H., MacKinnon, D. P., Flay, B. R., Hansen, W. B., Wang, E. Y. I., & Johnson, C. A. (1989). A multicommunity trial for primary prevention of adolescent drug abuse: Effects on drug use prevalence. *Journal of the American Medical Association, 261,* 3259–3266.

Penuel, W. R. (1995). *Adult guidance in youth development revisited: Identity construction in youth organizations* [On-line]. Hanover, IN: Hanover College Psychology Department. Available World Wide Web: http://psych.hanover.edu/vygotsky/penuel.html.

Perlmutter, M., Behrend, S. D., Kuo, F., & Muller, A. (1989). Social influences on children's problem solving. *Developmental Psychology, 25,* 744–754.

Perry, C. L., Grant, M., Ernberg, B., Florenzana, R. U., Langdon, M. C., Myeni, A. D., Waahlberg, R., Berg, S., Andersson, K., Fisher, K. J., Blaze-Temple, D., Cross, D., Saunders, B., Jacobs, D. R., Jr., & Schmid, T. (1989). WHO collaborative study of alcohol education and young people: Outcomes of a four-country pilot study. *International Journal of the Addictions, 24,* 1145–1171.

Perry, C. L., & Kelder, S. H. (1992). Models for effective prevention. *Journal of Adolescent Health, 13,* 355–363.

Pete, J. M., & DeSantis, L. (1990). Sexual decision making in young Black adolescent females. *Adolescence, 25,* 145–154.

Petersen, A. C. (1991, April). *Adolescence in America: Effects on girls.* The 1991 Gisela Konopka Lecture, University of Minnesota, Minneapolis, MN.

Petersen, A. C. (1993). Presidential address. Creating adolescents: The role of context and process in developmental trajectories. *Journal of Adolescent Research, 3,* 1–18.

Petersen, A. C., Kennedy, R. E., & Sullivan, P. (1991). Coping with adolescence. In M. E. Colten & S. Gore (Eds.), *Adolescent stress: Causes and consequences* (pp. 93–110). New York: Aldine de Gruyter.

Petersen, A. C., Leffert, N., Graham, B., Alwin, J., & Ding, S. (1997). Promoting mental health during the transition into adolescence. In J. Schulenberg, J. Maggs, & K. Hurrelmann (Eds.), *Health risks and developmental transitions during adolescence* (pp. 471–497). Cambridge: Cambridge University Press.

Petersen, A. C., Leffert, N., & Hurrelmann, K. (1993). Adolescence and schooling in Germany and the United States: A comparison of peer socialization to adulthood. *Teachers College Record, 94,* 611–628.

Peterson, G. W., & Leigh, G. K. (1990). The family and social competence in adolescence. In T. P. Gullotta, G. R. Adams, & R. Montemayor (Eds.), *Advances in adolescent development: Vol. 3. Developing social competency in adolescence* (pp. 97–138). Newbury Park, CA: Sage.

Pettit, G. S., Bates, J. E., & Dodge, K. A. (1997). Supportive parenting, ecological context, and children's adjustment: A seven-year longitudinal study. *Child Development, 68,* 908–923.

Phinney, J. S., Cantu, C. L., & Kurtz, D. A. (1997). Ethnic and American identity as predictors of self-esteem among African American, Latino, and White adolescents. *Journal of Youth and Adolescence, 26,* 165–185.

Phinney, J. S., Ferguson, D. L., & Tate, J. D. (1997). Intergroup attitudes among ethnic minority adolescents: A causal model. *Child Development, 68,* 955–969.

Pittman, K. J., & Wright, M. (1991). *Bridging the gap: A rationale for enhancing the role of community organizations in promoting youth development.* Washington, DC: Carnegie Council on Adolescent Development.

Pleck, J. H., Sonenstein, F. L., & Ku, L. C. (1993). Masculinity ideology: Its impact on adolescent males' heterosexual relationships. *Journal of Social Issues, 49,* 11–29.

Plotnick, R. D., & Butler, S. S. (1991). Attitudes and adolescent nonmarital childbearing:

Evidence from the National Longitudinal Survey of Youth. *Journal of Adolescent Research, 6,* 470–492.

Pomerantz, E. M., & Ruble, D. N. (1997). Distinguishing multiple dimensions of conceptions of ability: Implications for self-evaluation. *Child Development, 68,* 1165–1180.

Popowski, K. J. (1985). *Chicago area youth poll: Youth views on volunteering and service-learning.* Chicago: Cook County Sheriff's Youth Services Department.

Portner, J. (1994, October 26). Murder rate for young men soars, CDC says. *Education Week, 14,* 3.

Portner, J. (1997, October 15). Studies illuminate far-reaching ramifications of abuse of girls. *Education Week, 17,* 12.

Posner, J. K., & Vandell, D. L. (1994). Low-income children's after-school care: Are there beneficial effects of after-school programs? Special issue: Children and poverty. *Child Development, 65,* 440–456.

Pretty, G. M. H., Andrewes, L., & Collett, C. (1994). Exploring adolescents' sense of community and its relationship to loneliness. *Journal of Community Psychology, 22,* 346–358.

Price, R. H., Cioci, M., Penner, W., & Trautlein, B. (1990). *School and community support programs that enhance adolescent health and education* (Carnegie Council on Adolescent Development, Working Papers). Washington, DC: Carnegie Council on Adolescent Development.

Price, R. H., Cioci, M., Penner, W., & Trautlein, B. (1993). Webs of influence: School and community programs that enhance adolescent health and education. *Teachers College Record, 94,* 487–521.

Procidano, M. E., Guinta, D. M., & Buglione, S. A. (1988). *Perceived social support and subjective states in urban adolescent girls.* Paper presented at the annual meeting of the American Psychological Association, Atlanta, GA.

Pruitt, B. E., Kingery, P. M., Mirzaee, E., Heuberger, G., & Hurley, R. S. (1991). Peer influence and drug use among adolescents in rural areas. *Journal of Drug Education, 21,* 1–11.

Pryor, C. B. (1994). *Family-school bonding and student success.* Paper presented at the annual meeting of the American Educational Research Association, New Orleans, LA.

Quinn, J. (1994). A matter of time: An overview of themes from the Carnegie Report. *Voice of Youth Advocates, 17,* 192–196.

Ransford, C. P. (1982). A role for amines in the antidepressant effect of exercise: A review. *Medicine and Science in Sports and Exercise, 14,* 1–10.

Resnick, L. B. (1987). *Education and learning to think.* Washington, DC: National Academy Press.

Resnick, M. D., Bearman, P. S., Blum, R. W., Bauman, K. E., Harris, K. M., Jones, J., Tabor, J., Beuhring, T., Sieving, R. E., Shew, M., Ireland, M., Bearinger, L. H., & Udry, J. R. (1997). Protecting adolescents from harm: Findings from the National Longitudinal Study on Adolescent Health. *Journal of the American Medical Association, 278,* 823–832.

Reynolds, A. J. (1991). Note on adolescents' time-use and scientific literacy. *Psychological Reports, 68,* 63–70.

Reynolds, A. J., & Gill, S. (1994). The role of parental perspectives in the school adjustment of inner-city Black children. *Journal of Youth and Adolescence, 23,* 671–694.

Reynolds, J. W. (1995). Music education and student self-concept: A review of literature. In *Research perspectives in music education* [On-line]. Tallahassee: Florida Music Educators Association. Available World Wide Web: http://arts.usf.edu/music/rpme/rpmereyn.html.

Rhodes, J. E., Ebert, L., & Fischer, K. (1992). Natural mentors: An overlooked resource in the social networks of young, African American mothers. *American Journal of Community Psychology, 20,* 445–461.

Richardson, J. L., Dwyer, K., McGuigan, K., Hansen, W. B., Dent, C., Anderson Johnson, C., Sussman, S. Y., Brannon, B., & Flay, B. (1989). Substance use among eighth-grade students who take care of themselves after school. *Pediatrics, 84,* 556–566.

Richardson, J. L., Radziszewska, B., Dent, C., & Flay, B. R. (1993). Relationship between after-school care of adolescents and substance use, risk taking, depressed mood, and academic achievement. *Pediatrics, 92,* 32–38.

Richter, S. S., Brown, S. A., & Mott, M. A. (1991). The impact of social support and self-esteem on adolescent substance abuse treatment outcome. *Journal of Substance Abuse, 3,* 371–385.

Richters, J. E., & Martinez, P. E. (1993). Violent communities, family choices, and children's chances: An algorithm for improving the odds. Special issue: Milestones in the development of resilience. *Development and Psychopathology, 5,* 609–627.

Riley, T. L., & Karnes, F. A. (1994). A leadership profile of disadvantaged youth based on Leadership Strengths Indicator. *Psychological Reports, 74,* 815–818.

Roberts, W., & Strayer, J. (1996). Empathy, emotional expressiveness, and prosocial behavior. *Child Development, 67,* 449–470.

Robins, L. N. (1966). *Deviant children grown up: A sociological and psychiatric study of sociopathic personality.* Baltimore: Williams & Wilkins.

Robinson, R. B., & Frank, D. I. (1994). The relation between self-esteem, sexual activity, and pregnancy. *Adolescence, 29,* 27–35.

Rockwell, S. K., Stohler, R. F., & Rudman, L. E. (1981). *4-H's influence on advanced training, careers and leadership roles in adulthood.* Lincoln: University of Nebraska, Nebraska Cooperative Extension Service, Institute of Agriculture and Natural Resources.

Rodgers, J. L., & Rowe, D. C. (1990). Adolescent sexual activity and mildly deviant behavior: Sibling and friendship effects. Special issue: Adolescent sexuality, contraception, and childbearing. *Journal of Family Issues, 11,* 274–293.

Roehlkepartain, E. C. (1998). *Building assets in congregations: A practical guide for helping youth grow up healthy.* Minneapolis, MN: Search Institute.

Roehlkepartain, E. C., & Scales, P. C. (1995). *Youth development in congregations: An exploration of the potential and barriers.* Minneapolis, MN: Search Institute.

Roeser, R. W., & Eccles, J. S. (1998). Adolescents' perceptions of middle school: Relation to longitudinal changes in academic and psychological adjustment. *Journal of Research on Adolescence, 8,* 123–158.

Roeser, R. W., Midgley, C., & Urdan, T. C. (1996). Perceptions of the school psychological environment and early adolescents' psychological and behavioral functioning in school: The mediating role of goals and belonging. *Journal of Educational Psychology, 88,* 408–422.

Rogel, M. J., Zuehlke, M. E., Petersen, A. C., Tobin-Richards, M., & Shelton, M. (1980). Contraceptive behavior in adolescence: A decision-making perspective. *Journal of Youth and Adolescence, 9,* 491–506.

Rogers, T., Reighery, E. C., Tencati, E. M., Butler, J. L., & Weiner, L. (1995). Community mobilization to reduce point-of-purchase advertising of tobacco products. *Health Education Quarterly, 22,* 427–442.

Rohrbach, L. A., Graham, J. W., Hansen, W. B., Flay, B. R., & Anderson Johnson, C. (1987). Evaluation of resistance skills training using multitrait-multimethod role play skill assessments. Special issue: Drugs. *Health Education Research, 2,* 401–407.

Rohrbaugh, J., & Jessor, R. (1975). Religiosity in youth: A personal control against deviant behavior. *Journal of Personality, 3,* 337–346.

Role of religion. (1996, May 29). *Education Week, 15,* 4.

Romer, D., Black, M., Ricardo, I., Feigelman, S., Kaljee, L., Galbraith, J., Nesbit, R., Hornik, R. C., & Stanton, B. (1994). Social influences on the sexual behavior of youth at risk for HIV exposure. *American Journal of Public Health, 84,* 977–985.

Romig, C., & Bakken, L. (1992). Intimacy development in middle adolescence: Its relationship to gender and family cohesion and adaptability. *Journal of Youth and Adolescence, 21,* 325–338.

Rosenberg, M. (1965). *Society and the adolescent self image.* Princeton, NJ: Princeton University Press.

Rosenberg, M., & Simmons, R. G. (1972). *Black and white self-esteem: The urban school child.* Arnold and Caroline Rose Monograph Series. Washington, DC: American Sociological Association.

Rosenthal, D. A., & Feldman, S. S. (1991). The influence of perceived family and personal factors on self-reported school performance of Chinese and Western high school students. *Journal of Research on Adolescence, 1,* 135–154.

Rotter, J. B. (1966). Generalized expectancies for internal versus external control of reinforcement. *Psychological Monographs, 80* (No. 1, Whole No. 609), 1–28.

Rotter, J. B. (1975). Some problems and misconceptions related to the construct of internal vs. external control of reinforcements. *Journal of Consulting and Clinical Psychology, 43,* 56–67.

Rutter, M. (1979). Protective factors in children's responses to stress and disadvantage. In M. W. Kent & J. E. Rolf (Eds.), *Primary prevention of psychopathology. Volume III: Social competence in children* (pp. 49–74). Hanover, NH: University Press of New England.

Rutter, M. (1983). School effects on pupil progress: Research findings and policy implications. *Child Development, 54,* 1–29.

Rutter, M., Graham, P., Chadwick, O., & Yule, W. (1976). Adolescent turmoil: Fact or fiction? *Journal of Child Psychology and Psychiatry, 17,* 35–56.

Ryan, R. M., & Lynch, J. H. (1989). Emotional autonomy versus detachment: Revisiting the vicissitudes of adolescence and young adulthood. *Child Development, 60,* 340–356.

Ryan, R. M., Stiller, J. D., & Lynch, J. H. (1994). Representations of relationships to teachers, parents, and friends as predictors of academic motivation and self-esteem. *Journal of Early Adolescence, 14,* 226–249.

St. Lawrence, J. S., Brasfield, T. L., Jefferson, K. W., Allyene, E., & Shirley, A. (1994). Social support as a factor in African-American adolescents' sexual risk behavior. *Journal of Adolescent Research, 9,* 292–310.

Saito, R. N., Benson, P. L., Blyth, D. A., & Sharma, A. R. (1995). *Places to grow: Perspectives on youth development opportunities for seven- to 14-year-old Minneapolis youth.* Minneapolis, MN: Search Institute.

Saito, R. N., & Blyth, D. A. (1993). *The Twin Cities one-to-one local mobilization feasibility study.* Minneapolis, MN: Search Institute.

Sampson, R. (1993, April). *Family and community-level influences on adolescent delinquency in the city of Chicago.* Paper presented at the biennial meeting of the Society for Research in Child Development, New Orleans, LA.

Sampson, R. J. (1997). Collective regulation of adolescent misbehavior: Validation results from eighty Chicago neighborhoods. *Journal of Adolescent Research, 12,* 227–244.

Sampson, R. J., Raudenbush, S. W., & Earls, F. (1997). Neighborhoods and violent crime: A multilevel study of collective efficacy. *Science, 277,* 918–924.

Sandham, J. L. (1997, November 12). Philanthropy. *Education Week, 17,* 7.

Saucier, J. F., & Ambert, A. M. (1982). Parental marital status and adolescents' optimism about their future. *Journal of Youth and Adolescence, 11,* 345–354.

Scales, P. C. (1990). Developing capable young people: An alternative strategy for prevention programs. *Journal of Early Adolescence, 10,* 420–438.

Scales, P. C. (1991). *A portrait of young adolescents in the 1990s: Implications for promoting healthy growth and development.* Minneapolis, MN: Search Institute.

Scales, P. C. (1996). *Boxed in and bored: How middle schools continue to fail young adolescents—and what good middle schools do right.* Minneapolis, MN: Search Institute.

Scales, P. C. (1998). Poll finds youth are a priority, but many adults not doing enough to make a difference. *Source, 14,* 1–3.

Scales, P. C., Benson, P. L., Leffert, N., & Blyth, D. A. (1998). The strength of developmental assets as predictors of positive youth development outcomes. Manuscript submitted for publication.

Scales, P. C., & Blyth, D. A. (1997). Effects of service-learning on youth: What we know and what we need to know. *The Generator: Journal of Service-Learning and Service Leadership, 17,* 6–9.

Scales, P. C., Blyth, D. A., Berkas, T., & Kielsmeier, J. (1998). *The effects of service-learning on middle school students' social responsibility and academic success.* Manuscript submitted for publication.

Scales, P. C., Blyth, D. A., Conway, J. J., Donahue, M. J., Griffin-Wiesner, J., & Roehlkepartain, E. C. (1995). *The attitudes and needs of religious youth workers: Perspectives from the field.* Minneapolis, MN: Search Institute.

Scales, P. C., & Gibbons, J. L. (1996). Extended family members and unrelated adults in the lives of young adolescents: A research agenda. *Journal of Early Adolescence, 16,* 365–389.

Scheier, L. M., & Botvin, G. J. (1998). Relations of social skills, personal competence, and adolescent alcohol use: A developmental exploratory study. *Journal of Early Adolescence, 18,* 77–114.

Schorr, L. B. (1997). *Common purpose: Strengthening families and neighborhoods to rebuild America.* New York: Anchor Books/Doubleday.

Schorr, L. B., & Schorr, D. (1988). *Within our reach: Breaking the cycle of disadvantage.* New York: Anchor Press/Doubleday.

Schunk, D. H. (1995). *Social origins of self-regulatory competence: The role of observational learning through peer modeling.* Paper presented at the biennial meeting of the Society for Research in Child Development, Indianapolis, IN.

Scott, W. A., & Scott, R. (1989). Family correlates of high-school student adjustment: A cross-cultural study. *Australian Journal of Psychology, 41,* 269–284.

Search Institute (1998). [Profiles of student life: Attitudes and behaviors, aggregate sample, 1996–1997 school year]. Unpublished raw data.

Seifer, R., Sameroff, A. J., Baldwin, C. P., & Baldwin, A. L. (1992). Child and family factors that ameliorate risk between 4 and 13 years of age. *Journal of the American Academy of Child and Adolescent Psychiatry, 31,* 893–903.

Sexual behavior among high school students—United States, 1990. (1992, January 3). *Morbidity and Mortality Weekly Report, 40,* 885–888.

Seydlitz, R. (1991). The effects of age and gender on parental control and delinquency. *Youth and Society, 23*, 175–201.

Shaffer, D., Garland, A., Gould, M., Fisher, P., & Trautman, P. (1988). Preventing teenage suicide: A critical review. *Journal of the American Academy of Child and Adolescent Psychiatry, 27*, 675–687.

Shaklee, H. (1983). Sex differences in children's behavior. *Advances in Developmental and Behavioral Pediatrics, 4*, 235–285.

Shanahan, M. J., Elder, G. H., Burchinal, M., & Conger, R. D. (1996). Adolescent paid labor and relationships with parents: Early work-family linkages. *Child Development, 67*, 2183–2200.

Shanahan, M. J., Finch, M., Mortimer, J. T., & Ryu, S. (1991). Adolescent work experience and depressive affect. *Social Psychology Quarterly, 54*, 299–317.

Shaps, E., Battistich, V., & Solomon, D. (1997). School as a caring community: A key to character education. In A. Molnar (Ed.), *The constitution of children's character: Ninety-sixth yearbook of the National Society for the Study of Education, Part II* (pp. 127–139). Chicago: University of Chicago Press.

Shaw, S. M., Kleiber, D. A., & Caldwell, L. L. (1995). Leisure and identity formation in male and female adolescents: A preliminary examination. *Journal of Leisure Research, 27*, 245–263.

Sherif, M., Harvey, O. J., White, B., Hood, W., & Sherif, C. (1961). *Intergroup conflict and cooperation: The Robbers Cave experiment.* Norman: University of Oklahoma, Institute of Group Relations.

Sherrod, M. (1995). Student peer conflict management in California high schools: A survey of programs and their efficacy as perceived by disciplinarians. *Peer Facilitator Quarterly, 12*, 12–14.

Shilts, L. (1991). The relationship of early adolescent substance use to extracurricular activities, peer influence, and personal attitudes. *Adolescence, 26*, 613–617.

Shulman, S. (1993). Close relationships and coping behavior in adolescence. Special issue: Stress and coping in adolescence. *Journal of Adolescence, 16*, 267–283.

Shumer, R. (1994). Community-based learning: Humanizing education. *Journal of Adolescence, 17*, 357–367.

Silberman, M. A., & Snarey, J. (1993). Gender differences in moral development during early adolescence: The contribution of sex-related variations in maturation. *Current Psychology Developmental, Learning, Personality, Social, 12*, 163–171.

Silvestri, B., & Flay, B. R. (1989). Smoking education: Comparison of practice and state-of-the-art. *Preventive Medicine, 18*, 257–266.

Simmons, R. G., & Blyth, D. A. (1987). *Moving into adolescence: The impact of pubertal change and school context.* New York: Aldine de Gruyter.

Slee, P. T., & Rigby, K. (1993). Australian school children's self appraisal of interpersonal relations: The bullying experience. *Child Psychiatry and Human Development, 23*, 273–282.

Small, S. A. (1996). Collaborative, community-based research on adolescents: Using research for community change. *Journal of Research on Adolescence, 6*, 9–22.

Small, S. A., Silverberg, S. B., & Kerns, D. (1993). Adolescents' perceptions of the costs and benefits of engaging in health-compromising behaviors. *Journal of Youth and Adolescence, 22*, 73–87.

Smith, C., & Krohn, M. D. (1995). Delinquency and family life among male adolescents: The role of ethnicity. *Journal of Youth and Adolescence, 24*, 69–93.

Smith, T. E. (1990). Time and academic achievement. *Journal of Youth and Adolescence, 19,* 539–558.

Smith, T. E. (1992). Time use and change in academic achievement: A longitudinal follow-up. *Journal of Youth and Adolescence, 21,* 725–747.

Solomon, D., Battistich, V., & Watson, M. (1993). *A longitudinal investigation of the effects of a school intervention program on children's social development.* Paper presented at the biennial meeting of the Society for Research in Child Development, New Orleans, LA. Palo Alto, CA: William and Flora Hewlett Foundation.

Sommers, I., & Baskin, D. R. (1994). Factors related to female adolescent initiation into violent street crime. *Youth and Society, 25,* 468–489.

Spivack, G., Platt, J., & Shure, M. (1976). *The problem-solving approach to adjustment.* San Francisco: Jossey-Bass.

Spivack, G., & Shure, M. B. (1982). The cognition of social adjustment: Interpersonal cognitive problem-solving thinking. In B. B. Lahey & A. E. Kazdin (Eds.), *Advances in clinical child psychology* (Vol. 5, pp. 323–372). New York: Plenum Press.

Stacy, A. W., Sussman, S., Dent, C. W., Burton, D., & Flay, B. R. (1992). Moderators of peer social influence in adolescent smoking. *Personality and Social Psychology Bulletin, 18,* 163–172.

Stanton, W. R., & Silva, P. A. (1992). A longitudinal study of the influence of parents and friends on children's initiation of smoking. *Journal of Applied Developmental Psychology, 13,* 423–434.

Stanton-Salazar, R. D. (1997). A social capital framework for understanding the socialization of racial minority children and youths. *Harvard Educational Review, 67,* 1–40.

Stattin, H., Gustafson, S. B., & Magnusson, D. (1989). Peer influences on adolescent drinking: A social transition perspective. Special issue: Early adolescent transitions: Longitudinal analyses of biological, psychological, and social interactions. *Journal of Early Adolescence, 9,* 227–246.

Stein, J. A., Newcomb, M. D., & Bentler, P. M. (1992). The effect of agency and communality on self-esteem: Gender differences in longitudinal data. *Sex Roles, 26,* 465–483.

Steinberg, L. (1981). Transformations in family relationships at puberty. *Developmental Psychology, 17,* 833–840.

Steinberg, L. (1986). Latchkey children and susceptibility to peer pressure: An ecological analysis. *Developmental Psychology, 22,* 433–439.

Steinberg, L., Brown, B., & Dornbusch, S. M. (1996). *Beyond the classroom: Why school reform has failed and what parents need to do.* New York: Simon & Schuster.

Steinberg, L., & Dornbusch, S. M. (1991). Negative correlates of part-time employment during adolescence: Replication and elaboration. *Developmental Psychology, 27,* 304–313.

Steinberg, L., Elmen, J. D., & Mounts, N. S. (1989). Authoritative parenting, psychosocial maturity, and academic success among adolescents. *Child Development, 60,* 1424–1436.

Steinberg, L., Lamborn, S. D., Darling, N., Mounts, N. S., & Dornbusch, S. M. (1994). Overtime changes in adjustment and competence among adolescents from authoritative, authoritarian, indulgent, and neglectful families. *Child Development, 65,* 754–770.

Steinberg, L., Lamborn, S. D., Dornbusch, S. M., & Darling, N. (1992). Impact of parenting practices on adolescent achievement: Authoritative parenting, school involvement, and encouragement to succeed. *Child Development, 63,* 1266–1281.

Steinberg, L., Mounts, N. S., Lamborn, S. D., & Dornbusch, S. M. (1991). Authoritative parenting and adolescent adjustment across varied ecological niches. *Journal of Research on Adolescence, 1,* 19–36.

Steinberg, L., & Silverberg, S. (1986). The vicissitudes of autonomy in early adolescence. *Child Development, 57,* 841–851.

Steinberg, L. D., Greenberger, E., Vaux, A., & Ruggiero, M. (1981). Early work experience: Effects on adolescent occupational socialization. *Youth & Society, 12,* 403–422.

Stevens, C. J., Puchtell, L. A., Ryu, S., & Mortimer, J. T. (1992). Adolescent work and boys' and girls' orientations to the future. *Sociological Quarterly, 33,* 153–169.

Stevens, J. W. (1997). African American female adolescent identity development: A three-dimensional perspective. *Child Welfare, 76,* 145–172.

Stevenson, D. L., & Baker, D. P. (1987). The family-school relation and the child's school performance. *Child Development, 58,* 1348–1357.

Stice, E., & Gonzales, N. (1998). Adolescent temperament moderates the relation of parenting to antisocial behavior and substance use. *Journal of Adolescent Research, 13,* 5–11.

Stockhaus, S. H. (1976). The effects of a community involvement program on adolescent students' citizenship attitudes. (Doctoral dissertation, University of Minnesota, 1976). *Dissertation Abstracts International, 37,* 3545.

Stone, R. (1997). *The contribution of caring to community building.* Chicago: University of Chicago, Chapin Hall Center for Children.

Strassburger, L. A., Rosén, L. A., Miller, C. D., & Chavez, E. L. (1990). Hispanic-Anglo differences in academic achievement: The relationship of self-esteem, locus of control and socioeconomic level with grade-point average in the USA. *School Psychology International, 11,* 119–124.

Straus, M. A., & Yodanis, C. L. (1996). Corporal punishment in adolescence and physical assaults on spouses in later life: What accounts for the link? *Journal of Marriage and the Family, 58,* 825–841.

Strother & Associates (1990). *Youth investment and community reconstruction: Street lessons on drugs and crime for the nineties. Final report.* Rochester, NY: Author. (ERIC Document Reproduction Service No. ED 372 149)

Svedhem, L. (1994). Social network and behaviour problems among 11–13-year-old schoolchildren: A theoretical and empirical basis for network therapy. *Acta Psychiatrica Scandinavica, 89,* 4–84.

Swick, K. J. (1988). Parental efficacy and involvement: Influences on children. *Childhood Education, 65,* 37–42.

Switzer, G. E., Simmons, R. G., Dew, M. A., Regalski, J. M., & Wang, C. (1995). The effect of a school-based helper program on adolescent self-image, attitudes, and behavior. *Journal of Early Adolescence, 15,* 429–455.

Talmi, A., & Harter, S. (1998). *Pathways to better outcomes: Special adults as sources of support for young adolescents.* Paper presented at the biennial meetings of the Society for Research on Adolescence, San Diego, CA.

Tate, G. S. (1991). The institutionalization of youth participation through policy development: The missing step. *Future Choices, 3,* 91–92.

Taylor, A. R. (1991). Social competence and the early school transition: Risk and protective factors for African-American children. *Education and Urban Society, 24,* 15–26.

Taylor, L. C., Phillip, D. G., Hinton, I. D., & Wilson, M. N. (1992). *Influence of parental style and child duties on school performance of African-American students.* Paper presented at the annual convention of the American Psychological Association, Washington, DC.

Thomas, D. L., & Carver, C. (1990). Religion and adolescent social competence. In T. P. Gullotta, G. R. Adams, & R. Montemayor (Eds.), *Advances in adolescent development: Vol. 3. Developing social competency in adolescence* (pp. 195–219). Newbury Park, CA: Sage.

Thomas, J. W., Bol, L., Warkentin, R. W., Wilson, M., Strage, A., & Rohwer, J. W. D. (1993). Interrelationships among students' study activities, self-concept of academic ability, and achievement as a function of characteristics of high-school biology courses. *Applied Cognitive Psychology, 7*, 499–532.

Tierney, J. P., Grossman, J. B., & Resch, N. L. (1995). *Making a difference: An impact study of Big Brothers/Big Sisters.* Philadelphia: Public/Private Ventures.

Tosiello, M. (1994, February 6). Don't call us "teens." *Boston Globe Magazine*, 51.

Treboux, D., & Busch-Rossnagel, N. A. (1995). Age differences in parent and peer influences on female sexual behavior. *Journal of Research on Adolescence, 5*, 469–487.

Turner, R. J., Frankel, G., & Levin, D. M. (1983). Social support: Conceptualization, measurement, and implications for mental health. *Research in Community and Mental Health, 3*, 67–111.

Urberg, K. A., Degirmencioglu, S. M., & Pilgrim, C. (1997). Close friend and group influence on adolescent cigarette smoking and alcohol use. *Developmental Psychology, 33*, 834–844.

Urberg, K. A., Shyu, S., & Liang, J. (1990). Peer influence in adolescent cigarette smoking. *Addictive Behaviors, 15*, 247–255.

Urdan, T. C., & Maehr, M. L. (1995). Beyond a two-goal theory of motivation and achievement: A case for social goals. *Review of Educational Research, 65*, 213–243.

Vannatta, R. A. (1996). Risk factors related to suicidal behavior among male and female adolescents. *Journal of Youth and Adolescence, 25*, 149–160.

Vazsonyi, A. T., & Flannery, D. J. (1997). Early adolescent delinquent behaviors: Associations with family and school domains. *Journal of Early Adolescence, 17*, 271–293.

Vernberg, E. M., Ewell, K. K., Beery, S. H., & Abwender, D. A. (1994). Sophistication of adolescents' interpersonal negotiation strategies and friendship formation after relocation: A naturally occurring experiment. *Journal of Research on Adolescence, 4*, 5–19.

Viadero, D. (1997, May 7). Adventure programs found to have lasting, positive impact. *Education Week, 16*, 8.

Vilhjalmsson, R. (1994). Effects of social support on self-assessed health in adolescence. *Journal of Youth and Adolescence, 23*, 437–452.

Vincent, M. L., Clearie, A. F., & Schlucter, M. D. (1987). Reducing adolescent pregnancy through school and community-based education. *Journal of the American Medical Association, 257*, 3382–3386.

Visser, D. (1987). The relationship of parental attitudes and expectations to children's mathematics achievement behaviour. Special issue: Sex differences in early adolescents. *Journal of Early Adolescence, 7*, 1–12.

Vitaro, F., Tremblay, R. E., Kerr, M., Pagani, L., & Bukowski, W. M. (1997). Disruptiveness, friends' characteristics, and delinquency in early adolescence: A test of two competing models of development. *Child Development, 68*, 676–689.

Wagner, E. F. (1993). Delay of gratification, coping with stress, and substance use in adolescence. Special section: Motivation and addictive behaviors. *Experimental and Clinical Psychopharmacology, 1*, 27–43.

Waldron, I., Lye, D., & Brandon, A. (1991). Gender differences in teenage smoking. *Women and Health, 17*, 65–90.

Walker, G. (1997). Foreword and summary. In M. A. Gambone, *Launching a resident-driven initiative: Community Change for Youth Development (CCYD) from site-selection to early im-plementation* (pp. i–vii). Philadelphia: Public/Private Ventures.

Walker, K., Taylor, E., McElroy, A., Phillip, D., & Wilson, M. N. (1995). Familial and ecolog-ical correlates of self-esteem in African American children. In M. N. Wilson (Ed.), *African American family life: Its structural and ecological aspects. New directions for child development, 68* (pp. 23–34). San Francisco: Jossey-Bass.

Walker, L. J., & Taylor, J. H. (1991). Family interactions and the development of moral reason-ing. *Child Development, 62,* 264–283.

Walker, L. S., & Greene, J. W. (1987). Negative life events, psychosocial resources, and psy-chophysiological symptoms in adolescents. *Journal of Clinical Child Psychology, 16,* 29–36.

Wallace, J. M., & Williams, D. R. (1997). Religion and adolescent health-compromising be-havior. In J. Schulenberg, J. L. Maggs, & K. Hurrelmann (Eds.), *Health risks and develop-mental transitions during adolescence* (pp. 444–466). Cambridge: Cambridge University Press.

Wang, M. Q., Fitzhugh, E. C., Westerfield, R. C., & Eddy, J. M. (1995). Family and peer influences on smoking behavior among American adolescents: An age trend. *Journal of Adolescent Health, 16,* 200–203.

Warr, M. (1993). Parents, peers, and delinquency. *Social Forces, 72,* 247–264.

Waters, E., & Sroufe, L. A. (1983). Social competence as a developmental construct. *Develop-mental Review, 3,* 79–97.

Weigel, D. J., Devereux, P., Leigh, G. K., & Ballard-Reisch, D. (1998). A longitudinal study of adolescents' perceptions of support and stress: Stability and change. *Journal of Adolescent Research, 13,* 158–177.

Weinfurt, K. P., & Bush, P. J. (1995). Peer assessment of early adolescents solicited to partici-pate in drug trafficking: A longitudinal analysis. *Journal of Applied Social Psychology, 25,* 2141–2157.

Weinstein, R. S., Soulé, C. R., Collins, F., Cone, J., Mehlhorn, M., & Simontacchi, K. (1991). Expectations and high school change: Teacher-researcher collaboration to prevent school failure. *American Journal of Community Psychology, 19,* 333–363.

Weist, M. D., Freedman, A. H., Paskewitz, D. A., Proescher, E. J., & Flaherty, L. T. (1995). Urban youth under stress: Empirical identification of protective factors. *Journal of Youth and Adolescence, 24,* 705–721.

Weithorn, L. A., & Campbell, S. B. (1982). The competency of children and adolescents to make informed treatment decisions. *Child Development, 53,* 1589–1598.

Weitz, J. H. (1996). *Coming up taller: Arts and humanities programs for children and youth at risk.* Washington, DC: President's Committee on the Arts and the Humanities.

Wentzel, K. R. (1991). Relations between social competence and academic achievement in early adolescence. *Child Development, 62,* 1066–1078.

Wentzel, K. R. (1993a). Motivation and achievement in early adolescence: The role of multi-ple classroom goals. *Journal of Early Adolescence, 13,* 4–20.

Wentzel, K. R. (1993b). Does being good make the grade? Social behavior and academic com-petence in middle school. *Journal of Educational Psychology, 85,* 357–364.

Wentzel, K. R. (1994). Family functioning and academic achievement in middle school: A social-emotional perspective. *Journal of Early Adolescence, 14,* 268–291.

Wentzel, K. R., & Feldman, S. S. (1993). Parental predictors of boys' self-restraint and motiva-tion to achieve at school: A longitudinal study. *Journal of Early Adolescence, 13,* 183–203.

Wenz-Gross, M., Siperstein, G. N., Untch, A. S., & Widaman, K. F. (1997). Stress, social support, and adjustment of adolescents in middle school. *Journal of Early Adolescence, 17*, 129–151.

Werner, E. E. (1993). *A longitudinal perspective on risk for learning disabilities.* Paper presented at the annual conference of the Learning Disabilities Association of America, San Francisco, CA.

Werner, E. E. (1994). Overcoming the odds. *Journal of Developmental and Behavioral Pediatrics, 15*, 131–136.

Werner, E. E., & Smith, R. S. (1992). *Overcoming the odds: High risk children from birth to adulthood.* Ithaca, NY: Cornell University Press.

Wheelock, A. (1992). *Crossing the tracks: How "untracking" can save America's schools.* New York: New Press.

Whitbeck, L. B. (1987). Modeling efficacy: The effect of perceived parental efficacy on the self-efficacy of early adolescents. *Journal of Early Adolescence, 7*, 165–177.

Whitbeck, L. B., Conger, R. D., & Kao, M. Y. (1993). The influence of parental support, depressed affect, and peers on the sexual behaviors of adolescent girls. *Journal of Family Issues, 14*, 261–278.

Whitbeck, L. B., Hoyt, D. R., Miller, M., & Kao, M. Y. (1992). Parental support, depressed affect, and sexual experience among adolescents. *Youth and Society, 24*, 166–177.

Whitbeck, L. B., Simons, R. L., Conger, R. D., & Lorenz, F. O. (1989). Value socialization and peer group affiliation among early adolescents. *Journal of Early Adolescence, 9*, 436–453.

Wigfield, A., & Eccles, J. S. (1994a). Children's competence beliefs, achievement values, and general self-esteem: Change across elementary and middle school. *Journal of Early Adolescence, 14*, 107–138.

Wigfield, A., & Eccles, J. S. (1994b). Middle grades schooling and early adolescent development: An introduction. *Journal of Early Adolescence, 14*, 102–106.

Wigfield, A., Eccles, J. S., Mac Iver, D., Reuman, D. A., & Midgley, C. (1991). Transitions during early adolescence: Changes in children's domain-specific self-perceptions and general self-esteem across the transition to junior high school. *Developmental Psychology, 27*, 552–565.

William T. Grant Foundation Commission on Work, Family and Citizenship (1988). *The forgotten half: Pathways to success for America's youth and young families.* Washington, DC: Author.

Williams, R. M. (1993). *The effects of required community service on the process of developing responsibility in suburban youth.* Unpublished doctoral dissertation, University of Nebraska, Lincoln.

Williams, S., & McGee, R. (1991). Adolescents' self-perceptions of their strengths. *Journal of Youth and Adolescence, 20*, 325–337.

Wills, T. A., McNamara, G., Vaccaro, D., & Hirky, A. E. (1996). Escalated substance use: A longitudinal grouping analysis from early to middle adolescence. *Journal of Abnormal Psychology, 105*, 166–180.

Wills, T. A., Vaccaro, D., & McNamara, G. (1992). The role of life events, family support, and competence in adolescent substance use: A test of vulnerability and protective factors. *American Journal of Community Psychology, 20*, 349–374.

Wilson-Sadberry, K. R., Winfield, L. F., & Royster, D. A. (1991). Resilience and persistence of African-American males in postsecondary enrollment. *Education and Urban Society, 24*, 87–102.

Windle, M. (1992). A longitudinal study of stress buffering for adolescent problem behaviors. *Developmental Psychology, 28,* 522–530.

Windle, M., Miller-Tutzauer, C., Barnes, G. M., & Welte, J. (1991). Adolescent perceptions of help-seeking resources for substance abuse. *Child Development, 62,* 179–189.

Wright, L. S., Frost, C. J., & Wisecarver, S. J. (1993). Church attendance, meaningfulness of religion, and depressive symptomatology among adolescents. *Journal of Youth and Adolescence, 22,* 559–568.

Yamoor, C. M., & Mortimer, J. T. (1990). Age and gender differences in the effects of employment on adolescent achievement and well-being. *Youth & Society, 22,* 225–240.

Yap, K. O., & Enoki, D. Y. (1994). *In search of the elusive magic bullet: Parent involvement and student outcomes.* Paper presented at the annual meeting of the American Educational Research Association, New Orleans, LA.

Yates, M., & Youniss, J. (1996). A developmental perspective on community service in adolescence. *Social Development, 5,* 85–111.

Yogev, A., & Ronen, R. (1982). Cross-age tutoring: Effects of tutors' attributes. *Journal of Educational Research, 75,* 261–268.

Youniss, J., & Haynie, D. L. (1992). Friendship in adolescence. *Journal of Developmental and Behavioral Pediatrics, 13,* 59–66.

Youniss, J., Yates, M., & Su, Y. (1997). Social integration: Community service and marijuana use in high school seniors. *Journal of Adolescent Research, 12,* 245–262.

Zeldin, S., & Price, L. A. (1995). Creating supportive communities for adolescent development: Challenges to scholars—An introduction. *Journal of Adolescent Research, 10,* 6–14.

Zelnik, M., Kantner, J., & Ford, K. (1981). *Sex and pregnancy in adolescence.* Beverly Hills, CA: Sage.

Zill, N., Nord, C. W., & Loomis, L. S. (1995). *Adolescent time use, risky behavior, and outcomes: An analysis of national data* [On-line]. Rockville, MD: Westat. Executive summary available World Wide Web: http://aspe.os.dhhs.gov/hsp/cyp/xstimuse.htm.

Zimmerman, M. A., Copeland, L. A., Shope, J. T., & Dielman, T. E. (1997). A longitudinal study of self-esteem: Implications for adolescent development. *Journal of Youth and Adolescence, 26,* 117–141.

Zimmerman, M. A., Salem, D. A., & Maton, K. I. (1995). Family structure and psychosocial correlates among urban African-American adolescent males. *Child Development, 66,* 1598–1613.

Zimmerman, R. S., Sprecher, S., Langer, L. M., & Holloway, C. D. (1995). Adolescents' perceived ability to say "no" to unwanted sex. *Journal of Adolescent Research, 10,* 383–399.

Zitzow, D. (1990). Ojibway adolescent time spent with parents/elders as related to delinquency and court adjudication experiences. *American Indian and Alaska Native Mental Health Research, 4,* 53–63.

Index

rates for, 58; well-being of, 65. *See also* Race/ethnicity

Age: and achievement motivation, 129–130; and boundaries/expectations, 91–92; and commitment to learning, 128–130, 139; and conflict resolution, 69; and constructive use of time, 112; and empowerment, 51, 59, 69; and moral reasoning, 156–157; and positive identity, 207; and positive values, 156–158, 164; and safety, 69; and social competencies, 186–187; and support, 41–42

Aggression/aggressiveness: and adult role models, 79, 88; and bad behavior, 158; and boundaries, 79; community-appropriate patterns of, 83–84; and conflict resolution, 25, 177, 185, 191–192; and marital conflict, 32; and peers, 80; and positive values, 158; and social competencies, 176–177; and support, 25; and Zapotec Indian youth, 83

Alcohol use/abuse: and adult role models, 79; and boundaries, 77, 78, 79; and conflict resolution, 177; and driving, 8; and empowerment, 65–66; and family boundaries, 77; and parental support, 33; and peers, 80, 89; and planning/decision making, 175, 181, 190; and positive values, 152, 164; prevention programs, 65–66; and religion, 103, 160–162; and resistance skills, 176; and risky behavior, 8; and school, 27, 78; and social competencies, 175, 176, 177, 182; and sports, 102, 104; and use of time, 103; and work/jobs, 55, 60. *See also* Substance use/abuse

Altruism: and peers, 80; and positive values, 159, 161–162; and religion, 161–162; and service to others, 57

Annie E. Casey Foundation: Plain Talk Initiative, 13

Antisocial behavior: and conflict resolution, 177, 185, 191–192; and empowerment, 65; and lack of self-control, 40; and neighborhood support, 38; and parental support, 40; and peers, 81, 86; and religion, 162; and risky behavior, 8; and social competencies, 177; and use of time, 103–104

Anxiety: and achievement motivation, 122; and marital conflict, 32, 33; and parental support, 33; and school, 26; and support, 24–25, 26, 27

Appalachian youth: and resiliency, 204–205

Asian American youth: and academic success, 83, 84, 126–127; and group identity, 183; and positive values, 156, 160; in Search Institute survey sample, 7; and tobacco use, 84. *See also* Race/ethnicity

Asset building: for boundaries/expectations, 93–94; for commitment to learning, 142–146; in communities, 12–13, 14, 217–218; for constructive use of time, 113–114; for empowerment, 71–73; for positive identity, 209–210; for positive values, 167–171; and prevention/intervention, x, 16–17; for social competencies, 188–192; for support, 45–47. *See also* Developmental assets

Athletics. *See* Sports

Australian youth, 62, 84, 104, 135

Autonomy: and boundaries, 76, 87, 93; and empowerment, 50, 51; and family support, 28; and parental support, 33; and resistance skills, 176; and responsibility, 76; and risky behaviors, 110; and self-esteem, 206; and support, 22, 28

Big Brothers/Big Sisters program, 46

Bisexual youth. *See* Gay, lesbian, and bisexual youth

Black youth. *See* African American youth

Boundaries-and-expectations assets: adolescent experience of, 91–92; and age, 91–92; and aggression, 79; and alcohol use, 77, 78, 79; asset building for, 93–94; and autonomy, 76, 87, 93; and consistency, 95; and curfew, 76, 85; defined, 6, 75–76, 92–93; and delinquency, 79, 87; and drug use, 79; and family support, 43; and gender, 82–83, 92; and independence, 85; listed, 2, 77; and prosocial behavior, 77, 79; and race/ethnicity, 83–84; and responsibility, 76; and self-control, 86; and self-efficacy, 79, 93; and self-esteem, 77, 79, 93; and self-regulation,

About the Authors

Peter C. Scales, Ph.D., senior fellow at Search Institute, is a developmental psychologist, author, speaker, and researcher who is widely recognized as one of the nation's foremost authorities on children and families, family life education, and policy development. Among his previous positions, Dr. Scales has served as director of national initiatives for the Center for Early Adolescence, University of North Carolina at Chapel Hill; chair of the Alaska Governor's Commission on Children and Youth; and research director, Syracuse University's Institute for Family Research and Education. In addition to numerous scientific articles and chapters, Dr. Scales is author of more than a dozen books and monographs, most recently including *Boxed In and Bored; How Middle Schools Continue to Fail Young Adolescents—and What Good Middle Schools Do Right* (Search Institute) and *A Portrait of Young Adolescents in the 1990s* (Search Institute/Center for Early Adolescence); he is the coauthor of *Growing Pains: The Making of America's Middle School Teachers* (National Middle School Association). He earned his doctorate and master's degree in child development and family relations from Syracuse University, and his bachelor's degree in psychology also from Syracuse University.

Nancy Leffert, Ph.D., senior research scientist at Search Institute, is a developmental psychologist, licensed independent clinical social worker, researcher, author, and speaker who specializes in development during adolescence and childhood. She is the 1992 recipient of the Hershel Thornburg Dissertation Award by the Society for Research on Adolescence. Dr. Leffert has previously served in several positions at the University of Minnesota and as director of the Child and Youth Problems Clinic, Family Service Association of San Diego County. In addition to many scientific articles and chapters, Dr. Leffert is coauthor of *Starting Out Right: Developmental Assets for Children* (Search Institute), *Shema: Listening to Jewish Youth* (Search Institute), and *Making the Case: Measuring the Impact of Youth Development Programs* (Search Institute). She earned her doctorate in child psychology from the Institute of Child Development, University of Minnesota, and her master's of social work and bachelor's degree from California State University at San Diego.

About Search Institute

Search Institute is an independent, nonprofit, nonsectarian organization whose mission is to advance the well-being of adolescents and children by generating knowledge and promoting its application. The institute conducts research and evaluation, develops publications and practical tools, and provides training and technical assistance. It collaborates with others to promote long-term organizational and cultural change that supports the healthy development of all children and adolescents.